The Diary of A Compulsive World Traveler

Bill S. Ashley

Library of Congress Control Number:		2011913437
ISBN:	Hardcover	978-1-4653-4394-9
	Softcover	978-1-4653-4393-2
	eBook	978-1-4653-4395-6

Print information available on the last page.

Rev. date: 03/29/2016

To order additional copies of this book, contact:
Xlibris
1-888-795-4274
www.Xlibris.com
Orders@Xlibris.com
593250

Dedication

This book is dedicated to all the fellow world travelers I have met while satisfying my compulsion to see the world.

Introduction

My family moved to a tenant farm when I was about six years old. We didn't have the same kind of income that other families had. We lived in a small house with no electricity, no indoor plumbing, and no running water. We used a wood stove, a fireplace, an icebox, and a nearby spring.

The parents of several of my classmates received a paycheck on a regular basis throughout the year by working at a public job, either at the local woolen mill or possibly at one of the several large tobacco companies in a nearby town. Our annual family income was basically once a year when we sold the tobacco. That income was supplemented through our delivery of milk, eggs, and butter to several families once a week.

I knew that we were poor, but I was determined that it wouldn't keep me from reaching any goal that I had set for myself. From a very early age, I had this urge to see other places. I am of the full understanding that people are born with a "travel gene."

When I was in the third grade, my family went to visit my elder sister who was living several hundred miles away. I was so excited about being able to go that it didn't even bother me that I was going to miss an entire week of school.

My father had two sisters who were married and lived in a town some thirty-five miles from us. When my father would announce on Saturday that wc were going to visit either of them on Sunday, I was excited just to be going somewhere.

When I was in elementary school, my father took me on a short twenty-mile round-trip train ride on an old steam engine train, and I remember the excitement of that short journey, as though it happened just yesterday.

In the fourth grade, my teacher was conducting our geography lesson and I remember her telling us about places in Europe and other foreign places. Most of the other students in the class were bored to death; some were sleeping through all this. I was excited to hear about these places and was determined that I would visit them someday.

My grades in school were always above average. My parents had made a deal with me—I could stay home and work on the farm or I could attend school. I only missed about twenty days of school during the entire twelve years. From the eighth grade through graduation, I didn't miss even one day.

When I was a senior in high school and graduation was approaching, I started mentioning the fact that I would like to go to college. Of course, my parents told me that we were poor, had no money, and that it would be impossible because we couldn't afford it.

As I was about to graduate from the junior college, I had made up my mind that I would continue my education at a senior college to obtain my bachelor's degree. I was able to do this through receiving a small scholarship, working in the tobacco fields in the summer, and also working in the school cafeteria.

As soon as I had departed from the gymnasium from my senior college graduation ceremony, I reminded my parents that four years ago they had said I couldn't go to college because we couldn't afford it. I held out my diploma and was proud to say that I had completed it and it was paid for.

My college roommate, whose family seemed to be on an equal economic level as mine, and I had reason to celebrate this occasion. We drove to Florida and were staying in the Titusville area. The area was in close enough proximity to Cape Canaveral that we were able to see missiles being launched. We were walking along the beach near the launching area until we saw a barbed-wire fence and a sign that indicated if we went any further, we could be shot. We decided that we had gone far enough.

1962

The First Trip to Europe

In September following my college graduation, I began my teaching career in the business department of a high school. At the end of my second year of teaching, I had planned to go to North Carolina and spend the summer with my elderly parents.

However, several fellow teachers had made plans to go on a trip to Europe that was being sponsored by the state education association. I had been in North Carolina with my parents for a week or two and kept talking about this trip that these other teachers would be taking. I guess my mother was getting tired of hearing about it, and she said, "Well, why don't you just go on the trip with them?" My response was "I am so glad you said that because I leave next week for the trip."

My uncle had cosigned a loan at the local bank for $600 to pay for the trip. I took a sixteen-hour bus ride from North Carolina to New York to save money. Then, the flight from New York to London was six hours, and it was the first time I had ever been on an airplane.

The year prior to this, I had been writing checks to make monthly payments on a car and begrudged every one of them. The year after the trip, I was writing checks to pay for the trip, and it didn't bother me at all.

Upon arrival in England our group was driven to Stratford-upon-Avon, where we went to a performance of one of Shakespeare's plays. After almost two continuous days of travel, it was rather difficult to keep one's eyes open during the performance. The hotel in Stratford used names of Shakespearian characters instead of room numbers. The name of my room was Ariel, Prospero's slave in *The Tempest.*

The next day, we visited the city of Oxford and the university on our way back into London. The excitement really perked up with seeing Big Ben, The Tower of London, Westminster Abbey, Buckingham Palace, and several other tourist sights.

We left England on an overnight boat ride to Amsterdam. I can remember standing in a small room at the Diamond Exchange in Amsterdam the next day and feeling the room move as a result of being on the boat overnight.

I couldn't believe I was finally looking at all the wonderful canals in this city. It was a treat to be able to see people going to work or school on their bicycles and to see that there were even special lanes just for bikes.

From Amsterdam our motor coach headed south through the Black Forest in Germany.

It is possible to meet a variety of travelers when traveling with a group. It is difficult sometimes to determine who has traveled extensively and who hasn't been away from home very much. As we were approaching one area in Germany, our bus driver announced that just ahead on the left we would see where Konrad Adenaur lived. As we passed, I overheard the lady in front of me explaining to her daughter—"Oh, look! That's where Eisenhower lives!"

We were able to take a Rhine river cruise from Cologne to Koblenz and view all the beautiful castles along the way. We proceeded through Lichtenstein on our way to Austria. I marveled at being able to see the ski jump in Cortina d'Ampezzo, where the Olympics had been held. We also visited the city of Innsbruck.

Venice was the next highlight of the trip with all its beautiful canals and churches. The members of our group were given instructions as to when to be ready to leave for a tour of St. Mark's Cathedral. I told our guide that I thought I had seen enough churches by this time and that if I was confronted with another one, I might just lose my religion. She convinced me that this is one I must see. I conceded and was grateful to her later that she had insisted. It was beautiful, and I really enjoyed seeing The Bridge of Sighs.

From Venice, we traveled down the east coast to the city of Ravenna. The vivid blue mosaics there would impress anyone and leave them with an indelible remembrance. We then stopped in Assisi and toured the famous cathedral and monastery there. We were able to spend a night in the small country of San Marino.

The anticipation was really building in the hope that the next day I would be able to finally see the Colosseum and the ancient Forum in Rome. Next to Amsterdam, this was the most exciting city on the tour for me. Seeing all the ancient buildings here for the first time can almost bring chills of excitement. We toured the Vatican and were able to walk through the Sistine Chapel. Our group went to see the opera Aida at the ruins of Caracalla, and this was actually my first authentic opera. What a place to start!

We had an option for an excursion to Naples and the Blue Grotto. This was an additional treat! By this time, we had to begin our journey north to Florence. We visited the cathedral, the Uffizi Gallery, the Ponte Vecchio shopping bridge, and, of course, the famous statue of David.

We then drove to Pisa and saw the leaning tower. Our tour continued with an overnight stay in Milan. The next day we drove along the Italian Riviera, which has to be one of the most beautiful spots in the world. In Monte Carlo, we were able to see the castle, the casino, and all the large yachts in the harbor.

Our first night in France was in Nice. I was traveling as a single person and for some reason I kept getting very large rooms for one person. My room in Nice was a large circular one on the second floor just over the lobby. It was so large that I went out and bought several bottles of wine and had a party in my room for the other members of the group.

While driving through Provence, we were able to walk on the bridge at Avignon. We all remember singing about this when we were in our French one class, don't we?

Paris was our last stop on this tour, and as they say—we usually save the best till last—the Eiffel Tower, Notre Dame, Basilica du Sacré Cœur, and the Arch of Triumph. So my first major trip had come to a close, and I knew that from that day forward, I would be traveling at every opportunity possible in order to further educate myself on how the other people around the world lived and how it differed from my way of life.

When I arrived back in North Carolina from this trip, I was in dire need of a haircut. I went to the local barber shop directly from the bus station. They saw my piece of luggage and I suppose they didn't know whether, I had been somewhere or was getting ready to run away from home. I told them that I had just returned from a trip to Europe. The looks on their faces were as if I had told them that I had gone to the moon. I must say they seemed impressed and then began asking a lot of questions as to where I had been and what I had seen.

1965 TO 1967

Canada, Mexico, Jamaica, and Venezuela

In 1965, I obtained a job in Alexandria, Virginia, as the coordinator of the work-training program for students in the business department. It was an interesting area to have this job as each year I would have a student or two working on Capitol Hill, at the Pentagon, and several other government agencies, insurance companies, banks, etc.

After completing my first year in this job, while living in Washington, D. C I was able to travel to Canada during the summer of 1966 with a friend. We visited the Niagara Falls, Toronto, Ottawa, Montreal, and Quebec.

On our drive from Montreal to Quebec, we had an accident. A person driving a motorcycle came over into our lane and then proceeded to slam on his brakes. We had not alternative but to try to stop. There wasn't enough time. We hit the motorcycle and the driver came up onto our automobile and landed on the windshield. The police came and during the investigation, we exchanged information.

We were able to find a place in Quebec that repaired our broken windshield. We also telephoned the insurance company to determine the condition of the driver. The last thing we heard was that he was still in the hospital. We were determined that we weren't going to let this event spoil our vacation. We made a pact that we wouldn't mention it again, until we arrived back in Washington, D. C.

At Christmastime of 1966, my friend and I went to Acapulco. We stayed at a small hotel, which at the time was almost on the outskirts of the downtown area. We had been to the beach for the entire first day of our trip. Upon our return to the hotel, we decided that we should have a drink to celebrate our first day in Mexico. My friend went downstairs to get some ice. I was lying on the bed and suddenly, I thought I heard someone trying to break into the room. The glass-sliding doors began to shake. Then, I noticed the pictures on the wall begin to move! We were having tremors from an earthquake!

When my friend returned with the ice, I asked him if he felt it. He said the water in the swimming pool began to wave. That is as close as I have ever been to an earthquake and I hope I never get any closer.

This December, our Acapulco trip coincided with the honeymoon of Lynda Bird Johnson and Chuck Robb. We saw them one night when we went to Las Brisas for dinner. Well, the travel bug was beginning to really wake up!

In 1967, I went to Jamaica where I was able to drive for the first time "on the other side." My friend and I drove around the entire island. It was nice to see a five-mile stretch of beach in Negril, without a single hotel! Of course, now it is filled with them. We toured the rum factory in Savannah La Mar. It was exciting to drive through the banana plantations in the eastern part of the island.

There was an exclusive resort on the northern side of the island, near Port Antonio, that we had read about and decided that we would try to go and have Christmas dinner. It was pouring. As we drove up to the security entrance booth, we were directed to the lobby. Upon arriving, we were offered drinks and hors d'ouvres. After meeting several people from different countries, we were directed to an area where we would be served an excellent meal. The conversation during dinner revealed that the dinner was being paid for by the management, for the guests who were staying at the resort. At the end of the meal, we separately excused ourselves to go to the rest room. Then, we just got into the car and drove away. We had inadvertently and successfully crashed our first party!

We flew from Jamaica to Caracas, Venezuela. Our flight was severely delayed and we were not expected to arrive in Caracas until late in the evening. We discovered that there was a group of government workers and people who were relatives of politicians on our flight. They insisted that they give us a ride from the airport to our hotel, since all the banks at the airport would be closed and that there would be no way of obtaining cash or getting a taxi. I was in one automobile and my friend was in another. We were traveling into the city at a very high speed. It was New Year's Eve and when we arrived at the hotel, they hopped out of the cars and began throwing fireworks. Naturally, the hotel personnel looked at us with trepidation as if to say that they didn't know whether they wanted us to stay there or not.

Each day after sightseeing, we would go to the same restaurant on the walking street for coffee and dessert. We would have the same waiter every night and this helped in making us feel as if we were locals. Small world story: about two years later, the same friend I had been traveling with and I were invited to a new restaurant that was opening in Washington, D. C. We had only just been seated, when I looked at my friend and said, "You are not going to believe this." We had the same waiter that we had had in Caracas two years before.

After those few days in Caracas, we rented a Volkswagen and drove through the jungles to Puerto la Cruz. At several places during the drive, we saw snakes crossing the road. It is then that one hopes that the car doesn't break down. It would not have seemed uncommon, if we would have seen Tarzan swinging across the road.

Upon arriving in Puerto la Cruz, we parked the car next to the hotel and went in to register. Upon completing the registration process, we said that we needed to go out and move the car, since it was parked in a "no parking" zone. The hotel clerk became amused and said that we didn't have anything to worry about. He said to just leave it there—that the city has a certain amount of money to use for signs, but nobody obeys them. Another thing that we discovered is that no one stops for a red light—they just zoom right on through!

Each day there, we would go our separate ways and make arrangements to meet somewhere for lunch. During those hours, we would explore the city and it was a perfect way to be forced into using the only Spanish that you know.

We were on the beach and a couple of the locals came to talk to us, as they had determined that we were tourists from another country and it gave them an opportunity to practice their English. Later that day, they invited us to go with them in their car to have lunch together. That is when we had positive proof that drivers do not stop at traffic signals! We felt fortunate to get back to the beach in one piece.

The hotel where we were staying had a New Year's Eve party at the roof garden. We met several people there who were from the United States, Trinidad, etc. It was a great way to begin the New Year.

How to Fit Christmas in With Travel

One of the great advantages of teaching is the amount of time one has for vacation. Any time the school was to be closed for a holiday, I would usually be contemplating as to where I might go to spend those days. It was convenient to leave the country at Christmas time, when we would have at least two weeks vacation. I had heard of the saying "Christmas in July" many times. Well, evidently a little bell went off in my head and I decided that I would begin having a Christmas-in-July party and allow myself to travel in December. I continued to have these parties for twenty-five years.

My friends would look forward to them. I received a call one year from friends who lived out-of-town. They were planning a trip to Europe for the summer, but needed to know the dates for Christmas-in-July party for that year so it wouldn't coincide with their European plans. For the Christmas-in-July party in 1976, there were people in attendance from California, Florida, New Jersey, New York, Virginia, Washington, D. C, Maryland, and North Carolina.

Themes for these parties began to emerge. One year, I had Hawaii as a theme. I made lighted palm trees for the patio. The centerpiece for the dining room table was a gigantic display of fresh fruit and orchids.

"The gift" was the theme for another year. The entire front of the house was decorated to look like a giant Christmas gift. In the patio, there was a Santa's sleigh filled with gifts along with two other huge gifts that had lights for the ribbon and the bow. Even the centerpiece for the dining room table resembled a Christmas gift and was made using about seventy-five red anthuriums.

Friends began asking me what the theme was going to be the coming year, but I wouldn't reveal it. The invitations were mailed from places to coincide with the theme. For example, one year I was going to use the deer as the theme. I called the postmaster at the post office in Deer Isle, Maine, and explained to him what my request was and he conceded to have me mail the invitations there and they would postmark them with the Deer Isle stamp. For other years, they were mailed from North Pole, Alaska; Christmas, Florida; and Bethlehem, Pennsylvania.

As the twenty-fifth year of these parties was approaching, I was determined that I would do something special. This was also to be the last one, since I was going to retire that year and from that time on I would have Christmas in December and travel in July.

I was able to obtain a permit from the National Park Service to have a formal catered sit-down breakfast on the mall adjacent to the Capitol. The cocktail hour and breakfast began on a Sunday at 8:00 a.m. There were sixty-four in attendance and the brass ensemble from the Air Force band played Christmas music during the party. Two hours after the party began; tourists began arriving to go to the museums. When they heard Christmas carols being played in July their facial expressions would have a confused look. The party received a four-column write-up in the *Washington Post* along with two pictures.

1968

The Holy Land

In December of 1968, I traveled to Portugal, Spain, Italy, Israel, Turkey, and Greece for the Christmas vacation. Upon arriving at the hotel in Lisbon, my friend discovered that he had inadvertently picked up the wrong suitcase at the airport. It was filled with baby clothes, baby powder, diapers, etc. We called the airline and were able to get the bag to its proper owners and retrieve his bag.

On our flight from Barcelona to Rome and just about fifteen minutes into the flight, the plane hit some major turbulence and the plane suddenly dropped about two hundred-feet. Of course, we had just been served our meal and upon arriving in Rome, we discovered that we even had garden peas in our pockets from the ordeal.

As we were sightseeing in Athens, we encountered our first offer to go to a bar and have a drink. Naturally, this was to lure us in, order drinks, bring on the ladies, and then expect you to pay a large tab. I'm sure this has happened to many other travelers as well. Once this has happened, you never let it happen again. I really enjoyed seeing the Parthenon and other historical sites in Athens and buying gifts to bring back for relatives.

Now it was time for the highlight of our trip, which was to be in Israel and be in Bethlehem for Christmas. We took a local bus from Tel Aviv to Jerusalem early in the morning. Since it was just a year following the war, there were several very young people getting on the bus carrying submachine guns. We were able, though, to do our sightseeing in Jerusalem, Bethlehem, and Hebron.

We were supposed to fly out to Nicosia, Cyprus, and then to Cairo. However, while going through customs, my friend forgot to tell them to stamp the Israeli stamp on a separate piece of paper. At that time you could not enter Egypt, if you had an Israeli stamp in your passport.

We went to the American Embassy and asked what could be done. We were told that they could stamp over it, but that when we arrived in Cairo, they would know what had been done and would put my friend in jail. And since I was traveling with him, they would assume that we had both been to the same place and I would be put in jail as well.

We had what in 1968 was termed an "excursion fare" plane ticket. The price of the ticket was based upon your furthest point and you could have as many stops along the way as you wanted and the price stayed the same. So we decided that we would fly to Istanbul, Turkey and go to Egypt at another time.

We learned later that the day we flew from Tel Aviv, there were several El Al planes blown up. Fortunately, we were on Pan Am. It was good that we didn't know this until later!

In making our way back to the United States, we spent a couple nights in Nice, France. On the morning of our return, we looked at the airline tickets and discovered that the departure time was much earlier than what we had anticipated. We obtained a taxi from our hotel and started to the airport. Just down the street from the hotel there was a fire and we were diverted to another route. Then, a few miles later, the taxi pulled off to the side of the road and stopped. It seems the driver had put a blanket over the engine the night before to keep it from freezing. Yes, it had actually snowed that night in Nice! Well, he forgot to take the blanket off and the blanket was burning! We finally made it to the airport and found that our flight had already left. Fortunately, because of it being New Year's Day, an additional flight had been added to Paris. We were able to get to Paris and made our connection back to Washington just in time to go back to work the next day.

1969

South America and Back to College

The time that I had spent in Venezuela in 1967 had whetted my appetite to see more of South America. So in 1969, this trip was practically a circumnavigation of the South American continent. This adventure began in Bogota, Colombia. After selecting a hotel for the stay, we made arrangements through the hotel for an English speaking guide for our touring.

From Bogota, we flew through Quito, Ecuador and Lima, Peru to Santiago, Chile. One of the first things we noticed here was the number of blond people. We were apprised of the fact that many settlers from Sweden had migrated here several years prior—thus, blonds in Chile. We were able to take a train ride through the vineyards and spend a weekend in Vina del Mar.

From there, the journey took us to Buenos Aires. After seeing most of the sights in Buenos Aires, we took a train ride and spent the day in Mar del Plata. Our next stop was in Rio de Janeiro with a stop over in Sao Paulo. Rio, of course, is a beautiful city and there is so much to see and do. We took in all the obvious sightseeing venues including Pan de Azucar, Christ the Redeemer statue, Copacabana Beach, etc.

The highlight of this stop was to be in Rio for New Year's Eve and see the celebration on the beach. The voodoo people come down from the hills, build large mounds of sand on the beach, and cover them with gladioli and candles. So for five miles down the beach, one could see candles burning. The people would go into chants and collapse. At the strike of midnight, they gathered all the flowers and walked into the water with them. This was to signify that they were getting rid of all their problems and sins from the previous year and were ready to start anew with the New Year.

I had decided that I needed to return to college to obtain a master's degree in business education. This prevented me from traveling as much as I would have liked.

By the time I had finished this degree in June of 1970, I had decided to continue my studies and accumulate several hours of work toward my doctorate. I was the first in my family of six children to finish high school and now I had obtained my master's degree. My father had died in 1968. I knew that he was proud of what I was doing with my life because every time I would go home and be in our small downtown, he would make sure to introduce me to his friends and let them know that I was a teacher.

My mother came to attend the graduation. However, upon returning to my residence from that affair, she let me know that she had been to a graduation for me in the eighth grade, to another in high school, another for junior college, and yet another in senior college. After having been to this one she said that I could graduate as many more times as I wanted to, but she felt that she had been to enough graduations for me.

I returned to Rio for Christmas the following year. It was great to get away to a place that I felt I knew my way around, was warm, and no classes to attend! The last day there, it had been about 101 degrees. I flew overnight to New York and when I arrived there it was one degree.

1971

Russia

In 1971, a friend of mine who had never been to Europe before left a few weeks before me and toured Europe. We met in Vienna and began our sightseeing trip. From there we flew to Moscow. It was such a delight to be able to be in a communist country and see how the people lived.

We were able to meet several people and it seemed that they had just as many questions they wanted to ask us as we had to ask them. Fortunately, we met several students in the park by the Bolshoi who wanted to practice their English.

We were told by these students that there were probably police in the park and if they saw them talking to us for any length of time, they could probably ask questions. So we left going in one direction and they left going in the opposite direction, but we met on the other side.

They were able to take us to an apartment that was usually occupied by the parents of one of the students. Since those parents were on a mission out of the country, he was able to invite us in. They wanted to know things that were related to school, to dating, marriage, etc. They were also interested in learning the procedures we had to go through in obtaining permission to leave our country and be able to visit another. We were told that if they wanted to leave their country for any reason they had to apply. Usually, it would be denied and you would just apply again.

These students seemed startled to learn that when students graduate from high school in the United States they are allowed to move to another city or state without asking. They were just as much in awe to learn that single people here are able to have their own apartment and don't have to live with their parents.

We were told by the employees at the Intourist hotel that the tickets for the Bolshoi had been sold out. However, if we were to go there and stand out front, we would find people who would want to get rid of their tickets. We saw *La Traviata* and sat in box seats up front for $1.

Shopping in Moscow in 1971 was limited. Even in the state run stores, a lot of the shelves were bare. If you found something in Gum, their big department store, you had to let them know what you wanted and they would write a receipt for it. Then, you would take the receipt to a cashier and pay. You would be given a receipt and would then be able to go back and stand in line again to pick up your merchandise.

We saw many people standing in line in the street to purchase bread or milk.

Another interesting observation while we were in Moscow, near Red Square, was that there were drinking machines for water or juice. Everyone used the same glass. The machine had a brush that when the glass was placed over it, it would rotate to clean the glass and prepare it for the next person.

I purchased something in the gift shop at the hotel. When the cashier gave me my change I saw that it included a pack of matches for cigarettes. I asked why and he said it was because he didn't have any small coins for my change and this would make up for it. That makes sense, doesn't it?

We left Moscow on an overnight train to Leningrad. Upon arriving the next morning, we made our way to the hotel to freshen up. It was intriguing to see this city in all its splendor—the Peter and Paul Fortress, the naval museum, and the Hermitage Museum. We did go to Pushkin and saw the palace there.

I saw a watch in a shop in the lobby of the hotel that I liked. I didn't want to rush into something, see another I liked better, and wish I had not bought it. So I asked the shopkeeper regarding their hours of being open. I was told that they are open every day from early morning till late at night. The day that I was leaving, I went to the shop to buy the watch. Of course, it was closed. I asked the person in the newspaper kiosk nearby if it would be open later and also told him that I had been told that they were open every day. So why isn't it open today? He said that maybe the person just didn't feel like coming to work today. Fortunately, I was able to find another watch at the airport that I liked just as much. It cost about $5 and it is still working!

While my friend and I would take the local trams to get around the city, we noticed that many of the workers along the tracks were women. They were all dressed in long dresses and head scarves. The brooms and other pieces of equipment seemed to be quite antiquated.

We struck up a conversation with a gentleman in Leningrad. He was an instructor of music in the evening school. He told us that if he tried to begin teaching music that would be too closely compared to what would be heard in the west; he would be asked to stop. He said that his wife worked in a factory that produced women's clothes and the same thing applied there also. If the factory began making women's clothes that had too much of a western flair to it, they would be asked to stop. We asked this gentleman if he own a television. The look on his face resembled that of someone that you had just asked if he owned his own jet plane. He said that the only way that his family could own a television would be to save a little each month until they would save enough money to purchase one. This might take a long time.

One night while in Leningrad, we went to the Kirov for a ballet. We arrived back at the hotel at 10:00 p.m. and went to the restaurant to have our dinner. Another couple who had been at the ballet was there at the same time. Fortunately, they were from Sweden and spoke Russian. The sign at the entrance to the restaurant indicated that the closing time was 11:00 p.m. We were met at the entrance and were told that the restaurant was closed. The Swedish couple kept insisting to the point that we were allowed to enter. However, when we tried to order we were told that the kitchen had closed down and we wouldn't be able to have certain items on the menu. We had to settle with ox tongue and champagne for dinner.

Our next stop was Helsinki. Since it was the summer time, it didn't really get dark until about 10:00 p.m., and the sun was up very early the next morning. Our tour of the city included the government house, the cathedral, the railway station, etc. We enjoyed seeing the Sibelius monument. The Temppeliaukio Church was constructed in 1969 and is literally built into a rock. It is sometimes just called The Rock Church.

Stockholm was a charming city. There we met a couple of Swedes that became our tour guides. They took us on a train ride away from the city, for a visit to the beach. We were unaware, however, that the beach would be a "grassy beach." The one thing that impressed us so much about this beach was that it was so clean. During that period of time most of the people, including me and my friend, were smokers. At the end of the visit, we noticed everyone picking up the cigarette butts and placing them in trash bins, thus a clean place for the next day.

In Oslo, we did two or three days of sightseeing and decided that we would really like to see the fjords. We took a train from Oslo to Flam. My friend and I were very casually dressed—ratty jeans, tee shirts, tennis shoes, and somewhat long hair. Not long after we had settled into our compartment, a man and woman who were dressed much more formally joined us. We could tell that their first thought was—do we really have to share a compartment with these guys? After about three hours on the train, the gentleman decided to go to look for food. Upon his return, he informed his wife that there was no café car on this train. Not long after that, my friend and I decided it was time to eat. We opened our bags, which had bread, cheese, ham, and wine. We suddenly became good friends.

We took the cable down to Flam and spent the night there. The next morning we boarded a ship that took us on a tour through the fjords and ended in Bergen. From there, we took the train back to Oslo.

Now it was time to head off to Copenhagen. We met a person there who was born in the United States and had lived in Denmark for several years. He was great in showing us around the city. We both found it interesting that here was a person who had been born in the United States and he could speak Danish fluently. Not only that, he told us that he was able to detect whether a person speaking English was from Denmark, Norway, Sweden, etc. One cannot complete the visit to Copenhagen without going to the Tivoli amusement park. There, we were able to see the legendary Marlene Dietrich.

It was time to make our way to Amsterdam. Since I had been there in 1962 on my first trip to Europe, I delighted in being able to be the tour guide for my friend. This city has always been one of my favorites. It seems so genteel walking early in the morning along the canals and watching the people on their way to work on their bicycles, andall this while taking in the wonderful architecture of the buildings that are five hundred years old.

Our final stop on this trip took us to London. Again, I had been there once and was glad to be the tour guide again. While there, we decided to go to Westminster Abbey. It just so happened that upon arriving we were told that we could not go in because they were just getting ready for a special mass for the first black person who had sat in Parliament. The next hour was extremely exciting to see all the dignitaries arrive in their antique Rolls Royce automobiles to attend the service. By this time, we were told that once the service began we would be able to enter the Abbey and sit in any of the seats near the rear. When the service was over and the dignitaries were leaving, we had the great fortune of being able to shake hands with Harold MacMillan, the former Prime Minister of England. He asked where we were visiting from and welcomed us to England.

1972-1975

USA—Pacific Ocean—Hawaii

From 1972 through 1975, there were not a lot of extended trips. I had purchased a townhouse and travel priorities moved to a lower level. I had decided that I could forgo extensive trips for at least two years. After that, the second mortgage would be paid off and the travel doors could fling open again.

During the summer of 1972, two friends of mine and I drove across country. We left Washington, D. C just after Hurricane Agnes came through this area. We drove first to Chicago arriving there around the fourth of July. It was so cold that while walking around we were placing our hands on the sidewalk in order to warm them up.

Just before arriving in Denver, we drove through a terrific hailstorm. The hail was just about the size of ping-pong balls. We expected the automobile to have dents in it, but it didn't. From Denver we drove to Salt Lake City, where we visited the Tabernacle and saw the lake. We decided that we would leave and drive through the desert at night since it wouldn't be so hot. We arrived the next morning in Lake Tahoe. We did some sightseeing around the lake that day and saw the city of Reno.

From Lake Tahoe we drove to Burlingame, California, where one of our friends had an apartment. We had finally arrived safely to our destination. This was a fantastic way to see the country and be able to recognize the major differences between the topography of different states.

My friend made a big point of the fact that it is always hot and humid in Washington, D. C, but it is never hot in California. Well, the first day we were there, it was about one hundred degrees. The next day it was even hotter. So of course, we teased the friend about it never being hot there! The next day the fog came into San Francisco and we went to visit Muir Woods. We almost froze! The high that day was about sixty-five degrees and we were dressed for the one hundred degree days we had just suffered through.

In the summer of 1973, the second mortgage was paid off and the travel doors beckoned once again. I took a circle tour of the Pacific Ocean with a group of about fifteen travelers.

The trip started in Hawaii and continued through Japan, Taiwan, Hong Kong, Singapore, Australia, New Zealand, and Tahiti. I had never really had an urge to visit Hawaii. I felt that if I wanted to see palm trees I could just go to Florida. Well, I was wrong! Since that visit, I have now been to Hawaii thirteen times.

Tokyo was another exciting city for me. It was great to experience a completely different lifestyle, different religions, and different foods. I started school when I was five years old. Most of the other students in my class were almost a year elder than me. So for twelve years, I was always looking up at everybody. I couldn't believe that I was standing in The Ginza district in Tokyo and looking around me and discovered that I was the tallest person that I saw! Wow! Did that make me feel good!

While in Japan, we had two options in choosing how to go to Osaka. We could go by bullet train or we could fly. Fortunately, I chose to fly. The day we did this, it was extremely overcast and the people who took the bullet train were not able to see Mount Fuji at all. Those of us who chose to fly were above the clouds and could see it clearly!

After a brief stay in Taipei, we were off to explore Hong Kong. One of the highlights there was the ascent to Victoria Peak. The view of the city from there is spectacular. Riding across to Kowloon, one experiences the Star Ferry. The harbor there is always busy. There were many Chinese junks in the river at that time. Of course, the river doesn't look the same now with all the modern and expensive yachts.

Our group was taken to a place where we would be able to have clothes made and they would be delivered to our hotel later or the next day. Upon returning to the bus, everyone was trying to find out what the others had purchased. There was a lady in our group who was extremely obese. When asked what she purchased she relayed her experience there. She said that she went into the little room to be measured. One little guy took the measuring tape as far as he could and his friend picked up where he left off. While this was happening, they were giggling. So she said that the only material that they had enough of to make an outfit for her was a bright gold color and she declined because she thought people would mistake her for a Buddha.

Our hotel in Singapore was very nice. I had heard about how clean the city was and it became obvious that the saying was true as I walked through the parking lot of the hotel and didn't see one piece of trash.

We were in the bar of the hotel one evening and they asked the overweight lady to sing. As it turned out, she had a wonderful voice and they tried to get her to stay and do a television show. Of course, she told them that she couldn't because of having to leave with the travel group and eventually returning to her hometown in the United States. Sydney was the next place on our agenda and I was really looking forward to seeing the Opera House. The Queen of England had just been there the year before for its opening. We went to a performance there.

We also went to the Taronga Zoo and I was able to see my first kangaroos and koalas. When we arrived at the area to view the kangaroos, we were somewhat embarrassed as three kangaroos were in the middle of a three-way affair! We didn't know whether to laugh or ignore it. Either way, we did have a big chuckle from our first views of the kangaroos. The koalas are a little bit more low-key in that they usually sit in a tree eating eucalyptus and get a lot of sleep.

Our next stop was in Auckland, New Zealand. In New Zealand we had a side trip to Rotorua where we were able to see the hot mud bubbling up from the earth along with the strong odor of sulfur. We also had occasion to visit the caverns with their glowworms.

The last stop of the tour was in Tahiti. Someone in our group had discovered through their preparations for visiting here that the airport landing could be hazardous. It seems that with the extreme humidity the runway can be overly slick and can cause a plane to slide. There isn't much room for error because of the short length of the runway. We were told that a plane had just gone off the end of the runway and into the ocean the week before we arrived!

We toured the island and saw the Gauguin Museum. The French painter lived in Tahiti for some time in the late nineteenth century. It was now time to head back to the airport and return home with many more memories from another successful learning adventure through travel.

For Christmas vacation in 1973, I chose a trip that included Las Vegas, Hawaii, and San Francisco. This particular trip offered a choice of hotels and one could choose from plan A, plan B, or plan C. There wasn't much difference in the prices, so I chose the most expensive one. I was glad I did because when we would arrive in a city, the people on plans B and C were dropped-off at their somewhat two-star hotels and then I would go to a much better one.

Strangely enough, I kept running into people that I knew. When mentioning this to a restaurant manager in Kauai, he told me that his mother was the manager of the restaurant where our group was going the next day. He called her and told her that a friend of his was going to be there the next day and explained to her what I looked like. Upon entering the restaurant, the manager exclaimed my name and of course the people in the group were in awe and couldn't believe that I had yet again come across someone that I knew.

Part of the summer of 1975 was spent going to Munich. My friend and I rented a car so that we would be able to drive to all of Ludwig's castles. In doing so, we were on the autobahn when suddenly the windshield began to crackle until it had covered the entire surface. We pulled to the side and discovered that just ahead was a service station. We made it to the service station by remaining on the far side of the road. I had to keep my head outside the window to be able to see where we were going. We explained to the service station attendant what had happened. He then was on the phone calling the rental company. As he didn't speak English; the only thing I understood in his entire conversation was "windshield caput." The rental company sent a driver out with another car. In addition to seeing all the castles, we were able to drive to Innsbruck, Garmisch-Partenkirchen, and Nuremberg. It was nice to see the area where the passion play is presented every ten years.

1976

Communist Bloc Countries

In 1976, I talked a friend of mine into going with me on a trip to all the communist bloc countries in Europe. The United States was getting ready to celebrate its two hundredth anniversary and I said that the best was for us to appreciate our freedom would be to go to all these countries. We celebrated the anniversary on the mall in Washington, D. C, next to the Jefferson Memorial and enjoyed the fireworks display. The crowd for the celebration was estimated to be approximately two million people.

We departed the next morning for Prague. We enjoyed seeing all the sights of Prague including the Jewish cemetery, the cathedral, the bridge, etc. There are, however, a couple of interesting stories associated with the trip. We saw a boat in the river that was being used as a hotel and we thought it would be nice to stay there. We inquired with the manager and he told us that we would have to go to the central part of town where the government had an office that would tell us what was available. At first, they told us that it was not possible because the hotel didn't have any rooms available. We told them that they did because we were just there and the gentleman told us that they did, but we would have to come here to make the arrangements. After several minutes of haggling, we were able to convince them and were able to move to that hotel for the next evening. The main reason one is told that there are no rooms is because they don't want to do the paperwork involved.

On a tour of the city, one of the members of the group asked the guide what was the policy in their country if a person wanted to travel to another country. The guide contemplated for a minute and answered that one can not leave the country until they are sixty-five years old and then the government doesn't care if you leave.

We took a train from Prague through Bratislava to Vienna. This was my second time in Vienna and I began to realize how much I liked to visit this beautiful city. There is so much to see and do here.

Our trip continued by train from Vienna to Budapest. We noticed as we were traveling along on the train that there were a lot of barbed-wire fences along the sides of the tracks. In preparing for the trip, we knew that certain places were forbidden to take pictures and we tried to obey these rules as much as possible. Of course, we didn't want to stay there longer than we had planned!

In walking around the city of Budapest, we would have young people coming up to us to find out where we were from. We really enjoyed seeing the Parliament House, the old city, Fisherman's Bastion, and St Stephen's Basilica. We were able to visit one of the elaborate Turkish baths while there.

The next stop in Belgrade was an experience in patience. Upon an early arrival after an overnight train ride, we approached the office for hotel accommodations to discover that no one in the office spoke English. However, there were two young boys there who were children of an American military personnel stationed nearby and were able to interpret for us. We were extremely grateful to them.

After we were settled into our room at the hotel, we went to the front office to inquire about the possibility of doing a city tour. We were told that they didn't handle that at this particular hotel and that we should go out of the hotel to the right, make a right turn at the corner, and there would be another hotel just down the way there that would be glad to help us. We went there and were told that they didn't do it, but that if we went up the street, turned left, there would be a hotel there that would help us. We told them that those were the people who sent us to them.

Now, they told us that we should go on a local tram to the center of the city. There was a tourist office that would be able to accommodate us. Upon arriving there, we saw an airline office and decided to go there and see if it were possible to get a flight to Dubrovnik. We were told, of course, that all the flights were filled and that would be impossible. So we went to the central tourist office and were told on the first floor that we should go to the third floor. Then, the third floor people told us that we should go across the street to a hotel and that there would be a gentleman in the lobby there who would be able to assist us. We were in luck! We discovered that the gentleman there at the tourist information desk had lived in the United States for several years and had come back to visit his family when he discovered that he then was not able to leave the country. We explained to him what we wanted and he assured us that he could do it. We came back to him the next morning and he had us an appointment for our city tour, flights to Dubrovnik, and a hotel in Dubrovnik! We asked him why we were sent from place to place. His response was that any of those people we came in contact with are being paid a set income for the month. If they book one city tour or if they book one hundred, they get paid the same thing.

Ordering food in a foreign country can prove to be a challenge with menus written in another language. Sometimes, it is easier just to be able to point to the plate of another diner and just say, "I'll have that." We went to an upscale restaurant in Belgrade for lunch. The waiters were in tuxedos and the menu was extensive—about ten pages. We were the only ones in the restaurant. What do we do! I finally pointed to several items and said that we will have two of each. When the waiter left the table, I looked at my friend and said, "Guess what's coming to dinner?"

Before we left for this trip, I tried to forewarn my friend that there would be times that one would just want to scream because things just do not happen logically. This was based upon my experiences in being in the Soviet Union prior to this trip. If one thinks about how illogical something could be, they seem to be able to go a few steps pass that. We also looked at this as a learning experience because if we had been part of an organized tour group, we probably would have never seen this side of their existence.

We enjoyed our stay in Dubrovnik. It is such a beautiful city and one is able to absorb so much more of the city by being able to walk everywhere! Our hotel had a small balcony that overlooked the Adriatic.

We met a couple guys there from the United States. We made plans to go to dinner together that evening. We went to a local restaurant in the central part of the city. We ordered drinks and the waiter asked if there was anything else we needed at the time. We told him that we would like more ice. He went away and returned with a big bowl of rice. We tried to explain that we didn't want rice, but we wanted more ice. He indicated that he really understood now and promptly returned with yet another bowl of rice. We gave up on that and just ordered dinner.

The guys had a rental car and we were invited to drive with them down the coast to Kotor the next day, which turned out to be a pleasant surprise with its natural beauty.

We flew back to Belgrade and connected to a flight that would take us to Sophia, Bulgaria. We arrived there late in the evening. On the way from the airport we were asked if we would like to exchange money on the black market. We decided that that would not be a good idea. We were taken to the office to make hotel arrangements. The lady there tried to get us to exchange money and we denied her offer also. She was able to get us a hotel nearby. We went out on to the street and tried to hail a taxi to take us to the hotel. We finally gave up and walked there through a park with our entire luggage. We later found out that taxis do not stop as they do in the United States. One must make a reservation for one.

Upon arriving at the hotel, we were asked for the voucher and our passports. Both of us were tired and my friend took a shower. I decided that, that was not a bad idea and did the same. When I came out of the shower, my friend was asleep and I thought that it was too early to go to bed. I left the hotel and went for a walk. When I returned to the hotel later, my friend was in the lobby with our entire luggage. I asked him why he was there and he explained to me that just after I left the front desk called and told him that we were in the wrong hotel. He wouldn't leave until I had returned. The taxi took us to another hotel, but not nearly as nice as the other one. The elevator only stopped on the even floors. Our room was on the third floor. We had to take the elevator to the second floor and walk up or take the elevator to the fourth floor and walk down. The room, however, was very large and had several chairs and sofas distributed all around. We were able to sightsee on our own.

I can remember that there were these big wide streets and almost no cars on them. It made it convenient for crossing the street. We were there long enough to see most of the city and then it was time to head back to the airport and fly to Bucharest, Romania.

After obtaining a voucher for our hotel and finding it, we decided to take the tram to the city center and try to find out what there was to see and do in the city at that time. We were told that the Moscow Circus was in town. We got on a tram to take us there. On the way the tram hit another and we had to wait and then get on another one. When we arrived at the arena where we were told the circus would be, it was closed. We tried to find someone who spoke English to find out why it was closed. We were told that the circus had already been there and that there was nothing happening there now. So we got on a tram to return to our hotel. This tram caught on fire and we had to take another back to our hotel. Yes, we were beginning to understand why we were making this trip. It was to make us appreciate where we lived and our freedom. It was in Bucharest that we had another interesting happening with our food order. We both ordered steak. When the order came to the table, we discovered that my plate had steak and my friend's plate had liver. Since my friend detests liver, we just exchanged plates and life goes on.

The train from Bucharest traveled north to the border of Russia. We entered from Ungheni (that is now part of Moldova) to Iasi (the Trans-Dniester, but then it was considered part of Russia). While the gauge of the train was regulated for the tracks in Russia, the customs official came on board to check our passports and belongings. The friend that I was traveling with was a pharmacist and had packed all the medications he thought we might need in a tennis shoe. The customs official, who didn't speak much English, picked up the shoe, looked at it and said, "Shoe very sick."

The train from there to Odessa was a local train with wooden seats. The weather was quite hot and all the windows were open. It wasn't long into the trip that we saw all these people eating cherries and spitting the seeds out the window. We thought that was a little crude. However, a few minutes later when they offered cherries to us, we began doing the same thing and it just felt natural. It's amazing how easily one adjusts.

We arrived in Odessa and made our way to our hotel. We had to leave our passports with the clerk at the front desk and were told that we could pick them up later. When I went to retrieve mine, the lady kept going through them and didn't seem to be able to find mine. She made a gesture using both hands up above her head in a circular motion asking me if I had curled my hair. It was then that I realized that the picture in my passport had been taken a few years prior, when my hair was naturally straight. Now, it was curly with a perm. Then she found it.

We spent the first day walking all over the city and enjoying sights like the beautiful opera house. The second day we went to the beach. It was the time in the summer when all the people were having their vacations. The beach was literally packed with people of all ages and sizes. Some of the bikini swim suits were not very flattering, to say the least.

There was a big fireworks show the evening we were leaving and we decided it was definitely for us. We had an overnight train from Odessa to Kiev. We were quite surprised that we were to be sharing our compartment with two ladies. Since they didn't speak any English and we didn't speak any Russian there was a lot of gesturing in order to communicate. I gestured that my friend and myself would sleep on the two top bunks and that they could sleep on the two bottom ones. They understood and nodded approval. The next morning the ladies left the room to go down the corridor to the restroom.

We got up and went to our restroom to freshen up, and got ready to arrive in Kiev. When we all four arrived back at our compartment, there was a lot of nodding and smiling. I could only assume that they were employees of Intourist and were there to make sure that they knew where we were.

Kiev proved to be a nice stop and we enjoyed seeing all the onion-shaped gold domes on the churches, the university, and other buildings of interest.

Ordering food from a menu written in the Russian Cyrillic alphabet can become a challenge. On this day, I just pointed in the menu and said that we would have two of these. My friend asked me what I thought we were going to have and I said, "I think we are going to have a shish kabob." And we did!

The only hotel available for us in Moscow, when we were making our plans, was the National Hotel at the end of Red Square. The hotel was exquisite with an over abundance of gold leaf, oriental carpets on the stairs, chandeliers, etc. We had a suite that consisted of a living area, a dressing room, a bedroom, and a large bath. We were instructed when we checked in that included with our room was a sightseeing trip for four hours each day and the use of a limousine for four hours each day. One day, we had chosen to take the limousine to the Archangel's Palace outside the city. As we were approaching, there were people coming up to the vehicle to see who was inside. We felt like royalty.

We found out that there was to be a performance of a ballet of Carmen, while we were there at the Kremlin Palace Theater. We went there without a ticket. However, we were able to find people there who had tickets and wanted to get rid of them. We paid $1 just like the Bolshoi in 1971.

This was the first time in Russia for my traveling partner and he was intent upon having borscht. As we were walking around the city, we discovered a buffet! Voila! We could actually see what we were ordering! He was able to get his borscht here.

We took the train from Moscow. However, this time it was in the daytime as opposed to the overnight that I hadin 1971. We stayed at the Leningrad Hotel, which was the same one I had stayed in in 1971. We were in awe by visiting the Hermitage museum, the many churches, and the palaces of the tsars. Based upon our learning experiences along the way and the communist way of doing things, it explained why most of the guards in the museums were asleep.

We had planned to take the train from Leningrad to Warsaw. However, in checking further we discovered that it was a twenty-four-hour train ride. By flying to Warsaw instead we would save an entire day. So we flew to Warsaw.

It is easy to decipher that this city was part of the communist bloc by the architecture of the "wedding cake" buildings, the lack of advertisements, and the overall drabness of the city. At night it was pitch dark because there were no signs illuminated. Why should there be when everything is owned and operated by the government.

We were on our way to breakfast on our last day there and we decided to go across the street to the railway station and get our train tickets for Berlin first and then come back and have breakfast. Bad idea! We arrived around 8:30 a.m. and were instructed to go to counter four. We got in line and waited. I would stand in line for about fifteen minutes and then my friend would stand in line for fifteen minutes. At ten o'clock we finally made it to the front of the line. However, just as we approached the window the lady who was working there decided it was time for her tea break. She left the window and sat at a small table and was completely oblivious to the fact that at that time there were at least forty people standing in her line. Finally, she approached the window and began speaking in Polish. We asked if she spoke English and the answer was no. We were sent to the gentleman at the door where we had entered. He accompanied us back to window four and interpreted. It was then that we discovered that we had to pay for the ticket up to the border in Polish currency and the other part in a foreign currency. This required us to leave momentarily and make a visit to the bank next door. When we finally finished our train ticket purchase, it was 12:30 p.m. It had taken us four hours to purchase a train ticket! I said, "When I go home, I am going to tell all the Polish jokes I want to and if someone says that I shouldn't—I will just say for them to go there and find out for themselves." Needless to say, we didn't have breakfast that day.

We shared the overnight train compartment with a lady and her daughter. Things were going all right until the daughter had an epileptic seizure. Later, she had yet another. I went to see if I could find someone to help. Finally, a worker from the train was there talking to the lady. Even though it was in Polish, by the tone in their voices, it was as though they were saying, "Poor thing." My friend, the pharmacist, said that this is what happens when you have free medicine. It usually means no medicine.

We almost missed our stop in Berlin. If we had gone to the next one, we would have been back in East Germany and that could have created yet another problem. We got off the train and took a taxi to our hotel. It was exciting being in Berlin and seeing the Brandenburg Gate, going through Checkpoint Charlie, etc.

After six grueling weeks of travel, we were anxious to get to Amsterdam and spend a week and do nothing but eat, relax, and be ready to return to the United States.

1977-1979

The United States

Sometimes it is good to take a little break from international travel and see parts of the United States that I haven't seen before. Most of 1977 was spent traveling to different sections of the states.

The year started out by driving to Philadelphia to see the Mummers Parade. Of course, knowing my luck, the parade was cancelled because of high winds. They were able to have it the following day. Other cities visited during the year, included New York for theater, Milwaukee to see the Midwest, Seattle to see the northwest, and Atlanta to see relatives.

This year for Christmas, I went to Puerto Rico. I also spent some time in California and Cape Cod this year. I went to Provincetown on Cape Cod for a week each year for about ten years. It is a great place to get away from the hustle and bustle of the daily grind. For Christmas of 1978, it was time to return to Rio. This time instead of staying in Copacabana Beach, I stayed in Ipanema.

For spring break in 1979, a teacher friend of mine and I went to Texas. We were able to fly down on the Concorde. At that time, Air France had a flight that flew into Dulles Airport outside Washington, D. C. Then, it changed to a Braniff flight and flew to Texas. I feel fortunate to have been able to fly on that plane, since it has since been taken out of service. We rented a car and were able to be in Dallas, Austin, and Houston.

The most memorable experience of that trip was the flood in Houston! We had theater tickets for the evening. We decided to go to a French restaurant for dinner that was near the theater. That way we could just walk to the theater afterward.

As we were progressing through our meal, the rain became much more intense. It was then that we noticed through the window next to our table that the people who were getting off the local bus were having to jump from the bus to get up to the sidewalk because of the water that had already accumulated in the street. The water kept coming up across the sidewalk and was actually approaching our window.

I told my friend that I was going to ask the waiter for a garbage bag in which we could put our shoes. My friend felt that it would be rude to ask a waiter in a French restaurant for a garbage bag, however, I didn't intend on wading through water with shoes on when I could avoid that situation.

We moved the car to a spot that was higher than any other spot we could find. When we arrived at the theater we saw employees with brooms trying to sweep the water out of the theater.

Several of the performers were unable to get to the theater. We were, however, invited in and those actors who had made it to the theater sang and did comedy routines, while we were served free champagne.

After about an hour, we decided to try to get back to the car. By this time the water in the street was already about knee-deep and rowboats were going down the street. Now, I was really glad that I had my shoes in the bag. We went into a bar for a drink and all the customers were barefoot and either had on shorts or had their pants rolled up above their knees.

We started driving to find our way back to the hotel, in a city in which we were unfamiliar. We drove two or three blocks down one street and found out that it was a dead-end street. By this time, there were two or three cars following us thinking that we knew where we were going. We got some strange looks from them as we started to retrace our way back to the main street.

We finally abandoned the car in a strip mall parking lot and walked from there back to the hotel. The sign in front of our hotel was on the national news the next night.

Needless to say, the car didn't smell any too fresh the next few days. That was my only visit to Houston, but it sure was one that I won't forget.

1979

Ireland, Wales, Scotland, and England

In August of 1979, I flew to Ireland with a friend. We started in Shannon on the west coast. After picking up the rental car, we first visited Bunratty Castle. Then, we drove through Tralee and continued toward Dingle Bay where we had reservations for a stay in a B and B.

On our way it seemed that the road kept getting narrower and narrower and the corn fields seemed to keep getting closer and closer. Finally, we saw a little store and decided to stop and show them the map and ask for directions. We asked the lady about the highway that circled this area, which we were hoping to drive and she replied, "Well, they keep putting that road on the map, but they have never gotten around to building it." We turned around and proceeded with plan B.

We finally arrived at the B and B in Dingle. It was a nice place; however, we didn't expect it to be as cold as it was. The blankets felt really good. After we left there we drove through Killarney, the Ring of Kerry, and on to the city of Cork.

We had told the gentleman at the airport at the car rental office where we would be driving. One of his suggestions was that when we were in Cork, we had to drive up into the hills and see the upscale resort that was there. Just after we arrived at the resort, we saw a large group of people on the veranda getting ready for a big group picture. This family was celebrating their fiftieth anniversary and there were people there from Europe, the United States, and Australia. A lady in the group spotted my camera with a long lens on it and asked if I would take some pictures of the group. It seems that they had just discovered that they had no film! (Now, I guess I'll have to start telling Irish jokes) I agreed and took several pictures. Since this was before the integration of digital cameras, I had the pictures developed and mailed her the pictures and the negatives so she could have additional ones made. I received an Irish woolen tie from her every year for Christmas for several years. These are truly the things that happen, when you travel that stay with you forever.

We stayed at Longfield House Hotel outside Cashel. The view from our room was overlooking a large pasture with cattle grazing. There was a pub in the basement, where the locals came to sing and have a pint or two. My friend and I were invited to join in with them and it was another memorable evening.

No one can visit Ireland without a visit to Blarney Castle and the Blarney Stone. Yes, we did climb up to the top and kissed the stone. We continued on and did a tour of the Waterford factory. It was fascinating to go through the factory and see how the items were made. It was also exciting to stroll through the gift shop and admire all of the items there. After having just seen how the items are made, it made you really appreciate their value.

We drove through Wexford and finally arrived in Dublin. After two or three days there, we took the ferry to Wales. There we picked up another rental car and drove to Ruthin. We stayed in Ruthin Castle, which was a real treat. There was a Renaissance Dinner in the lower level of the castle in which we participated. There was a Jewish couple sitting across the table from us who had just been married. We were eating with our fingers and the new bride said, "If my mother saw this, she would s . . . !"

The day we left Wales, we had a long drive. We drove through the countryside to Liverpool and on to Windermere in the Lake District. We spent an entire day just driving around the area. I wasn't aware how mountainous the area was. Since rain can happen in this area at any time, one is able to spot beautiful rainbows.

The next leg of the journey was the drive from the Lake District to Edinburgh. We didn't realize that we were going to be there during their annual festival. Therefore, nearly every room in the city was taken. We were finally able to find a B and B, a few miles outside the city. We were quite surprised the next morning to see the husband of the couple standing at the stove preparing the breakfast while using crutches. Yes, he had been grass skiing and had broken his leg just a few days prior to our visit. He cooked and his wife served.

We were fortunate in getting tickets for the military tatoo, which is one of the highlights of the festival. It is difficult to find the words to describe this affair. My camera really got a workout here.

On the way to Inverness, we were able to see Balmoral Castle, the home of the Queen. Along the highway were fields of heather all in bloom. After a day of sightseeing in that area, it was time to head south.

We stopped at Loch Ness to see if we could spot the monster—we didn't! When driving in Ireland, Wales, England, and Scotland, it is rare to be able to drive for a mile or two without seeing a castle. One is excited to see them at first and then after a week or two, you just looked and say to yourself that there is yet another castle. We did stop to see Inveraray Castle, the home of the Duke of Argyll.

Our next overnight was in Glasgow. Our hotel was in the center of the city that made it convenient for walking around sightseeing, choosing a restaurant for dinner, etc.

From Glasgow we drove through York, where we took the tour that allowed us to go to the top of the cathedral and see the city from there. In Stratford-upon-Avon, we toured the Anne Hathaway's cottage. In Bath, we were able to see the famous baths. From Bath we drove past Stonehenge, saw Salisbury Cathedral, and spent the night in Rye.

Rye is a quaint little town and in our early morning walk we were surprised to see little signs in front of the houses to let the milkman know how many quarts of milk to leave that day. We were tempted to change some of them, but our better judgment took over.

Today was to be the day that we were finally going to see the white cliffs of Dover. However, the one thing that I remember more vividly than anything else was the fact that I locked the keys in the car. Of course, in today's world, one would just take out their cell phone and call. This was 1979 and cell phones had not been thought of. We were able to get to a place and have them call the rental company and they came and opened the car.

On our way from Dover to London, we were able to stop in Canterbury and toured the cathedral there. We arrived in London and it was a pleasure after all the days and days of driving (on the other side) to turn the car in and just walk everywhere. It was also comforting to know that we had driven all that and had not had an accident.

The friend I was traveling with had never been to London. He had heard all the stories about London and the rain and the fog. Well, he was pleasantly surprised to be able to be there for an entire week and it was sunny every day.

1980

Greek Islands Tour, Egypt, and Morocco

In April of 1980, I took a Greek island cruise on the Stella Solaris. The cruise originated in Athens. My travel partner and I arrived in Athens a few days before the cruise was to begin. In touring the city with my friend, we were approached by a person wanting to take us to a nightclub. Voila! Here we go again! This had never happened to my friend and he wasn't aware of the outcome. I attempted to explain to him what was about to happen, but he insisted upon going. I told him that he could go and I would see him later. In about ten or fifteen minutes later, he came rushing out of the establishment. He couldn't believe what was happening and my only comment was—"I tried to tell you."

The cruise left Athens at the Piraeus port. The first stop on the cruise was at Dikili in Turkey. As is usual on many cruises, one has but a few hours to do some basic sightseeing and then it is time to return to the ship and be on the way to the next stop. The next stop in this case was Istanbul. Being here again brought back memories as to why I was here the first time. That, of course, was when I couldn't go to Egypt from Israel in 1968 and came here instead. My friend and I went out on our own for the day and took in the Blue Mosque, the Topkapi museum, and the covered bazaar.

The cruise progressed from Istanbul to Kusadasi, Ephesus, Rhodes, Lindos, Santorini, Mykonos, and back to Athens. We had some time for shopping in Kusadasi, toured the ruins in Ephesus, took the donkey ride from the shore to the top in Santorini, and witnessed the abundance of the strange windmills in Mykonos.

My annual summer Christmas party took place in July. A longtime friend of mine and I left a few days later and spent a week in Toronto. While there, we were trying to decide where to have dinner one evening. We looked in the yellow pages of the telephone directory and discovered that there was a restaurant nearby that served rijstaffel. This is an Indonesian dish whereby you are served many different kinds of food. We both had this meal in Amsterdam, but not together, and decided that it would be nice to have it together. In fact, when my friend had his in Amsterdam, he sent me a post card with a picture of the meal and wrote on the card that this meal would just be a snack for me!

We were at the restaurant and were sitting at a table with all the food in front of us, when another party came through and marveled at all the many food dishes in front of us. Later, the same party came through and marveled yet again that all the dishes previously filled with food were clean! Bon Appetite!

Canada had a national holiday one day while we were there. All the stores and places of interest were to be closed. We decided that this would be a perfect day to take a tour to Niagara Falls. While there, I picked up a few post cards of Niagara Falls covered with snow and hurriedly wrote them to send back to friends in Washington. Since the week before had been Christmas (in July) in Washington, this would have figuratively been New Year. Thus, the greeting on the cards said that we were spending New Year in Niagara Falls.

By December of 1980, I was ready to journey to Egypt. It just so happened that my travel agent had just booked another client to go to Egypt who was traveling alone. We agreed to travel together and save the single supplement. Our flight was to go through Rome to Athens and then on to Cairo. There was a strike of aviation workers in Rome and our flight was delayed. This meant that by the time we arrived in Athens, our scheduled flight had already departed. We had deplaned and were waiting to find out what was going to happen. We were instructed to get back on the same plane that we had been on since it was also going to Cairo. Our only concern was what would happen to our luggage. We were assured that our luggage would be put back on the plane and that we had nothing to worry about. Wrong!

Upon arriving at the airport in Cairo, we had about ninety people filling out lost luggage forms. So here we were in Egypt without any luggage. After a couple days, I went back to the airport to talk to someone who could try to tell me when we could expect the luggage to arrive. I was sent into the basement of the terminal. I couldn't believe it. It was just like a small city with dirt streets under the airport terminal and each block was enclosed with a wire fence. In walking through, believe it or not, I saw one of my pieces of luggage! By leaving the main terminal, I then had to go through customs again.

While touring, my two friends and I wore the same clothes for several days. After seeing the sights in Abu Simbel, we were in Aswan for a day. We were walking along and discovered a street sale. We found the essentials of underwear, socks, and toothpaste. We each also bought a gallibaya, the traditional long shirt worn by the Egyptians. When we showed up for dinner that night, we were a hit! Our other touring friends exclaimed at how fresh and clean we looked and smelled.

Our four-day Nile cruise took us to Kom Ombo, Esna, and Edfu. I had said that when I retired, I hoped to write a book including all the dumb questions that I had encountered in traveling, especially when in a group. I think that probably the best one came here when we were touring one of the temples. Our guide went out of his way to explain their religion and showed us where their god, the crocodile, lived. He also explained the hieroglyphics. He kept reiterating that this was two thousand years ago, that this was over two thousand years before Christ, etc. At the end of the tour, he asked if there were any questions and a lady from New York asked if these people were Christian! I could just see the guide wanting to hit his head up against the wall. Duh!

Our cruise terminated in Luxor. We went to the sound and light show there and it was one of the highlights of my traveling experiences. All of my life I had heard the term "another civilization," but it wasn't until I was sitting and listening to the commentary of this sound and light show that I then realized what another civilization really meant.

While walking down the main street in Luxor, I saw a large banner hanging across the street announcing an international rowing competition that was being held there. The son of a fellow worker had participated in the Olympics and I wondered if he might be there. I went into the adjacent hotel and asked if he were staying there. They looked at their register and said that he was. I asked if I could see him. A gentleman from the front desk escorted me to his room. Upon opening the door, he saw me standing there and couldn't believe it. Of course, when I returned from the trip, his mother couldn't believe that I had actually seen her son in Egypt.

The last night in Egypt was to be spent going to the sound and light show at the Pyramids. During that last day, I got the concierge at the hotel to make a telephone call to the airline office. He explained to them my dilemma regarding the other piece of luggage and that if I had not received my luggage by the time I returned from the sound and light show that I would be calling the tourism office of Egypt and reporting the situation. The threat evidently worked because when I arrived back at the hotel my other piece of luggage was sitting in the room. The one lesson I learned from this experience is that I always include an itinerary along with the names of hotels, etc. and have it in my checked luggage. I learned that the piece of luggage that had been missing had been from Athens to Cairo, back to Athens, to Rome, New York, back to Rome, Athens, and finally back to Cairo.

A friend of mine had arrived from the states and was going to accompany me for the remainder of the trip. We flew from Cairo through Tunis and Algiers to Casablanca. We spent a couple days in Casablanca sightseeing. We were trying to find a particular place and couldn't seem to find it on the small city map. I saw a policeman standing in the median between two heavily traveled streets. I asked if he spoke English and he said no. I tried to slowly ask him for the directions in my broken French. He consequently responded slowly as well, and strangely enough, I understood him. As we were walking away, my friend asked me, "Where did that come from?" and my response was, "high school French."

We went to pick up a rental car to use in driving around the country. We were asked if we needed a map. The gentleman showed us a very large map and said that it costs $5. We looked at the map and saw that 95 percent of the map was the Sahara Desert. Thus, we decided to forgo that and just try our luck. We drove then to Rabat, Meknes, Fez, Marrakesh, Agadir, and back to Casablanca.

In Rabat, we saw the presidential palace. That evening we had a traditional Moroccan dinner that was not only good, but extremely filling. There was so much of it that we hardly slept all night. We were so full we couldn't breathe!

We had driven from Rabat through Meknes to Fez. It had begun to get dark and we couldn't figure where the switch was for the lights in the rental car. We pulled into a service station and were asked if we wanted gas. We said no—we just want to learn how to turn on the lights in the car.

The electricity went out in the hotel in Fez that night. It was quite cold. Therefore, all the guests in the hotel gathered in the lobby where there was a big fire in the fireplace.

The next day while driving to Marrakesh, we noticed that in the higher parts there was snow. We stopped at an outdoor place to eat along the side of the road. There were pots cooking in the open air. We were told what each pot contained lamb, beef, or chicken. We chose one and sat at the outside table and had our lunch. These are the kinds of stories one relates to friends upon the return from a vacation and the first question is "and you didn't get sick!" Evidently, my stomach is made of iron because in all of my traveling I have been very lucky.

While we would be driving from one city to another, we would see many concrete obelisks along the road with arrows offering directions. These signs were written in Arabic and we would just look at them and say, "Why don't we just go this way?" It worked because we made our complete circle of the country without a map.

From Marrakesh we drove up into the Atlas Mountains, where we were able to see some of the Nubian people and where they live. From the top, the view was spectacular since you were looking into the Sahara Desert.

We drove to the coastal area of Agadir and spent some time on the beach. Then, it was time to head back to Casablanca and catch our flight back to the States.

1981

Arizona, New Mexico, and Hawaii

Spring break in 1981 was spent driving around Arizona and New Mexico with a fellow teacher. We went for a long jog on our first morning there. After both of us had showered, shaved, etc., we were off to the restaurant in the hotel for breakfast. I was looking over at the other side of the restaurant and saw a waitress that looked familiar. I mentioned it to my friend but he reminded me that we were about two thousand miles away from home. However, the waitress approached our table a few minutes later and gasped as she called my name. Yes, it was one of my former students! It is a small world after all.

The aunt of a very good friend lived outside Phoenix and I got in touch with her after arriving. She invited the friend of mine and me to join her the next day at her country club. She was elderly (in her late 80s), yet she still enjoyed driving her Chevrolet convertible that was at least twenty years old. We traveled to the country club with the top down. It was about 110 degrees. They always comment about how they have dry heat. I don't care if it is dry or not—it was still hot!

We drove through the desert area where we could see the large twenty-five-foot tall cacti on our way to Old Tucson. It reminded me of the scenes that we always saw when we would watch *the Lone Ranger, Hopalong Cassidy* as a kid.

My friend had an affinity for airplanes and had taken flying lessons. We went to the Pima Air and Space museum near Tucson. There are over 250 airplanes there on an area of more than 150 acres. My friend was ecstatic to say the least. The justification for choosing this area was the fact that it seldom rains here and the planes were not as likely to rust. I can only think of how many pictures he would have taken if it had been thirty years later with the introduction of the digital camera.

We continued driving across Arizona and into New Mexico until we were able to veer off and see El Paso, Texas. We knew we were definitely in cattle country when the waitperson at the restaurant brought a large tray of uncooked steaks to our table for us to choose which one we would like for dinner.

We were able to walk across the border there into Juarez, Mexico. With all the problems now related to the drug situation it is much more difficult to do and it is much more dangerous.

Our next stop was Albuquerque, New Mexico. There we were able to include a visit to Santa Fe. We enjoyed the smallness of this quant city and the adobe color of the buildings.

The first highlight upon arriving back into Arizona was the visit to the Petrified Forest National Park. Here the fossils date back to two hundred million years. It was definitely "another Kodak moment."

While driving west, not far from here, we stopped near Winslow to see one of the most famous craters in the world. It is almost two and a half miles in circumference and about 550 feet deep.

Both these stops help to build up the excitement for our next stop that we both had been looking forward to and that was the Grand Canyon. We were at the South Rim.

It was a thrill to finally see it in reality after having seen so many pictures of it through the years. It isn't possible to capture the enormity of the place and give it the justice it deserves through pictures. You have to see it to believe it.

Now it was time to drive back to Phoenix through the Red Rock Country with its many rock formations. This excursion had come to an end, but the memories of it will linger on forever.

This year was brought to a close by returning to Hawaii for Christmas. Several other friends were planning to be there, which made it much more meaningful.

1982

New York, Mid West, and Caribbean Cruise

Visiting friends in New York started off the 1982 year. While there, we were able to attend several Broadway plays and an opera. Soon after, it was time to head south and visit relatives in Georgia.

My niece was living in Denver at this time. In July, I flew out to visit. After a few days in Denver I rented a car and drove north through Casper, Wyoming, and saw the Black Hills National Park, the Custer statue under construction, and Mount Rushmore. I was able to see the state capitol building in Bismarck. I drove on to Minot for the evening. It was difficult finding accommodations since they were having their annual state fair here. I was able to find a room in an old hotel in the downtown area. I drove about sixty miles east of Minot and dropped in on the parents of a good friend who lived in the Washington area. I continued south from there through Nebraska and back to Denver.

While visiting in Denver, my sister from Georgia came to visit at the same time. We had sort of a family reunion since it was I, my sister, my niece and her husband, and my grandniece. In Colorado, we visited so many wonderful places in the state including the Royal Gorge and the Red Rock outdoor theater. We then did a large circle tour as we drove through the Grand Teton mountains; Yellowstone National Park; Jackson Hole, Wyoming; Butte, Montana; Pocatello, Idaho; and Salt Lake City, Utah.

In Jackson Hole, Wyoming, there was another "small world story." While standing there to watch the evening shoot out in the main town square, I looked across and saw another teacher from the same school where I taught. I said to my family, "I just saw someone I know, I'll be right back." They said, "We are not surprised because it seems that no matter where you go you always run into someone you know."

In December, I went to Puerto Rico with a friend and we took a Caribbean cruise. We went to Aruba, Curacao, Caracas, Grenada, and Martinique. Highlights of this cruise would be the colorful houses in Curacao, the volcano sight in Martinique, and the various herbs and spices in Grenada.

While we were driving around the island of Grenada, we would notice, for example, a new highway. We asked our guide about it and his reply was that it was being built by "them" (meaning the communist). We also saw trucks parked in the middle of the street. We asked why they would leave it in the middle of the street. His answer was that this was their way of letting us know they are here. Fortunately, a few years later the United States took care of that problem.

This cruise was my last big fling for a while, since I had just found out that I had been accepted to a graduate school where I would be able to transfer my graduate credits and by attending for two summers be able to complete my dissertation.

1983 and 1984

St. Louis, Missouri, Acapulco, and Florida

In June, I left for St. Louis and was there until August taking classes and meeting with my mentor to begin the preparations of my dissertation.

My niece and her husband from Colorado came to visit one weekend while I was there. The weekend they visited coincided with the Miss Universe pageant and the contestants were staying at the same hotel that the school was using for its students. On Sunday morning, we were leaving early to go sightseeing. One of the contestants was in the elevator wearing her nightgown. She had curlers in her hair and was carrying an iron. Even at this hour of the morning and dressed like that—she was wearing her sash and her tiara. I suppose it is the rule!

The students in the school decided to do a pool similar to those for the super bowl as to who would win Miss Universe. My roommate drew Reunion. He said that he didn't even know where Reunion was. We looked it up and discovered that it was a small island in the Indian Ocean. We were fortunate enough during that time to meet the contestant from Reunion. She let us know that there were more people in the hotel we were in than there was in her country.

Our first stop on our sightseeing endeavor was the famous Saint Louis Arch. We had entered the ticket entrance for the arch and while we were waiting to get our tickets, I spotted two coworkers. They were as surprised to see me as I was. A person must be on their best behavior at all times because you just never know who or when you are going meet someone you know.

I ended the year by going to Acapulco for a week with several friends. It was really great to get away and forget about the studies for a few days. Being the Christmas person that I am—I had taken several items with me. The maids in the hotel couldn't believe that the room had lights around the headboard of the bed, a macramé tree with lights on the wall, and lights on the balcony. They went to get all the other maids and brought them to our room to see what we had done. Feliz Navidad!

In January of 1984, I went to Florida to attend the Super Bowl between the Washington Redskins and the Oakland Raiders. It was a wonderful experience even though we lost the game. I had never seen them play so badly. I don't think they completed one play that was right!

I was back in St. Louis for another summer. After I completed my oral exams and was told that I would be graduating, I decided that it was time to celebrate by having a Christmas party. I had taken some Christmas decorations with me just in case. The lady at the hotel looked a little puzzled when I went to her and asked if it would be possible to get a Christmas tree. It was July after all! She found one though and we were able to have a tree. I invited several other students and they couldn't believe their eyes when they saw that the suite at the hotel had Christmas lights around the entrance door, a Christmas tree with lights, Christmas music, and there were Christmas goodies to accompany the drinks.

With my advance graduate degree out of the way, I was ready to fling open the travel doors again.

1985

Alaska and Hawaii

In the summer of 1985, I took a cruise to Alaska. It left from Vancouver and traveled the inner passage to Ketchikan, Sitka, and Juneau. I took a helicopter ride to the Mendenhall Glacier, where we were able to get out and walk on the glacier. It is about twelve miles outside of Juneau. Juneau happens to be the only United States capital that is not approachable by automobile.

With all the food one is confronted with on a cruise I had decided that I should spend some time in the gym. While there, I met the lady who worked in the gift shop. She asked me if I was a veteran cruiser. I told her that I had been on a Rhine river cruise, a Nile cruise, a Caribbean cruise, a fjords cruise, and a Greek island cruise. She then interrupted me and said, "Yes, you are a veteran cruiser."

There were about eighty Australians on the cruise. One lady from Australia heard about my having Christmas parties in the summertime and she said that she was so glad to see that someone else celebrated Christmas in the summertime like they did.

We left the ship in Skagway and took a bus through the Yukon Territory to Dawson. My seatmate for the bus ride was from Paris, France. She spoke just about as many words of English and I did in French. We did try to communicate as much as possible. I asked her if she had been to the United States before and she said yes. I asked where she had visited and the first word was "ca-lor-a-doo" with emphasis on the last syllable. Needless to say that ever since that occasion, every time I hear the word "Colorado," I think of her.

From there we drove west into Alaska and had our first stop in Tok Junction. Upon checking into the room at the hotel, I swatted about ten extremely large mosquitoes, which are called the national birds of Alaska. We were given a dogsled demonstration that evening near our hotel.

On our way to Fairbanks, we had a brief stop in North Pole, Alaska. Again, I had planned ahead. I knew that about two weeks after my arrival back home I would be having my summer Christmas party. That year the invitations were mailed from North Pole, Alaska.

Fairbanks was an interesting city. The first thing that most people think of when they hear Alaska is that it is cold. Well, in Fairbanks it was ninety degrees at almost 11:00 p.m. and the sun was still shining. I had never seen such huge flowers! With the sun being there for so many hours during the day, they just keep growing!

Upon entering Denali Park, our guide told us that we would not be able to see everything because the park is about the size of the state of Massachusetts. We did see quite a few animals; including caribou, big horn sheep, lambs, and moose.

On our drive from Denali to Anchorage, we were able to see Mt. McKinley. Our bus driver, who was a college student, did this for his summer job. He told us that his roommate had been doing this drive for two summers and had never seen the mountain because it was always fogged in. He was letting us know how fortunate we were to be here just once and it was crystal clear.

We toured Anchorage and then drove to Valdez. We were able to see the pipeline and the many glaciers that are in that area. We were on a boat ride to see the glaciers and there was a group of people who had joined us and they were so excited to see a mountain with snow on it and were takinga lot of pictures. We were wondering. "What could be so exciting about seeing a mountain with snow on it?" Then we realized that this was their first day in Alaska and they were acting just like we did on our first day.

Our trip came to an end and it was time to fly back to Seattle. I became aware of something at the airport there that I had not witnessed in any other place. There were several huge cargo planes there. Of course, they are used since most things have to be flown in from the lower forty. The tour guides in Alaska like to remind you that if Alaska were cut into two parts, Texas would then be the third largest state.

Well it is December again and time to head to Hawaii. Usually in doing so, I stop in San Francisco on the way and visit friends there. On the way back I stop in Sacramento and visit other friends there. However, in Hawaii my hotel room was the only one with Christmas lights on the balcony!

Mendenhall Glacier, Alaska 1985

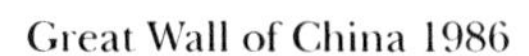

Great Wall of China 1986

Taj Mahal, India 1987

Fox Glacier, New Zealand 1989

Australia 1989

The Equator, Kenya 1990

Kikuyu Tribe, Kenya 1990

Bridge of the River Kwai, Thailand 1991

Mandalay, Burma 1991

Hawaii 1994

Sri Lanka 1994

Kulusuk, Greenland 1997

Skogofoss Waterfalls, Iceland 1997

The Antarctic 2003

1986

Vienna and Prague, China, Saint Louis, and Mexico

In 1986, I had arranged a trip to China through my travel agent for July. Not long after these plans were made I had determined that if I took a couple of days of personal leave in connection with the spring break I could have ten days off. I called him to ask if there were any bargain flights at that time for Budapest or Vienna. He was a little confused and said that he thought I was going to China. I told him that I was but that I had discovered a way of doing another trip prior to China.

A friend of mine and I flew to Vienna and spent four days enjoying the many sights of this beautiful city. We were able to get tickets for *Turandot* at the Staatsoper, which is the Vienna State Opera. It was a magnificent production. After the opera we went to the elegant Sacher restaurant behind the opera house in order to have their famous sacher torte for dessert.

We then took a hydrafoil on the Danube river to Budapest. I was able to meet a friend there that I had met when I was there in 1976. We spent four nights in Budapest and my friend conceded to be our tour guide. From Budapest we took the Orient Express train back to Vienna. We checked back into the same hotel that we have been to a few days before for two nights and then it was time to return to Washington. I had to get back because I only had three days before I was leaving for China.

The China trip started in Hong Kong. It was good to be back here and observe all the changes since my visit here in 1974. The Excelsior Hotel was in a completely different area than I had been previously, which made it feel like being in a new city.

Our touring included Repulse Bay, Aberdeen's Floating City, Victoria Peak, and shopping in Kowloon.

Our next stop was in Guangzhou (formerly Canton). Here we saw the Temple of Six Banyon Trees, the Liu Pong Pagoda, the local market, and the Sun Yatsen Memorial Hall. We also visited an Ivory Carving Factory. This city, as well as all the others we visited in China, was completely filled with bicycles! And as usual, there was always time for shopping.

We drove to the airport to catch a connected flight to Guilin. We were waiting and waiting, but we didn't know what for. In the meantime, a choir group from the United States began singing patriotic songs since back home at that time it was the fourth of July. It seemed that all the others in the airport were entertained by the singing and applauded exuberantly.

We then found out that there were horrendous downpours in Guilin and the airport was closed. Our tour director had to get on the telephone and make arrangements for us to be picked up from the airport and transported back to a different hotel. It seems that the hotel that had accommodated us previously was completely filled with other groups of newly arrived tourists. The next morning, our group returned to the airport and was able to finally make it to Guilin.

The highlight of Guilin is the cruise on the Li river. The extremely pointed mountainous structures are mind boggling. As soon as you begin to absorb your surroundings, you realize that these are the peaks that you have seen in so many paintings from China.

Shanghai was our next stop where we were able to see the Temple of the Jade Buddha, the museum of art, a silk factory, and observe the making of carpets by hand. We visited a commune and were able to see how these people live. For example, maybe four families living at the same place and they have their separate places for sleeping, etc., but the kitchen is used communally. We witnessed the mixing of medicines in the lab at the local hospital.

Children can volunteer to attend a Children's Palace after school hours or in the summer. There they can take classes in dancing, ballet, acting, music, art, and computers. Some of the students performed for us.

We flew to Xian and were able to see the terracotta statues that are the funeral vaults of Qin Shi Huang Di and had not been excavated until a couple years before our visit. At the time of our visit you were allowed to go in to see them; however, you were not allowed to take pictures. Fortunately, I knew my camera well enough that I turned it on and positioned it on a ledge for stability. When I was ready to snap the photo, I made a sniffling noise in order to stifle the sound of the shutter. Thus, no one knew I took the picture. It turned out great!

Our final stop in China was Beijing. The main attractions there, of course, are Tiananmen Square and the Forbidden Palace. The buildings that surround the square include the Chairman Mao Zedong Memorial Hall, the Monument to the People's Heroes, and the Great Hall of the People. The Forbidden City is entered through the north side of the square.

The pagoda-shaped Temple of Heaven was constructed in the early fifteenth century and was a place where the emperors would come to pray. There is a large adjoining park. I remember this because our bus dropped us off at one end and was going to pick us up at the other end.

After going through the monument we were visiting the gift shop. When one is in China, for any length of time, you begin to feel that every shop has the same items. However, while looking through this gift shop, I spotted a cloisonné clock that I fell in love with. I asked the price and decided to buy. However, my wallet with the credit card had been left on the bus. I ran from the gift shop through the park to the other end where I found the bus, retrieved my wallet, and returned to purchase the clock. Then I realized that I would need an additional bag in transporting it back to the United States. So I later bought a bag that fit it perfectly. It was well worth an inconvenience because the clock has turned out to be one of my most prized possessions from traveling.

It is not uncommon in the early morning to see several groups of Chinese people doing their *tai chi* exercises. It is almost as though they are in a trance as their movements are so fluent and graceful.

Our group was on its way to visit the Ming tombs and the bus had stopped so we could walk and take pictures of the statues that line the way. There was a mother and daughter sitting to the side of the road. As I was passing by, the little girl had a sad look of amazement on her face as if she was thinking—what kind of creature is this that is all white and has red hair! As I passed I said, "*ni how.*" (Chinese for hello). Instantaneously, her facial expression changed to a full smile and she responded, "*ni how.*"

The day we visited the Great Wall the sun was shining and it was a beautiful day. I have fair skin and sometimes use an umbrella for the sun. That day was one of those days. Others in the group were asking me why I had the umbrella. I said because of the sun. However, about an hour later and just as we were getting ready to turn around and make our way back to the entrance, a large black cloud appeared and it began raining heavily! Then, of course, I was asking them where their umbrellas were.

The Summer Palace was constructed for Empress Dowager Cixi. There are gardens, pavilions, temples, and lakes. The lake has a beautiful bridge that crosses it. There is also the Marble Boat which serves as a lakeside pavilion.

Our trip to China came to a close. We had a nice farewell dinner on the last night of the tour. My friend and I had previously made plans to fly to Tokyo at the end of the tour and be able to rest for a few days before returning home.

After having had Chinese food for lunch and dinner every day for three weeks it can get a little boring. Miraculously next to our hotel in Tokyo was a McDonald's! I told my friend that he could eat wherever he pleased that evening but that I knew where I was going to have dinner. They had the best hamburgers I had ever tasted! . . . And the French fries! Yummy!

While there we were able to visit the Tokyo Tower and the Imperial Palace with its manicured gardens, which I had visited twelve years earlier. We went to a Kabuki theater performance. We also did a round trip outside the city on the bullet train.

About three days after my arrival back home, I left on yet another trip. My roommate from St. Louis was living in Florida. He and I needed to be in St. Louis for an alumni meeting. We met in New Orleans and drove through Mississippi, Arkansas, Oklahoma, and Kansas. We ended our trip in St. Louis for the alumni meeting.

Growing up in North Carolina I thought I lived in the south until I drove through Mississippi and Arkansas. This is when I realized that this was really the south. We chose a restaurant in Little Rock for our Sunday night dinner. The waitperson came and inquired as to what we would like to drink. Both of us immediately spouted off that we would have a Bombay Gin martini and a Manhattan. She said, "You are kidding, aren't you? You can't have an alcoholic drink in Arkansas on Sunday!"

I was quite surprised to see the oil wells on the grounds of the state capitol in Oklahoma. One can't believe how flat part of our country is until you drive through Kansas. One of the reasons for this trip was that by doing so I could finally say that I had traveled in all of the fifty states!

On the first night in St. Louis, we sat around in one of the rooms chatting and catching up on what had happened to each of us since we graduated. At about 9:00 p.m. one of the ladies said that she just had to get to bed since it was one-hour time difference in time from where she lived and St. Louis. My friend began laughing hysterically! He told her that she only had a one-hour time difference. Then he proceeded to tell her that I had just been from Washington, DC to Vienna and Budapest for ten days. Three days later, I had gone to China for three weeks. And three days after that, we had just driven from New Orleans to St. Louis. My body didn't know where it was!

In December of 1986, I returned to Mexico with two friends. We started in Acapulco and proceeded through Taxco, Cuernavaca, and Mexico City to the Yucatan peninsula. Neither of these friends had been to Mexico before, so it was fun showing them around.

I tried to explain to them that the first time I had been to Cancun it was pristine with no hotels. Now, of course, it is just one resort after the other all the way down. We stayed in Merida and from there we were able to visit the ruins in Chichen Itza.

We later flew to Cozumel for a few days. While there, we took a day trip to Tulum. The tour consisted of flying to the mainland, taking a bus to the ruins and back, and returning to Cozumel by plane. The Mayan ruins in Tulum are very picturesque in that they are adjacent to the Atlantic Ocean coastline.

The plane ride from Cozumel to the mainland is only about five minutes. Two planes were being used to transport us. However, on our way back one of the planes had a mechanical problem. So they took half of the group first and the others had to wait for the plane to return in order to go back. While we were waiting, we noticed a person with a large box of turkeys that he was going to take back on the plane. I must admit that this was the first and only time I have been on a plane with a box full of turkeys. I suppose they were the club sandwiches for the next day.

1987

Bermuda and India

In the spring of 1987, I went to Bermuda for the first time with another friend of mine. There I took a tour of the island. In one area near the golf courses there were several large estates. We were told that some of the natives cherished being able to work at one of them because the owners were usually gone and they nearly had the place to themselves.

While walking on the main street on our first evening there, we noticed that even fine pieces of jewelry were still in the windows of the shops and there didn't seem to be any security system. We asked our guide about that and he told us that one advantage of living on a small island is that usually there is very little crime. If you were to steal something, where do you go?

One piece of information that I remember the guide talking about was their prison. He said that it is rarely used because people know that they don't want to go there. There is no air conditioning. There is no heating. You have a bowl of soup and maybe some crackers and that's it.

In late 1987, I went to India. My friend and I perused several brochures in determining what company to use. Just reading some of the brochures made you tired. We chose one of the most expensive tours because of the amount of time you were able to spend in each place. The other reason is that the accommodations for the tour used several former homes of maharajas as hotels. Consequently, there were only seven people on our tour. During our sightseeing excursions, we would encounter other tour groups that would have as many as forty people in the group!

In New Delhi, we stayed at the Taj Mahal Hotel. During our stay, there was a wedding at the hotel. The entrance gate to the hotel, the automobiles, and everything was covered with marigolds. One of the great features for our trip was that if a hotel had five restaurants in it, we could choose which one we wanted to go to, order from the menu, and just sign the check and it was paid for. We figured that we ate enough to pay for the trip!

New Delhi sightseeing included the government buildings, Emperor Humayun's Tomb, the Gandhi burial site, the flea market, and the stadium. From our hotel, at dusk you could see the smoke beginning to cover the city. We thought it was fog at first, but we found out it was smoke. Families would burn dung for cooking and also use it for heating their homes. Thus, the evenings would be filled with smoke.

It is fairly common given that at some time during a group tour you are going to attend a folklore show. These can be entertaining, however, after you have seen about twenty-five or thirty of them in various countries, they seem to become a little jaded.

At this point in our itinerary we made a slight diversion from India and flew to Nepal. We stayed in the Oberoi Hotel in Katmandu, which was very nice and even had a casino. On the first evening there, we were taken to a nearby restaurant for our introduction to Nepal. The dinner was very nice. The one feature that seemed to impress most of us was the baked Alaska for dessert. There was a lady in our group who was born in Ireland, but had lived in Bermuda for several years. She announced to the group that if any of us visited her in Bermuda, we would be treated to her baked Alaska!

In Katmandu, we first visited the Swayambhunath or Monkey Temple that dates back almost to two thousand years.

We drove to Bhaktapur (Bhadgaon), which wasn't that far from Katmandu. There we visited the museum and the Royal Palace. We also saw the cremation sights along the Bagmati river. This town is known for its pottery making. I remember seeing one large open square and it was completely filled with pottery for sale.

There was one day in Katmandu that was spent flying to see Mount Everest.

We then flew to Megauli. The airport in Megauli was memorable! It was a grass strip. Along either side at intervals were huge rocks that were painted white to indicate the edge of the runway. The plane then taxied back to the terminal, which was a small, open air, thatched roof structure. We deplaned using a handmade wooden ladder.

The Tiger Tops Lodge where we would be staying was a distance away. We started in an open air 4 × 4. We crossed at least two small rivers before arriving at the lodge. We were instructed to be in the lobby in about a half hour to go on a two-hour elephant ride. My stomach had been churning all day, which was unusual for one with an iron stomach! I don't know what I ate, but it didn't set well. I told my friend to go and I would find out later how it was.

The next morning, after breakfast, there was another elephant ride. My stomach had almost returned to normal. However, that morning my friend had the same thing I had had the day before. So I went on the elephant ride and he stayed at the lodge.

Mid morning we left in the 4 × 4 and drove about a half an hour toward our tented village for the next night. We were then transferred to a small boat for another half-hour ride. We walked for another half hour and finally arrived at our new home. We had no more begun to settle in, when a jackle ran across in front of me. Being so remote, there was no hot water. We had to walk a few yards from our tent to the showers. We had a small basin just outside our entrance for washing up a little or shaving. My comment was "for some reason this just doesn't seem like Christmas."

That afternoon we went for yet another elephant ride. We were in the middle of having our Christmas dinner when we were notified that a Bengal tiger had been spotted and that it would be necessary for us to pull off our shoes and walk toward the blind where the food had been placed there to attract it. Of course, by the time we got there it had left. We returned and finished our Christmas dinner.

The next morning we had to retrace our journey back to the lodge and on to the airport. We flew back to Katmandu and connected to our flight to Varanasi in India.

On our arrival, we were met at the airport by our guide for Varanasi and taken to our hotel. She was a very good guide and explained a lot about the way of life in India and how it differs from ours.

There was a couple in the group from New York. The wife of the couple was the kind of person who thinks that everyone in the world is just dying to be exactly like her. She tried to ask a question about the "poor" people. Our guide tried to explain to her that what was poor to her might not be poor to these people. I did notice that a lot of the people, both young and old, were smiling. It wasn't long into this conversation that I equated the life of these people to my early life. If this lady from New York had traveled to North Carolina during the early 1940s she probably would have thought the same thing about me and my family. However, just like so many of the people in India—no one ever told us that we were poor. This was our way of life and the only life we knew, so we were happy.

I also remember that the guide had told us that the color for mourning in India is white. The next morning we were to get up early and go to the Ganges for the early morning ceremony. When we arrived on the bus, the lady from New York made sure that we were all aware that she had such foresight and had packed a black outfit, which she thought was perfect for this occasion. Evidently she wasn't listening the day before when the guide explained that the color for mourning in India is white.

We arrived at the Ganges and were escorted into a small boat. We were given the lotus leaves with a candle in it. We were to release it into the river. It was quite a sight to witness this. When this was over, we disembarked from our small boat and were given a tour of the ghats where bodies were being cremated. My friend and I had seen through the thick fog last evening, near our hotel, a group of people carrying a wrapped body toward the river.

We drove to Agra and stayed at the Sheraton Hotel, which was centrally located with really good view. We went to see the Taj Mahal, which was practically the major reason for visiting Agra. We were fortunate to be there during a full moon and were able to witness the structure in moonlight conditions, as well as daytime.

In Agra, we also visited the Red Fort, which is a sixteenth century structure along the Yamuna river. The Peacock Throne was supposedly in this fort at one time.

We also visited the Pearl Mosque.

A few miles outside of Agra is Fatehpur Sikri, which was built by the Mughal Emperor Akbar in the sixteenth century and was the center of Agra at one time.

It consists of many monuments, temples, and a very large mosque. It is a UNESCO World Heritage Center.

When we left Agra and headed for our next destination, which was the Keoladeo Ghana Bird Sanctuary at Bharatpur. There we saw egrets, stork, green parrots, kingfishers, and eagles.

We had a long bus ride through the desert. We were going through a small town on our way. Suddenly there was a loud crash. We discovered that one of the young degenerates had taken upon himself to hurl a bottle at one of the windows of the bus. Fortunately, no one was hurt and window was only cracked.

We continued on until we reached our destination at the Rambagh Palace Hotel in Jaipur. This hotel had been a home of one of the maharajas. Our room was in one of the corners and the bedroom had a giant dome in the ceiling. The grounds at the hotel were exquisite. I remember also that the gift shop at the hotel had a wonderful selection of collectable items. I bought a signed miniature painting that I was told was painted with the hair from the tail of an animal. It was painted on ivory. It is kept in a glass exhibition case in my home and has a background light which reveals the thinness of the ivory.

In Jaipur, we toured the City Palace. The Palace of the Winds had a grill-like façade that facilitated the circulation of air. Behind the grillwork, the harem could rest comfortably while not being seen from the outside.

One of the highlights of visiting the Amber Fort was that you are taken from the entrance to the fort on an elephant. Some of the rooms in the Fort are completely covered in pieces of mirror.

Our hotel in Jodhpur was the Umaid Bhawan Palace Hotel. It also was a former home of another maharaja. In fact, the present one and his wife along with their two kids were living in fifty rooms of the palace at the time we were staying there.

We were invited for cocktails and dinner with a maharaja and his wife at the nearby Ajit Bhawan Palace. It was a wonderful experience. We were shown many of their possessions displayed throughout the palace and had dinner in an open courtyard.

Driving south from Jodhpur, we stopped at a Jain Temple that had been built in the fifteenth century. There were two hundred columns and no two were alike. We were also shown some of the erotic sculptures incorporated in the structure. I assume it was similar to what we would have seen if we had gone to Khajuraho. We had been scheduled in our itinerary to go to Khajuraho from Varanasi. However, we were told while we were waiting at the airport that there wasn't a plane for us. Now it was time to revert to plan B.

We stayed at the Lake Palace Hotel in Udaipur. As the name implies the hotel is in the center of a lake. It is the same hotel that was used in the James Bond 007 movie *Octopussy* with Roger Moore.

Our guide confided in me, my friend, and the lady from Bermuda that the hotel only had a few rooms with balconies and we had two of them. We were asked not to tell the other two couples since they didn't have one. I think this was in retaliation for something they had done at some of the previous hotels. They were intent on making sure that they got the best rooms available. At one hotel, our guide told us, they went to the desk two or three times to look at different rooms and then decided that the first one was the best.

One evening in Jodhpur, we had dinner at the City Palace. We had to take the boat from our hotel to the shore. We traveled to Bombay (now Mumbai) where we spent one night at the hotel that was bombed a couple years ago. We returned to the United States the next day.

On my first day back at work, one of my students asked me where I went to for the holidays. When I told her that I had been to India and Nepal she said “you must be rich” and my answer was “no, if I didn’t travel, I could be rich.”

1988

Vermont, Canada, and California

In the summer of 1988, I traveled to Stowe, Vermont, to visit two friends of mine. There we drove north alongside Lake Champlain to Montreal and Quebec. From Quebec we began our way south through Fredericton, New Brunswick. We stayed in Moncton, New Brunswick, where we were able to observe the high and low tides of the Bay of Fundy. From low tide to high tide, approximately two hundred billion tons of water comes into the bay. It is really phenomenal to see this. This fluctuation is the greatest of any tide in the world.

We spent most of our time in Nova Scotia in Halifax. However, we were able to drive to Peggy's Cove and saw the famous lighthouse there.

Of course, on Prince Edward Island the main attraction is the house of Anne of Green Gables. We also visited Woodleigh, a miniature village where there were several miniatures of famous structures including St. Paul's Church, Yorkminster, Anne Hathaway's Cottage, and the Tower of London. I understand that it has since been closed.

In driving back to Vermont we were able to drive through Maine. I remember a license plate on a local vehicle in Bar Harbor that read, "Welcome to Bar Harbor—now go home." We toured the Acadia National Park there.

I had a few days in Vermont before returning to Washington, D. C. This gave me an opportunity to see the Von Trapp family place and also the local skiing venue.

By the month of December it was time to go to California again. After a few days in Sacramento we had made plans to drive to Los Angeles. On the morning that we were to leave we had quite a surprise. It was actually snowing in Sacramento! We had flurries almost all the way to Los Angeles.

While there, I was able to visit some other friends who lived in Long Beach. Since it was that holiday time of the year, we were invited to several parties. We had hoped to go to the Rose Bowl Parade; however, we had not done our homework and didn't realize that they never have the parade if the first falls on a Sunday. That happened to be one of those years and we were leaving on Monday. C'est la vie.

1989

New Zealand, Australia, Hawaii, and London

A friend of mine had just retired from serving twenty-five years in the Navy and wanted to do something special to celebrate his retirement. He and another friend and I took an extended trip to New Zealand, Australia, and Hawaii.

After a couple of days of sightseeing in Auckland, we rented a car and drove south toward Rotorua. We visited the Rotorua Museum of Art and History that was located in an old bath house. Nearby we were able to visit the Waitomo Caves and see the glow worm grotto. People are taken inside in a small boat. When you are all the way in and it is completely dark, you begin to see the top of the grotto begin to glow. It is somewhat surreal in that you feel you are actually looking at the sky but the stars are blue.

We stayed in a hotel in Rotorua that was adjacent to the thermal area where the mud bubbles from the heat underneath. The scent of sulfur is quite prominent.

We arrived in Wellington, the capitol and were able to see the Parliament buildings and other government offices. Wellington has some of the most beautiful gardens of any city I think I have ever been in. There is a funicular that operates from the central business area to a suburb above. There is a small museum at the top. From there, one can begin meandering back down while walking through some of the beautiful gardens. There is an old cemetery along the way also.

We had to get rid of our rental car in Wellington. We then took the ferry from there to the south island. On the other side we picked up another rental and drove down the western side of the island to Nelson where we spent the night.

On our drive further down the south island the next day we realized how tropical it is here and alongside the highway were these large and beautiful fern trees.

The next day we had made a reservation to fly on to the Franz Joseph Glacier. Our female pilot landed and we were able to walk around and take pictures while on the glacier. As we continued our flight we were able to see Mount Cook, the Tasman glacier, and the Fox glacier. It had been a memorable experience.

In Queenstown we took another funicular in the evening and had our dinner in a restaurant high above the city. It was a spectacular view.

We signed up for a tour of Milford Sound. On flying there you are flying over what is called the Southern Alps. We took a cruise of the sound and were able to see several large waterfalls.

We drove to Dunedin, which is almost at the southernmost point of the island. The architecture of some of the homes there with the grill work reminded me a little bit of New Orleans. From there we drove up to Christchurch. Christchurch is another wonderful city to walk in and absorb all of their parks, flowers, and fountains along the Avon river.

A friend of mine in Washington had friends in Christchurch. When he learned that I was going to be there he made contact with his friends and let them know that a friend of his was going to visit. In the meantime, we communicated several times before I arrived. Of course, this was before the cell phone era and communication was somewhat different to say the least.

Upon arriving we contacted one of them. We were invited to dinner. It was nice to be able to put faces to the information that had been generated through our letter writing. My friends and I invited them to go to dinner with us the next evening. Since they were more familiar with their city than us we allowed them to choose a restaurant. It just so happened that the restaurant they chose had a story behind the name. The person had wanted to open a restaurant that seated forty people. He looked and looked and couldn't find anything. He finally found a place that was perfect, but it would only accommodate thirty-four people. Thus, he named the restaurant Six Chairs Missing.

Our tour of New Zealand had come to a close and it was time to fly back to Auckland and connect with our flight to Sydney, Australia. We spent a few days in Sydney and again I acted the tour guide since I had been there previously. Our taxi driver to the Opera House didn't have much difficulty in surmising that we were Americans. His one comment was that he didn't think he could ever be able to drive on the other side.

After we finished our sightseeing here we got our rental car and drove to Canberra.

It was August, which is their wintertime. By the time we were ready to go to bed in Canberra, we were glad to feel some heat and have the extra blanket! It was nice to see the Capitol buildings and the War Memorial there.

We then drove to Melbourne where we were able to tour the old Olympic stadium that was used in the 1956 games. Flinders Station, their railway station, is one of the must-see tourist sights here. Parliament House is interesting to see in the daytime; however, it is much more interesting to see it at night when all of it is illuminated with hundreds of white lights.

When we told the people in Melbourne that Tasmania was our next stop, they immediately warned us that we had better take our "woolies" with us because it was going to be even colder there. It was!

Hobart is a port city and serves as the capitol of Tasmania. After touring here we departed to explore the remainder of the island. Our first stop was the site of the Port Arthur penal colony. British and Irish criminals were imprisoned here during the mid nineteenth century.

Launceston is the second largest city in Tasmania. Both my friends and I were surprised at its size. We did a lot of walking throughout the city to try to get a feel of the people who live there and what their way of life was.

During my early travels I prided myself upon being in a new place and being able to look through the yellow pages of the local telephone directory in order to choose a place to have dinner. In Launceston, I chose a place because it was located in an old Victorian house. However, I was a little skeptical of the name that was "The Pampered Pussy." We were surprised at all the floral arrangements in the house and were told that the higher-ups in government had been there that day for a big luncheon meeting.

In all our travels around this island we weren't privileged enough to have witnessed seeing one of their illustrious Tasmanian devils.

We flew from Hobart to Adelaide, the capitol of South Australia. After having been in Sydney and Melbourne, the city of Adelaide was much more low keyed. It was a pleasant change of pace yet completely different from being in Tasmania.

Our next leg of the journey was to fly to Alice Springs. I am so glad that I finally got to see this area of Australia. Climbing Anzac hill just across from our hotel provided an excellent overview of the entire area.

We rented a car in Alice Springs to drive to Ayres Rock. In renting a car for that purpose you have to sign a form indicating that you agree not to drive at night. There are so many animals crossing the road and there had been so many accidents that you were not allowed driving through that area at night.

Just outside Alice Springs we went to Simpson's Gap and the Standley Chasm. These natural rock formations are a must-see. The narrow gorges are extremely high and the sun only reaches the bottom for a few minutes during the day.

The one thing that amazed us on our drive to Ayres Rock was the number of camels we saw. We arrived in Ayres Rock in time to see the rock and do some climbing. We were able to witness the changes of color as twilight emerged. The next morning we were able to go back and see those changes at daybreak. Then, it was time to drive back to Alice Springs.

We flew to Cairns and there took a day tour of the barrier reef. We went to Green Island and did some snorkeling on the Norman Reef. The next day we went on the Kuranda railway that has been working since 1891. The many curves that it makes on its way up contribute to an extremely enjoyable journey and allow you to be able to see the beautiful scenery. By the end of the journey you realize that you are in a rain forest.

One of my friends had to leave us here in order to return to the States because of employment obligations. So for the remainder of the trip, there were just the two of us.

We flew to Brisbane from Cairns. Brisbane is the capital of the state of Queensland. We did the usual sightseeing in the center of the city. Then it was time to make a little diversion, and we headed to the Lone Pine Sanctuary. There we were able to cuddle with the koalas, see numerous kangaroos, and many, many different kinds of birds.

The next day we took a bus tour for the day to the Gold Coast. This area reminded me a little of Miami Beach. There were many high-rise apartment buildings, large hotels, and large shopping centers.

Upon leaving Brisbane, we flew back to Sydney and connected with our flight to Hawaii. My friend who had just retired from the military made it possible for us to be able to stay at the military hotel there. It was nice to be able to relax for a week by the pool after six busy weeks of sightseeing. In fact, we had our photos developed, and by the time we arrived back home our photo albums were complete.

One would think that after all that traveling you would be ready to not travel for a while. No way. That year in December there were six of us who traveled to London for Christmas and New Year. We saw at least six theater performances that week. The weather was a little rainy, but enjoyable. The Christmas decorations in London were as if Charles Dickens had come back and said that this is really the way it should look.

The headlines in the London newspaper on the day after Christmas announced that it had been warmer in London for Christmas than it had been in Key West, Florida. And I had teacher friends who had chosen to go to Key West that year. They said it was freezing!

1990

Kenya, Tanzania, Zambia, and Zimbabwe

In the summer of 1990, I did a photographic safari in Kenya and Tanzania. The tour began in Nairobi. Here I saw the Kenya National Museum, the city market, several mosques, and the important government buildings.

We stayed at the historic Norfolk Hotel. The original one was home to Ernest Hemingway and Theodore Roosevelt whenever they visited. Up to the time of my stay in 1990, we were told that many heads of state stayed at this hotel.

In all of my travels I have had a misplaced bag only twice and both times were when I was on my way to visit Africa. The first time, as you might remember, was on my way to Cairo in 1980. Now here again I was without luggage. Fortunately, I have learned to pack enough essentials to be carried with me to be able to exist.

Our first introduction to the countryside of Kenya was in the Masai Mara Reserve at the Keekorok Lodge. The first night there I was awakened during the night with a noise on the other side of the wall. Being brought up on a farm, I was familiar with the sound of a cow eating grass, and I knew exactly what it sounds like. I stood up on the bed and looked out through the screen at the top and there was a group of zebra grazing. One of the rules at the lodge was that we were not to walk between our rooms and the reception area without an escort. The escort carried a rifle.

In this reserve we saw lions, elephants, cape buffaloes, rhinoceros, and cheetah. I have always loved to see a giraffe even in a zoo. As we turned around the corner driving, suddenly we saw several of them casually eating the leaves off a tree—wow, another Kodak moment!

One of the highlights of this trip was the balloon ride over the reserve. We had to be up very early in order to catch the early morning breeze just right. There is such a surreal feeling gliding along and everything is so quite. As you look down you see a drove of wildebeest migrating. Then, you look in the other direction and you see a group of elephants. During the entire trip we saw many animals. Upon landing we were treated to a champagne breakfast—almost worth getting up early!

We visited a Masai village and were able to see how they live. Many of the men are herders. Most of their attire resembles a blanket and usually in bright red colors.

The ladies also wear a lot of red and fabrics consisting of very bright patterns. Beads are a prominent part of their attire.

The Lion Hill Lodge adjacent to Lake Nakuru was our next stop. Each room was a separate entity almost like having your own little house. Each house was named after a flower. My abode was named Acapanthus. Here were able to spot spider monkeys, waterbucks, cormorants, impala, and flamingoes.

On our visit to Aberdare National Park we had some entertainment and photo ops with a member of the Kikuyu tribe. Our lunch that day was at the Outspan Hotel.

All this was on our way to Treetops Lodge. This place is known for watching the elephants. However, there is one more important fact of interest. Queen Elizabeth and Prince Phillip were visiting here in 1952. While here her father, King George VI, died. The next morning when she came down for breakfast they informed her that she was now the Queen of England. This is also the place where Prince William brought Kate Middleton to propose in 2011.

Our guide did a demonstration of the Coriolis force at the equator. Buckets of water were placed several feet north and south of the equator. He placed a straw in the bucket on the north side and as the water was drained the straw began rotating in a clockwise direction. When he proceeded to the bucket on the south side and did the same thing the straw rotated counterclockwise.

The Mount Kenya Safari Club was a real treat. Not only were the grounds well manicured, the food was excellent. Each room was equipped with a fireplace. In the evening while you are in the dining room an employee of the establishment enters your room and starts a fire. How comforting it is to walk in the chilly air from the restaurant and enter your warm room with the fire crackling. The Mount Kenya Safari Club was the only place on the trip that we had been asked to bring a coat and tie for dinner. Miraculously my misplaced bag arrived that day!

The Mount Kenya Safari Club was the dream child of the late Hollywood actor William Holden. Some of the animals roam the grounds of the lodge. Animals here include giant turtles, bongo, dik-dik, cranes, monkeys, and the hornbill.

Our last stop in Kenya was the Amboseli National Park. From this park you have great views of Mount Kilimanjaro.

The Ngorongoro Crater in Tanzania is the world's largest volcanic crater with unbroken walls. It is 7,500 feet above sea level, is 102 square miles in area, and is two thousand feet from the rim to the floor. Our lodge here was right on the top of the rim looking down into the crater.

Our safari here made it possible to see lions, zebras, hyenas, hippopotamus, cape buffalo, rhinoceros, and hartebeest. It was here that I saw more flamingoes than I had ever seen in my life. There would be times when the entire sky above you would be a sky of pink! Yes, another Kodak moment!

The Olduvai Gorge was a place where the Leakey family performed excavations in the 1920s. Here we saw wild dogs going after other animals and succeeding. At the same place we saw a leopard eating a hyena.

When traveling around through Kenya and Tanzania we saw many, many acacia trees. They are highly recognizable because of the flatness on top. There are many baobab trees also.

Our accommodation in another part of the Serengeti was the Lobo Lodge. It was built into kopje, which are huge rock formations. It was a beautiful lodge and the architecture of it fit in perfect with its surroundings.

I will never forget the first morning there as I casually opened the drapes in the room there was a large cape buffalo standing on the other side as if to say—what are you doing here, this is my home!

In close proximity of the lodge I was able to spot several small animals including monkeys, rock hyrax, etc. In fact, I have a picture of a monkey pulling a sheet across the rocks that it had stolen from the housekeeping department.

There were two vans in our entourage. One day as we were on our way from one spot to another, I caught sight of a cheetah. The other people didn't believe me at first but I told them that I was sure. Before we turned around to go back, we fast forwarded to the van in front of us to bring them back with us. Sure enough, when we arrived back at the place there were three cheetahs. One member of our group took about forty pictures just to make sure he got a good one. This was really the age before digital cameras.

We stayed at the Seronera Lodge at our next stop. Here, we were able to see some of the usual animals that we had seen at other places. However, there were a lot of lizards and blue rocco.

We stopped when our guide had spotted a leopard in a tree. It was really difficult to see it at first because nature seems to be on their side. I think we waited almost an hour to see it move but it was too busy eating a gazelle. We also passed an ostrich farm. At the Lake Manyara Lodge we saw a fish eagle and a kingfisher.

Arusha is a city that is considered to be the center of Africa because it is halfway between Johannesburg and Cairo. Near the town is the Arusha Mountain Village. This is where we stayed and had great views from here of Mount Kilimanjaro.

This was the last stop for the group. They were leaving to return home and I was planning to go to Victoria Falls. I flew from Nairobi through Lusaka, Zambia to Harare, Zimbabwe. I stayed at the Meikles Hotel in Harare. A local guide there was thrilled to be able to show me around the city. From there I flew to Victoria Falls where I stayed at the old and historic Victoria Falls Hotel.

A nice stroll behind the hotel brings you to the edge of the falls. The way the falls are situated it creates a large amount of mist. While I was taking photos I slipped. I had a small cut on one hand but the frightening part of this ordeal was that I was only about six feet from the edge. If I had gone over, my friends back home would have never known what happened since I was traveling alone. Back at the hotel the staff was extremely helpful in cleaning the cut on my hand and making sure that it was taken care of.

In the afternoon I had agreed to take a plane ride around the falls. The small plane would accommodate two people in addition to the pilot. The pilot would tilt the plane to one side to alleviate the taking of photos. Then the plane would be tilted to the other side in order for the other person to have the same advantages. The photos came out great and it was the highlight of the visit.

That evening there was entertainment at the hotel, which included singing and dancing. This was a good send-off since I would be flying out the next day and heading home.

The plane for our departure was a 747. This was the first time that I had been on a 747, where it was necessary to walk up a set of stairs to board the plane. As one walks up the stairs it becomes obvious at the size of the engines when you are this close to them!

During those days smoking was allowed on planes. Even though I usually didn't smoke on a flight I would choose the smoking section because you usually didn't have any small children. On a long flight that is important.

There was a lady sitting in the center section on the opposite aisle from me with two or three empty seats in between. I asked her where she was from and she said, "Australia." I asked what part and she said that she was from Tasmania. When I further asked if she was from Hobart or Launceston and she asked, "You have been there?" Then she asked me where in Australia I had visited. I told her that I had been in Sydney, Canberra, Melbourne, Tasmania, Adelaide, Alice Springs, Ayres Rock, Cairns, the Barrier Reef, Brisbane, and the Gold Coast. Her response was that I had been in more of Australia than most of the Australians.

1991

Thailand, Burma, Laos, Cambodia, Vietnam, and Washington Opera Appearances

The big trip of 1991 was arranged, as usual, by my travel agent. He worked through a company in New York to set up the itinerary. This company had their main offices in Bangkok. The visa for Thailand was obtained prior to leaving. The other visas, we were told, would be made available to me in Bangkok. It wasn't anything unusual for me to be traveling as a group of one.

I stayed at The Windsor Hotel in Bangkok. The various sights I was able to see included the Temple of Emerald Buddha, the Temple of Golden Buddha, the Vimanmek Palace, the Royal Gardens, and the Marble Temple. The Golden Buddha weighs over five tonnes and was made from pure gold.

The traffic in Bangkok was even horrendous in 1991! You can sit for what seems to be an eternity without moving. There were many more tuk-tuk taxis being used then than at the present time.

The tourist office in my hotel could arrange excursions. I had a one-day excursion to Kanchanaburi. This place is well known for the Bridge of the River Kwai. On the way to this area we stopped at a war cemetery. We were able to see where there had been a prisoner of war camp during the war. Nearby was the *Jeath* (Japan, England, America, Australia, Thailand, and Holland) War Memorial.

The death railway was built between 1942 and 1945 and was used to transport more than sixteen thousand prisoners.

My hotel in Bangkok was used as my basic headquarters for this trip as you will be aware of during the following dialog.

I flew from Bangkok to Rangoon (or Yangon) for a one-week stay in Burma (Myanmar). My hotel in Yangon was centrally located in the downntown area. I visited the Shwedagon Pagoda. This pagoda is supposed to be the most religious shrine in the entire country. The architecture is strictly Burmese and it contains a lot of gold and jewels.

Other places of interest include the Railway Station, the Reclining Buddha, the National Museum, and the large market. I saw a wooden fu dog statue that I really liked. I asked how much it was and converted that amount to dollars. In doing so, I realized that it was too expensive. It was approximately $100. As we walked away, my guide asked me if I really wanted it. I said yes. She went back and got it. I ask her how much I had to pay for it, and she said it was about $10. There was a huge gold restaurant sitting on the Royal Lake that was built to look like a royal barge. It was called the Karaweik Hall or Royal Barge Restaurant.

The next morning I had a flight to Pagan (Bagan). The Thiripyitsaya Hotel in Bagan was quite modern compared to the one I had in Yangon. There I was able to tour the magnificent ruins of Pagan, one of Asia's most remarkable archeological sites. It seemed that there were small pagodas and structures of varying sizes as far as the eye could see.

Some of the larger temples there included the Shwezigon Pagoda (1076), the Shwegugyi Temple (1140), the Amanda Temple (restored in the late eighteenth century), the Thatbyinnyu Temple (twelfth century), the Manuha Temple (1059), the Dhammayangyi Temple (c. 1165), and the Htilominlo Temple (1218).

Driving through the farming area was like going back in time. Any equipment being used in the fields was antiquated. In a local village we saw people alongside the river doing their laundry by hand and taking their baths. I visited a lacquerware factory and also saw young boys weaving bamboo to be used in housing construction.

I flew from Bagan to Mandalay. In Mandalay I saw the Royal Palace, Mandalay Hill (one thousand steps to the top), the Atumashi Monastery, the Shwenandaw Monastery, and the Kyauktawgyi Pagoda. The Kuthodaw Pagoda is known as the world's largest book for its stone slabs with Buddhist scriptures on them.

I was taken to an embroidery factory to see items being made by hand and to a silk weaving factory.

I returned to Yangon for one night and flew back to Bangkok the next day. While back at the hotel in Bangkok, a gentleman came to the hotel from the Adventures in Paradise office with my visas for Cambodia and Vietnam. I asked about the visa for Laos and was told that there would be someone at the airport in Vientiane with that visa. I was a little apprehensive to say the least, but everything worked out like a charm.

When I arrived at the airport in Vientiane, a gentleman was standing there with a large card with my name on it. He assisted me with my luggage and we went outside to meet my driver. It is rather nice to sightsee and have your own English speaking guide and a chauffeur.

Kumcha, my guide, took me to the Presidential Mansion, the war memorial, Wat That Luang, Wat Si Saket, and Wat Prakeo National Museum. We also visited the hospital.

The black and white television in my hotel room only received one or two stations. I will never forget turning it on and seeing *Leave It to Beaver* and *I Love Lucy* in Laotian.

The next morning I had a flight from Vientiane to Phnom Penh in Cambodia. Upon arriving I was taken to the Hotel Cambodiana that was located alongside the Mekong river.

My guide had informed me not to exchange money at the hotel. He would take me to a place that afternoon for that. We stopped at this store and I went in to cash $50. The stack of Cambodian bills was at least five or six inches high. Rubber bands were used for each $5 worth. The $50 in Cambodian bills was then placed in a brown paper bag.

We toured the Silver Pagoda and the National Museum. We then proceeded to the elephant village for an elephant ride. In that area I saw a lot of men with missing arms and legs. Some had one arm and some had none. Some had one leg and some had none. Once you have walked through the killing fields, it begins to explain what you have just seen.

The civil war there with the Khmer Rouge left enormous numbers of people killed. The Choeung Ek Memorial is a stupa that is filled with skulls that were found in the area. It seemed a little morbid in looking at this structure yet at the same time it reminded you of just what happened and makes you feel grateful for where you live.

The next morning I had a short flight from Phnom Penh to Siem Reap in order to visit the ruins at Angkor Wat. One of the highlights was the Temple of Bayon, which is a massive stone structure with many towers. I had my lunch at what was at that time the only hotel there.

The next few hours were spent just exploring the vast area of the entire complex. This was indeed another Kodak moment! Then, it was time to head back to the airport and fly back to Phnom Penh where I would have a much needed day at leisure.

I flew from Phnom Penh to Ho Chi Minh City in Vietnam the next morning. That day was also a free day. The Caravelle Hotel was just across the square from my hotel. This hotel had been used by military and heads of state whenever they would visit. I understood that some high-level meetings had been held at that hotel also. I had dinner there that evening and the food was distinctively French, but the prices were Vietnamese.

The old building that stood almost in the middle of the square had been converted into a theater. Just up the street were the old Rex Hotel and the City Hall.

My guide came to the hotel the next day and we drove to the beach town of Vung Tau. During the drive, it was interesting to observe the lack of automobiles. Most of the traffic was large carts being pulled by young boys.

Back in Ho Chi Minh City the next day we saw the Presidential Palace (no pictures allowed), a lacquer factory, and the old American Embassy. There was a floating hotel in the river that had been brought there from Australia. In Australia it had been a hotel at the Barrier Reef.

One of the most exciting things, while in Ho Chi Minh City, was to tour the Cu Chi tunnels that were used during the war. The Viet Cong used these tunnels for communications networks, a hospital, cooking, and just as a place to hide.

Nearby was a War Museum. My guide refused to go in because he felt that everything in it was a lie—all propaganda. He said that I could go if I wanted to but he would be outside when I finished.

Now it was time to fly back to Bangkok, my home away from home. Of course, when I arrived back at the Windsor Hotel, I felt like family by this time. And it was comforting to know that the next day was another "free" day!

I flew from Bangkok to Chiang Mai. Later in the day we ascended the Doi Suthep Mountain by road and visited the temple near the summit. That evening we had an excellent dinner in their oldest public house.

We visited another elephant training camp, had lunch at the Mae Kok River Lodge, and then boarded a long boat for a ride to Chiang Rai. I spent three nights there.

This area is referred to as the Golden Triangle because at one point you are able to see Laos, Myanmar, and Thailand at the same time.

From Chiang Rai I flew to Phuket for a three-night stay at the Banthai Beach Resort.

Each day I would sign up for a tour. I met another tourist at the hotel from Switzerland. He and I would go on our day trips together. One day we did a tour to the Andaman Sea and we were able to see several caves and grottoes. Another day we traveled by long boat to "James Bond Island" or Phang Nga Bay where the 007 movie, *Man with a Golden Gun,* was filmed.

It was time now that I began working my way back to Washington, D. C. I started by flying to Hong Kong where I stayed for three nights at the Park Hotel. It was really good to be back in Hong Kong for the third time. A new culture center had been built since my last visit and that was good to see. A trip to Victoria Peak is a must no matter how many times you're in this city.

From there I flew to Seoul, Korea and spent three nights at the Hamilton Hotel. I really enjoyed walking in this town, seeing all the sights, and shopping. One large department store that I visited here collapsed a year or so later and many people were killed.

I flew from Seoul through Tokyo to San Francisco and back to Washington. I remember waiting in the terminal in San Francisco and feeling like a zombie after the long overnight flight. On the flight back to Washington I was surrounded by several businessmen who had been to California for a business trip. One gentleman kept complaining about how much he hated this long flight. He had said that more than once. As we were landing at Dulles he was saying it again. It was then that I turned to him and told him that this was the shortest flight that I had had in two days.

In the fall of 1991 there was a small diversion from travel. I appeared as a supernumerary in the Washington Opera production of *Don Carlo.* This experience was exhilarating and it allowed me to meet prominent opera singers from all over the world. It also satisfied that little urge one has to be on stage. This fascination was so strong that it lasted for almost ten years.

Between tours I would try to find time to pursue this endeavor. To do so does, however, take up a lot of one's time. The rehearsal period is usually over a period of two weeks. Then the performances are over a period of three weeks. Thus, there is a block of about five weeks that must be relegated to this endeavor in order to be able to accomplish it.

From 1991 through 1999 I was fortunate enough to appear with the Washington Opera in the *Marriage of Figaro, Carmen, Der Rosenkavalier, Mefistofele, La Boheme,* and *Dangerous Liaisons.*

I also was a supernumerary in the production of *Tosca* at Lisner Auditorium, the full length production of *Manon* by the American Ballet Company in the Eisenhower Theater of the Kennedy Center, two Rossini operas at the Barns of Wolf Trap, and the *Magic Flute* at Wolf Trap.

1992

Amsterdam and Brussels, Baltic Cruise, and Costa Rica

In the spring of 1992, I traveled with two friends to Amsterdam and Brussels. While in the Netherlands we were able to enjoy the many fine art galleries, museums, and canals in the city of Amsterdam. We took tours outside Amsterdam to the old city of Volendam, to The Hague, and to Madurodam, which is an outdoor miniature display of the country of the Netherlands. Surprisingly enough this miniature display even included the airport complete with jumbo jets.

We took the train to Brussels. One of the things that anyone looks forward to in visiting this city is its chocolate! And we did! We also did our sightseeing to the usual spots, which included the beautiful gardens near the Royal Palace, the central square with its outstanding architecture, and the Atomium monument that was built for the expo held there in 1958. No one can visit the central square without searching for the Manneken Pis, which is a small statue of a boy urinating.

We did a one-day trip from Brussels to Bruges. I really enjoyed seeing this old city. However, a strange happening I remember was my friends and I decided to visit the church and it was on a Sunday. We arrived at the door and there was a sign there that read "closed on Sunday." Figure that one out!

When another school year end is coming to a close, the one thing that will be the topic of discussion among fellow teachers is the question—where are you going for the summer? I revealed that I would be going on a Baltic Cruise. One teacher asked what cities would be included in the tour. After going down the list that included St. Petersburg I was asked if I had ever been there before. My answer was that I had been to Leningrad two times, but they changed the name to St. Petersburg so I had to go back again.

The ship for the cruise was part of the Kristina Cruise Line of Finland. The cruise started in Helsinki. We toured the Russian Orthodox Church, St. Isaacs Cathedral, and several other places nearby which I had toured on a prior visit in 1971.

The next stop was in St. Petersburg. Our first day was spent going to St. Isaacs Cathedral, the Hermitage, and to the Naval Museum.

We were taken to another museum later that day. I had a strange feeling that I had been to this museum before, but many things had changed. I noticed as we were walking to the top floors that all the small niches along the way were empty. Of course this was where the busts of former government leaders had been before and had been removed. Upon exiting the museum there was a guard standing outside. I approached him and told him that I had been here several years prior and I wanted to know if this wasn't the same museum that in the courtyard before it contained several military tanks, etc. His response was that I had a very good memory.

I took some spare time to walk over to the area near the Aurora ship to the hotel where I had stayed in 1971 and 1976. The name of the hotel during those two visits was the Leningrad Hotel. Now, it is known as the St. Petersburg Hotel.

It was good being back here for the first time since their reign of communism had ended and to observe the many things that had changed. The most obvious one was the new flag! Then I began noticing people along the streets selling various kinds of things, which would not have been possible in the years before.

Part of our two days here was to travel to Pushkin and tour the palaces there. At some point during our sightseeing, I overheard another tourist mention the words Connecticut Avenue to one of his friends. My ears perked up because, of course, Connecticut Avenue is a major thoroughfare in Washington, D. C.

It wasn't until we had returned to our ship and we were preparing to depart St. Petersburg when I came in contact with the person that I had overheard. I asked him where he was from and his answer was indeed Washington. He seemed to think that I looked familiar but couldn't place how or through whom he would have known me before. Finally two and two were put together and he realized that he and his friend had attended one of my summer Christmas parties with a mutual friend of their's and mine. Another small world story!

We sailed away from St. Petersburg and were on our way to Tallinn, Estonia. This was to be the first place on our tour that I had not visited before. The highlight of being in this city was the walk through the old city and being able to absorb the exquisite architecture of the buildings. We saw the Alexander Nevsky Cathedral and the Herman Tower and Palace.

As we approached the city of Riga, the capital of Latvia, I remember the recently built very modern bridge with many cables. Among the sightseeing in Riga, we saw the Dome Cathedral, the Opera House, the Government Offices, the Monument to Liberty, and the theater district. As we were walking along one street the Presidential limousine drove past with the country's flags on the front. We were told that it was probably on its way to a memorial service.

We visited a beach along the south side of the Baltic Sea and were told by our local guide that this area was the place where much of the Latvian amber is found. Amber is essentially fossilized pine resin; however, some pieces have small fragments of leaves or small insects inside. It is said that amber jewelry with an insect inside is more valuable than plain pieces.

We drove from Riga to Vilnius, the capital of Lithuania. There we saw the Parliament and the Science museum. There was a huge memorial park here dedicated to those who died for freedom. A section was also for those from World War II.

From Vilnius we drove to the port in Kaliningrad where we were able to rejoin our ship. Before leaving there were saw the walled city, the museum, and the stock exchange.

The small island of Visby was our next stop. There we enjoyed strolling through the Botanical Gardens and the Old Town before we had to return to the ship to sail to Stockholm.

In Stockholm, we visited the Nordic Museum and the Vasa Museum. We saw their Opera House, the Parliament, and the Palace.

Christmastime of 1992 was spent in Costa Rica. There we were able to tour most of the country seeing the volcanoes, a butterfly sanctuary, hummingbirds, etc.

1993

Northwest United States and Canada, New England Cruise, and Paris

As a kid, in North Carolina, I had always dreamed of being able to play the piano. I had subconscientiously said to myself that when I retired, I would take up piano lessons. Our school was closed for a long weekend in February for Presidents Day. Upon returning to work on Tuesday, I was asked how I spent the weekend. They were surprised when I told them that I went out on Sunday to buy a mattress cover for a bed and bought a piano! SinceI had taken the first step, it was time to go to the next one, which was taking piano lessons.

In April, I drove from Seattle to Banff, Lake Louise, Jasper, Edmonton, Calgary, Spokane, and back to Seattle. It was really great to see this part of the country. Lake Louise is like a fairyland, unbelievable. As I drove back into the United States, I was in awe of Glacier Park. It was also a treat driving through to Missoula, Montana to see the area where the movie, *A River Runs through It*, took place.

During the summertime I went on a one-week cruise from Boston to New York. On that cruise my friend of mine and I spent one night in Boston prior to boarding the ship. The cruise went to Provincetown, Martha's Vineyard, Nantucket, New Bedford, Newport, Block Island, and on into New York.

I had been to Provincetown many, many times, yet it was good to have a while there and see how much it had changed. It was good to finally see Martha's Vineyard and Nantucket after having read so much about the people who live there. We found it interesting that McDonald's had wanted to open a franchise there and the residents said no. Seeing the "cottages" of Newport, Rhode Island was probably the highlight of the cruise.

Since I would be retiring in December of 1993, I decided that I would go to Paris for a week for Thanksgiving. My coworkers asked why I was going then when I could just wait another month and go when I retired. My response was that for retirement I had to rehearse.

We went to Versailles Palace and gardens, Notre Dame Cathedral, and some of the other major sights in Paris. Since I had been to Paris a few times previously, I suggested to my friend that we obtained a rail pass that would allow us to travel outside the city. On the first morning using our train pass we were going to take the train to Lyon. We couldn't believe it when we left our hotel to discover that it was snowing! Fortunately, it didn't last very long. We enjoyed the high speed of the TGV train. We walked around the city of Lyon, had a nice lunch, and took the train back to Paris.

The next day we took the train to Reims, had our lunch there and toured the famous cathedral and again returned to Paris.

And the next day we took the train to Roeun where we toured that city's famous cathedral and saw the spot where Joan of Arc was burned at the stake.

Now that I had completed my rehearsal for retirement I felt that I was ready. This would be my first year of celebrating Christmas in Washington in December. It would double as the celebration of my retirement, which would occur on December 31 at midnight.

1994

Florida and Southern United States World Tour to Celebrate My Retirement!

It was a great thrill to awake on the morning of January 2, 1994, and realize that I didn't have to go to work after having taught for thirty-four years! It was doubly exciting to immediately turn on the television to hear that it had snowed and they were trying to determine whether or not school would be closed or delayed for two hours. What a convenience to just be able to turn the television off and roll over for another short snooze.

In February of 1994, I decided it was time to get out of the cold weather of Washington and go to Florida for a week or two. I was really getting absorbed into my piano lessons by this time and I actually found a place in Florida where I could rent a keyboard for the time I was there in order to be able to practice. My piano teacher was impressed!

In April, a friend of mine from Brooklyn came down to Washington to visit. We then drove through Virginia, North Carolina, Tennessee, Mississippi, Louisiana, Alabama, Georgia, South Carolina, and back to North Carolina. During this trip, I was able to visit a lot of relatives and at the same time see areas of the country I had not seen before.

Highlights of this trip (other than family) included Biltmore House in Asheville, the Grand Ole Opry in Nashville, the civil war cemetery in Vicksburg, and the antebellum homes in Vicksburg and Natchez.

I visited friends in New Orleans. The weather in New Orleans can be extremely hot and just as humid. I remember seeing a t-shirt in a window there that read—"it's not the heat, it's the stupidity!" However, to compensate for this New Orleans can boast of having many, many excellent choices of eating facilities.

By the time I retired in December of 1993, I had already been in over hundred countries. However, I had been to a place and returned—to another place and returned—and so on. I had always promised myself that when I retired I would go on a trip around the world by myself. Well, that time had come!

My travel agent had taken my plans and had made all my airline and hotel reservations before I departed. On the day the big journey began, it started out with my arriving at the airport in Washington, D. C. I approached the check-in counter and handed my airline tickets to the clerk. I was asked how many people would be traveling with me and I said that I was traveling alone. The clerk then said she asked me because she was wondering why there were so many tickets in the packet. I told her that I was leaving to go on a trip around the world by myself. At that point she indicated that she was beginning to hate me already. A few minutes elapsed and she inquired as to how many bags I had to check-in. I told her that I only had two carry-on bags. She excused herself to the adjacent clerk and explained what was happening. They both agreed that upon my return I should come to the airport and teach a class in how to pack a bag for a trip. She then gave me my boarding pass and told me from which gate the plane would depart. She further informed me that I had just made her day and that she had upgraded me to first class. So I began my trip with a first class flight to California.

Three days were spent in Sacramento visiting a childhood friend of mine. While I was there we went to Yosemite National Park for a visit. I had never been there before and was really impressed and grateful that I had finally had the chance to visit this beautiful national park.

That entire excursion to Yosemite was not without a little excitement. While my friend was driving through the park and we were looking at all the sights, the car veered a little to the right and hit a curb. Unfortunately, both tires on the right side had a blowout. We waited for a while and a park ranger approached. After explaining what had happened he telephoned to seek assistance. After what seemed to be an eternity a tow truck finally arrived. We had to be towed about twenty miles.

There were three adults along with four dachshunds riding in the car. The tow truck driver had us ride in the tow truck and the dogs stayed in the car. We finally were able to get two new tires on the car and be on our way. For some reason these are the very things that you never forget about in your traveling experiences.

My friend took me to the airport in Sacramento. That day I was to fly to Los Angeles and on to Honolulu. I had no more arrived at the gate when there was an announcement saying that this flight was overbooked and they needed volunteers to go on a later flight.

The announcement indicated that if you volunteered, you would leave thirty minutes later and fly through San Francisco and on to Los Angeles. I went to the desk and explained to the clerk what my plans were—Los Angeles and then Honolulu—and asked if it would be possible to go on the later flight and instead of flying on to Los Angeles if I could fly from San Francisco to Honolulu. She checked the computer and indicated that it was possible. I waited to leave on the later flight, arrived in Honolulu two hours before I had originally planned, and the airline gave me $300 for going on the later flight. I was beginning to think that if this kind of luck continued, I was going to have a wonderful trip around the world.

I arrived in Honolulu and stayed at the Inn on the Park Hotel where I had stayed before. My room had a wonderful view of Diamond Head.

A longtime friend of mine who lives in Honolulu volunteered to give me a tour of Oahu and possibly take me to see things that I hadn't seen on previous trips. We went to the zoo and on the other side of the island; we walked through a Japanese cemetery. Another friend who previously lived in the Washington, D. C area was now living in Honolulu. We were able to meet and have lunch together.

The next day I flew to Manila where I stayed at the Admiral Hotel on Roxas Boulevard. I made arrangements through the tourist bureau at the hotel to have a group tour the next day. There were eight in our group and we were from seven different countries. We toured Fort Santiago. We saw the Coconut Palace that had been built for the Pope on his visit there, but he refused it. We saw the Manila Hotel where MacArthur, Eisenhower, and others had stayed. Their buses around town are called Jeepneys because they look like jeeps, but are ornately decorated. We did a Palace tour and were able to see Imelda's shoes. We were told that this was the last month that they couldbe viewed.

I went to the Manila American Cemetery and Memorial outside the city. There are over seventeen thoudsand military buried here. The father of a fellow teacher was buried here. I found his grave and was able to take pictures and bring them back to her.

Brunei was my next stop where I stayed at the Sheraton Hotel in Bandar Seri Begawan, the capital of Brunei. Here we saw several large mosques, even a floating mosque.

The Sultan of Brunei is one of the richest men in the world. His palace is supposedly the largest residential palace in the world. It contains almost 1800 rooms. He also maintains a palace for his second wife.

Living in Washington, D. C we are accustomed to seeing many pictures of the President on the walls of government offices, banks, etc. In the Sheraton Hotel here I noticed the picture of the Sultan and just below it was the picture of his two wives.

Just outside the city we saw a village of people who live in houses that are built on stilts in the river. They use boats to go back and forth to the city.

While reading a small newspaper at the hotel in Brunei I noticed that there had been a bomb explosion in Colombo, Sri Lanka. It concerned me since that was to be the next stop on my trip. I called the American Embassy to determine if any restrictions had been placed upon going there since I was to be there in a couple days. I was told that as far as they knew there had been no restrictions. However they told me that if I came to the embassy the next day they would further look into it. They did and printed out a sheet for me, which didn't indicate any restrictions upon going.

My flight took me through Singapore and I had a long layover before my flight to Sri Lanka. I discovered at the airport in Singapore that it was possible to go on a free city tour by bus. Upon returning to the airport you have a place where you can take a shower and then be ready for your ongoing flight. Why can't other airports be so obliging?

My hotel in Colombo was the Ceylon Intercontinental Hotel overlooking the Indian Ocean. The front desk at the hotel was extremely helpful in assisting me in arranging for an English speaking guide and driver for the next two days.

Just as I was picked up the next morning at the hotel, I told the driver about the article that I had read in Brunei and asked if the bomb explosion had been here. He responded by saying "No, it wasn't here, it was at the hotel across the street." I felt much better now!

Some of the sights in Colombo included the Government Headquarters, the floating temple, a new Convention Center, the Chinese Embassy, and a snake charmer. Yes, just walking along the street and here were the snakes in several little baskets. I didn't hang around since I have always said that there are only two kinds of snakes I detest; live ones and dead ones.

The following day I was driven to Kandy. On the way there we visited a batik factory. Every hour it seems that the terrain would change. There would be rice paddies. Later there would be banana trees. It went from flat to mountainous.

We stopped at the elephant baths and witnessed the elephants being washed. And yes, I rode an elephant here. I could then attest to the fact that I had ridden an elephant in Kenya, Tanzania, Nepal, India, Cambodia, and Sri Lanka!

It was great to be able to see the town of Kandy in the mountains. I walked through the botanical gardens and of course, took photos of the main temple.

I had to be at the airport early the next morning for my flight to Kuwait. The clerk at the airport wasn't going to allow me to board since I had not reconfirmed my reservation. I explained that I had tried to telephone over the weekend and that the offices were closed. While I waited, I thought about what would happen if I couldn't get on the flight. But not to worry, just at the last minute I was told that I could board the plane.

My visas for various countries had been obtained in Washington before I left. When I went to the Embassy of Kuwait to obtain a visa the gentleman told me that I had to be invited to be able to go there. I explained to him that I was going on a trip around the world by myself and that I had a friend who was working in Kuwait. I wanted to stop there and visit for a couple days. He then pushed a piece of paper through the window and told me to write an invitation letter with the purpose of the trip and the dates and sponsor myself. I wrote it and was told to come back in two days and pick up the visa.

The Safir Hotel was near the Kuwait Towers that had been seen many times on television during the war. During the day I took a tour of the city. We went to see Victory Square, the Planetarium, the National Museum, the Presidential Palace, and the state mosque. The National Museum had been severely damaged during the war.

By the time I was to continue my trip, the friend I was to visit in Kuwait had been transferred back to the United States. He gave me the names and telephone numbers of a couple who lived in an apartment building near the hotel. I called them and was invited to visit them.

After we visited for a while we left their apartment building to go out for dinner. As we were leaving the garage it was pouring rain! Yes, the only place on my world tour it rained was in Kuwait. These friends said that it had not rained there in about a year. All the dust on the street became mud. I commented that in the morning there would be a lot of dirty cars. I was told that I would probably not see any dirty cars. It seems that when these people moved there they were contacted to determine if they would like to have their car washed. They said that that would be nice about once or twice a week. They were told that that would not be possible because they would do it every day. What a service!

There was a lot of big gas guzzling cars being driven around the city. However, gas was about 10 cents a gallon.

My world trip continued from Kuwait with a stop in Bahrain. I stayed at the Delmon Hotel and was able to walk about the downtown area. The gold souk was in a four or five floor building and completely filled with everything gold.

In Manama, the capital of Bahrain, I visited the Beit Al Qur'an Museum where I saw ancient copies of the Koran, the Koran Museum, and the Grand Mosque. We visited a camel farm, saw the Tree of Life on the highest spot on the island, and visited the oil museum. We were shown several wind towers that are used for ventilation. The afternoon tour took us across the new causeway that had just been opened that connected Saudi Arabia to Bahrain.

After checking into my hotel in Rome, I decided to go for a walk and have my dinner before I returned. I had not walked but a few blocks from the hotel when I was approached by a gentleman who asked me if I spoke English. Then, he wanted to know where I was from. Once he found out that I was from the United States he seemed comforted that he had found someone who spoke English. He had asked me for directions, but then he wanted me to go with him to a place for dancing. I thought—oh, here we go again! I told him that I had had a long day, that I had people back at the hotel waiting for me, and that I was very hungry.

He insisted that he take me to a small restaurant where we had dinner. I volunteered to pay my part, but he said no and he paid. Upon leaving he again began talking about going to a club. I then said good-bye and walked the other way. I figured two people can play this game and I got a free dinner out of it. A similar situation happened the next night and I got another free dinner—I think I am either getting good at this game or I am a very lucky person.

I spent the next two days walking around the city of Rome and enjoying the sights that I had seen in 1962 and in 1968.

Flying from Rome to Munich to make my connection for a flight to Madrid and being able to look out of the plane and see the snow on the Alps suddenly reminded me that I had literally been around the world and was slowly making my way back home.

Madrid was my last stop on the world tour. There I visited the Royal Palace, the Prado Museum, and Retiro Park. In the park were the Valazquez Palace, the Crystal Palace, and acres and acres of beautiful gardens.

My flight from Madrid to Washington culminated this wonderful experience! I had taken nineteen flights, had flown over twenty-eight thousand miles, and had fulfilled my promise to myself of taking a trip around the world. It's a big world—not a small world.

Being a teacher for so many years had always prevented me from even thinking about the possibility of taking a vacation in September. It would be like a priest announcing that he was going to take a vacation at Easter or Christmas.

I had always wanted to see the fall foliage in New England. This being my first year of ever being able to take a trip in September I decided that this was the time to do it. A friend of mine and I flew up to New Hampshire where we rented a car. We visited people in New Hampshire who had previously lived in Washington.

We left our hotel in Meredith and drove all over New Hampshire and Vermont. We had arrived at just the perfect time. The mountains were spectacular in their varying shades of yellow, orange, and red. I was finally able to say that I had taken a trip in September!

Before it was time to begin all the Christmas decorating that year, I made up my mind that it was time to fulfill the invitation that was made by the lady from Bermuda while we were in Nepal. The friend who was with me on the trip to India and I went to Bermuda and was able to go to her home and have the Baked Alaska that we had been promised when we were in Nepal.

Between all this I was able to squeeze in enough time to be a supernumerary in *The Marriage of Figaro* with the Washington Opera.

In December of 1994, I had another Christmas-in-December party and celebrated my first year of retirement.

1995

Acapulco, California, and London

I began the year 1995 with a one-week trip to Acapulco in January. In February, I went to Palm Springs and San Diego. I stayed in Palm Springs for a few days and remember taking the aerial tramway to the pinnacle of Mt. San Jacinto. It is about six thousand-feet high and the temperatures up there are at least forty degrees lower than they are down in Palm Springs.

I arrived in San Diego a day earlier than I had planned. I drove to the Coronado Hotel and inquired if they had accommodation for a single for one night. They did and by doing this I was fulfilling another wish. I called a close friend in Washington and told him what was happening. He said that in the evening I had to have dinner in the Crown Room of the hotel.

As I was walking from the hotel I noticed a sort of an art deco theater. I then saw on the marquee that the play *She Loves Me* was playing. A year or two before this the same play was playing on Broadway and I really wanted to see it and never got around to it. I went to the box office to inquire about the possibility of getting a ticket for that evening. The lady at the box office checked and told me that there was a seat on the far side in the upper section. Upon further scrutiny she discovered that someone had canceled and there was a single seat in the front row.

She further explained to me that the performance this evening would be the opening evening for the "new" theater. It had been undergoing a complete makeover. Furthermore, since it was a special occasion there would be a reception at the Coronado Hotel after the performance in the Crown Room with the cast of the play.

After having lived in Washington for several years and knowing the prices of theater tickets, I was beginning to wonder how much all of this was going to cost. I inquired about the price of the ticket. When she quoted the price to me, I couldn't believe how inexpensive it was.

An official of the theater appeared on the stage to welcome everyone to the new theater and indicated that he wanted to introduce a couple who had donated a lot of money for the makeover. It wasn't until that moment that I realized that I was sitting next to them in the front row.

The play was enjoyable and the reception in the Crown Room was an evening I will never forget.

The next day I talked to my friend in Washington and the first thing he wanted to know was whether or not I had dinner in the Crown Room. When I told him that it had been closed for the evening he was really disappointed until I told him the real story. I told him about my luck with the theater and that I actually got to go to a reception in the Crown Room with lots of food and the cast of the show.

In February of 1995, I was a supernumerary in the American Ballet's full production of *Manon* and in March of 1995, I was in *Carmen* at the Kennedy Center with the Washington Opera. Denyce Graves, the world renowned opera singer, was the Carmen for this production. She was born in Washington and the city has always been happy to claim her as one of their own.

In June of 1995, I took my elder sister to London for a week for her seventy-fifth birthday. She had never been to Europe and was overly excited about the trip. She had just had knee replacement surgery a few months prior to this. However, she never once asked me to slow down or say that she was tired. We went to Buckingham Palace, Westminster Abbey, Hampton Court Palace and gardens, and Windsor Castle. I made a photo album for her as a memento and she not only still has the album, she still talks about how excited she was to have been able to go on the trip.

Since I have two living sisters I couldn't do something for one and not do something for the other. So I gave the other sister money for her and her husband to go on a vacation of their choice for a week.

In November of 1995, I had my all-time favorite supernumerary appointment at the Kennedy Center. I was asked to be the doctor in *Der Rosenkavalier*. Eric Halverson, who sings at the Met in New York, was the lead singer. I was on stage for about twenty minutes.

First, I had to enter to assist in his being stabbed. In approaching him I had to push four of the opera chorus members out of the way. I placed my medical bag down in front of him. I looked to see where the stabbing was and made a gesture that I didn't see anything in the area that the quartet who was standing behind the chair was pointing to.

I then proceeded to pull out a large magnifying glass from the bag. It was only after closer inspection with the magnifying glass that I made the gesture to let them know that I knew where the location of the stabbing was. I then pulled out a large hyperdermic needle. He became alarmed and tried to leave the stage. I had to retrieve him. I then had to take some liquid ointment from the bag and place some on his arm which made him scream. Before I returned the ointment to the bag I sampled a little myself and indicated that it wasn't bad.

This brought us to the final phase, which was putting a sling around his arm and neck. I was instructed to go offstage and bring him back something to drink. Of course as I returned the wrong person grabbed the drink. Disgustedly, I leave.

1996

Australia and Italy

In March I went to visit a friend in New Mexico. I had enough time there to really get the feel of the area around Albuquerque. I was able to go to an opera in Santa Fe before returning to Washington.

I arrived back just in time to be a supernumerary in the Washington Opera production of *Mefistofele* with Samuel Ramey. I was to be a "hell pusher" for a float that was to be pushed around the stage. The float had a giant pot on it with Adam and Eve in their garden attire that consisted of a fig leaf. My red full-length caftan was sprinkled with small mirrors. The headdress had two large red devil horns which didn't help in maneuvering the stairs in the tower of the set.

My travel agent was to attend a travel convention in Australia. He invited me to go with him. In addition to the meetings in Sydney, the group saw the usual spots including the opera house, had a picnic at Macquaries Point, visited the sight for the Olympics, and took an all-day trip to the Blue Mountains outside Sydney.

After the convention in Sydney, another travel agent from Australia had planned an extended trip. We stayed at the Como Hotel in Melbourne. It was a really nice hotel and we had a wonderful suite on the top floor with a nice Japanese garden on the roof just outside our room. There had been a big tennis tournament in Australia just before we were there. We were told that Boris Becker, Monica Seles, and Andre Agassi had been guests at this hotel for that tournament.

We were given an inside tour of the opera house where we were able to try on costumes from operas and have a group picture. The group saw the other major tourist sights there.

We then flew to Cairns where we stayed at the Kewarra Beach Resort. One day was spent on an Ocean Spirit cruise to Michaelmas Cay to enjoy that area of the barrier reef. We took a train trip to Kuranda. I had been there before in 1989, but this time the skyrail had opened. It covers almost five miles.

The next big trip for 1996 was to Italy. A friend of mine and I flew to Milan where we picked up a rental car and drove to Lake Como. We stayed at the Hotel Villa Flori that was situated on the lake. The breakfast room at the hotel was absolutely exquisite. It felt so good to sit there in the morning to have a leisurely breakfast as you witnessed the sun arising on the other side of the lake.

One day, while there, we drove around the lake to see some of the beautiful homes. Villa Carlotta was one of them. It was built between 1690 and 1743. We drove to Lake Lugano in Switzerland, to Lake Maggiore, and also to Lake Gorda.

We spent a night in Verona on our way to Venice. We saw the tomb of Juliet in Verona, the war memorial, the old city gate, the Castel Vecchio, the large arena, and of course the balcony of Romeo and Juliet.

Our hotel in Venice was just a block or two off St. Mark's Square. In the square are St. Mark's Cathedral and the Doge's Palace. High tides flood the area nowadays. We saw Rialto Bridge and many other sites along the Grand Canal.

From Venice we drove to Florence. The Bonciani Hotel was in close proximity to the major attractions. We toured the Cathedral, the National Museum, Boboli Gardens, and the Pitti Palace.

We drove from Rome to Pisa where were able to walk to the top of the Leaning Tower. We walked around the central square in Siena and then drove to San Gimignano. I was hoping to see a friend of mine who was going to be spending the summer here. However, when I was there he had gone to Russia to see relatives. The countryside in Tuscany is breathtaking with large fields of sunflowers and vineyards.

We spent two or three days in Rome exploring the sites and eating our way into oblivion.

The day we were leaving we were going to drive to Tivoli's Villa d'Este Gardens.

We had looked at a map and had determined the best way to exit the city to be on our way to Tivoli. That worked for several blocks; however, we approached an intersection where we needed to turn left. Of course the sign indicated that a left turn at this intersection wasn't allowed. What to do? If we turn right, we will most definitely get lost. As soon as the light turned green, I said to my friend, "Hold on." I made a quick jag through the pedestrian walkway and made my illegal turn. We made it!

Today, one would only have to use their GPS with their destination keyed in and just sit back and listen to the directions.

As we were driving through a somewhat lengthy area of forest, we kept seeing ladies standing beside the highway. The first time or two it didn't click. Upon seeing several others we surmised that they were prostitutes. Both of us had read about encounters where these people would agree to take you into the woods and suddenly their brothers would appear. They would proceed to rob you, beat you up, and sometimes even take your car. We decided it wasn't worth it.

The gardens were just as spectacular as I had remembered them in 1962 on my first trip to Europe thirty-four years before.

We continued on our journey to Sorrento. We stayed at the Cristina Hotel that was high up on the hill with a fantastic view of Mt. Vesuvius and the Bay of Naples.

We drove up the hill toward the hotel, found a place to park, and were in the process of getting out of the car when a couple saw that we were Americans. They said "you didn't actually drive in Italy, did you?" We let them know that we had just finished driving over two thousand miles in Italy and had had no problems. They couldn't believe it!

We could get the train near out hotel, which made it convenient going back and forth to the ruins at Herculaneum and Pompeii.

From Naples one day we took the ferry over to Capri. We walked around the island, had lunch, and returned. We had planned to take the trip into the Blue Grotto; however, with extremely high tides and wind that day, it was closed.

The highlight of being in this area was the drive down the Amalfi Coast. I have visited places all over the world and I must admit that I feel this is probably the most beautiful place I have ever visited. The curvy highway lends itself to magnificent views at every turn. Suddenly you realize that you are approaching a small town that just seems to be hanging on the side of the mountain when in the other direction it is nothing but scenery of blue sea.

We were in Positano, Amalfi, and Ravello. Ravello overlooks the Bay of Salerno. The gardens at Villa Rufolo are exquisite. Greta Garbo used to come here to get away from everything and relax.

We ended the trip by arising early, going to the airport, and taking a flight to Paris. The reason for this was that my birthday coincided with the conclusion of our trip. I had told my friend before we left for the trip that I wanted to be able to get up in Sorrento and say, "I think I'll just fly to Paris for my birthday!"—which I did.

I returned to Washington the next day and soon began rehearsals for *La Boheme.* Things can become a little strange when you are being fitted for your costumes.

For some reason the lady didn't particularly like the shirt they had chosen for me. She didn't like the tie either. Both of them were replaced. Then we proceeded to put on a vest, a jacket, and a topcoat. Next, I was given a large scarf and was instructed as to how they wished it to be worn. She said that I should put it on in such a way that you wouldn't be able to see anything under it. Duh! Why all the fuss about the shirt and the tie!

I actually had three roles in this opera. In the opening scene, I passed through a crowded street pushing and cranking a music box. I returned to cross the scene again as a coal man carrying an empty bag. As I returned to cross yet again the bag had been filled and I had obtained a few coal smears on my face.

When that scene was finished I had to retreat to the dressing room, get rid of the coal smudges, and change my costume in order later reappear as old man in the snow. As the curtain rose at the beginning of the act, I was to slowly walk across from one side to the other rubbing my hands together and over my arms to indicate the intense coldness in the air.

As the curtain rose on the first night of performances, there was a thunderous round of applause. Even though I knew that the applause was for the set I couldn't help but to think that it was for me being that I was the only person on stage at the time.

In a flash it occurred to me that I could pause, face the audience, and take a bow. However, in an instantaneously quicker second flash I was reminding myself that if I did that it would probably be the last time I would be able to walk across that stage.

1997

Gulf Coast, Iceland, and Turkey

In April of 1997, I took a trip across the Gulf Coast from New Orleans to Tallahassee and back. I drove to Baton Rouge where I was able to see that capitol city for the first time. The capitol building is thirty-four floors tall and is the tallest state capitol building in the United States. From the observation deck one can see the Mississippi river nearby.

In this area there are several large plantation homes. I toured Greenwood in St. Francisville. It was built in the early 1800s and is in the Greek revival style of architecture. The nearby Afton Gardens was a treat with its meticulously manicured hedges, flowers, and statues.

Rosedown Plantation and gardens is considered to be one of Louisiana's most distinguished museum homes. It encompasses fourteen historic plantation buildings, twenty-eight acres of gardens on approximately two thousand acres.

Some of the other plantation homes visited include Rosemont in Woodville, Mississippi; Oakley Plantation, which was the home of John James Audubon; Destrehan Plantation; Nottoway Plantation, used as a B and B; Oak Alley Plantation, which is probably the most publicized; Tezcuco Plantation Home; Houmas House Plantation and Gardens, which was used in the movie, *Hush . . . Hush, Sweet Charlotte*; and the San Francisco Plantation House.

I drove to Biloxi, Mississippi, where I was confronted with more large homes built along the beach. I toured Beauvoir, which was the last home of Jefferson Davis, President of the Confederate States of America. On view was the caisson for Jefferson Davis and a confederate cemetery.

The only thing that detracted from this area was the huge casino that had been built there.

Pensacola, Florida, had an old opera house where Sarah Bernhardt had appeared. There were several old buildings in the downtown area worth seeing. There is also the Museum of Naval Aviation.

It seems that no one could go to Pensacola without a visit to McGuire's Irish Pub. It was extremely fascinating to see. The entire ceiling and most of the columns were covered with dollar bills that people had signed and stapled to the wall or ceiling. There were also signed pictures of political figures, sports stars, movie stars, etc., who had dined there. There was even a letter from the Governor to help out a sailor who was being kicked out of the Navy for having stolen one of the dollar bills. With the Governor's help, the charges were dropped.

Driving along the coast toward Panama City, I could not believe how white the sand was at the beaches and the consistency was almost like confectioners' sugar.

By this time I had finally made it to the easternmost point of my excursion, which was Tallahassee. There I saw the capitol, the gardens, and the Vietnam Memorial.

In retracing my steps back to New Orleans I stopped in Mobile, Alabama. This city has several large old houses in its downtown area. Most of them it seems are occupied as law offices. The major plantation here was Oakleigh, which is a Greek revival mansion built in the early 1800s.

My only night of culture on this trip was a performance of *The Odd Couple* sponsored by the University of South Alabama. Starring in this performance was Jamie Farr and William Christopher, who had both acquired notoriety through their portrayals in *M*A*S*H.*

Bellingrath Gardens, located a few miles west of Mobile, is a real treat and one of the highlights of the trip. Mr. Bellingrath was one of the first franchise holders for Coca Cola, thus his fortune. It covers about sixty-five acres.

The summer of 1997 was spent completing a circle tour of Iceland. The tour started in the capital city of Reykjavik. The most prominent building in the city is the 244-foot tall Lutheran Church of Iceland, Hallgrimskirkja. It is named after an Icelandic poet. Our tour group drove passed the Hofdi House, which was the sight of the disarmament talks between Gorbachev and Reagan.

Most of the electricity and hot water in Iceland comes from hot volcanic water and is piped into large distribution stations. I had dinner in a revolving restaurant that was situated directly above the city's hot water supply.

There were so many volcanic mountains, lava fields, geysers, and waterfalls that it would be impossible to mention all of them. Some of the most prominent waterfalls would include: Gullfoss, Godafoss, Svartifoss, Skogofoss, and Seljalandsfoss.

We visited a place where there had been an earthquake and the earth split. One section is on one plane and just beside it the other section that is several yards higher. The difference between the two is similar to looking at a wall where it just goes straight up as if one part either fell or the other part rose.

Several of our hotels during our stay are used as schools in the wintertime. They are boarding schools because most of the students would have to be bused long distances from their homes to the school and with the harsh weather it would be impossible to go back and forth. Some of the students may go for a long period of time during the school year without seeing their parents.

Drangey Island is in the Skagafjordur (Skaga fjord) and is the result of an earthquake many, many years ago. It is inhabited by an enormous number of birds, especially the puffin. The noise as one approaches is almost deafening.

There was a church adjacent to the Hotel Reynihlid, which was our hotel near Lake Myvatn. After our dinner that evening, we were fortunate to be able to attend a very pleasant baroque concert in the church. As the concert was coming to a close around 10:00 p.m. the sun was still shining. I even remember taking a picture of the bar behind the hotel at 11:30 p.m. and the sun was still shining then also.

Namaskard is an area near Lake Myvatn where sulphur was mined. The earth around these hot mud springs consists of many different colors. At some locations it almost gives you a feeling of what it would be like standing on the moon.

We were at the Leirhnjukur Volcano where an eruption had occurred in 1984 and the earth was still hot. At the point one begins to wonder why we are standing there!

Our group was staying at the Hotel Egilsbud in Neskaupsstadur. In the evening we took a boat out through the fjord and docked in order to have a barbecue picnic dinner in a natural cave-like structure formed by volcanic lava.

For several days on our excursion we had been reminded that there are almost no trees on the island. Well, this evening our navigational guide proceeded to light a big bonfire. My question to him was that if there were no trees on the island, whose furniture are we burning.

On our way back to shore and to the hotel, the guide asked me if I would like to steer the boat. Since I had actually owned a boat at one time while living in Washington, I felt quite competent in accepting this challenge.

Some of the people in the group didn't realize that I was navigating the boat until they realized that the person whom they were involved in conversation with was the person who should be manning the boat! He just said, "Oh, Bill is taking care of that."

We visited the Maritime Museum of East Iceland in Eskifjordur. It was an interesting museum and had on display an old typewriter, molds used for making chocolates, an old doctor's office complete with an operating table and various medical instruments, and an old dentist office.

The Vatnajokull Glacier is Europe's largest glacier. The Jokulsarlon lagoon is formed from the melting of this glacier. We had to don our special life jackets and went on a cruise of the lagoon. The boat moves slowly through the lagoon and as it does we have giant icebergs floating next to us. They throw out a beautiful blue color. It really isn't blue, just as I was told when later I went to the Antarctic. It appears blue because that is the only color of the prism the human eye picks up.

We drove up to a lodge near Eyjafjallajokull. We had an hour or two where we were able to go out on a quasi-jet ski. This is the volcano that erupted in 2010 and caused havoc in most of Europe because of the volcanic ash.

I took a one-day trip from Reykjavik to Greenland. We flew to the Inuit Village of Kulusuk. On the way there the pilot would tilt the plane in order for us to be able to take photos of the endless mountains and hills covered with snow and ice.

The local population of Kulusuk gave us a seal-spearing demonstration, a sled dog demonstration, and a musical performance. We were able to see how they dry the seal skins. We were told that we were lucky that this particular day was the hottest day they had had all summer and it was almost fifty degrees.

Being the traveler that I am, there is no direct way home. From Iceland I visited Amsterdam for a couple days, took the train to Luxembourg where I the caught a flight back to Washington. Strangely enough, on that flight home we flew over Iceland.

After returning from Iceland I was a 'super' in two Rossini operas at the Barns of Wolf Trap outside Washington. As soon as these performances were over, it was time to "hit the road again!"

In September of 1997, I revisited Turkey. The trip didn't start off well. My flight had been delayed and by the time I arrived at the airport, all the other tour participants had been transported to our hotel. I called to find out what I should do. I was told to get a taxi to the hotel and make sure I kept a receipt and I would be reimbursed. I used the ATM machine and obtained Turkish currency. I think the receipt showed that I had about five million Turkish Lira. However, upon arriving at the hotel I was informed that the taxi ride was two million Turkish Lira—easy come, easy go!

Our first day of sightseeing was to the usual places in Istanbul. One of the places we saw that I hadn't been to previously was the Dolmabahce Palace. The ceremonial hall, the crystal staircase hallway, the salon, and the ambassador's room—all were unbelievable!

The next day we left Istanbul by bus and began our journey. Our first stop was at a small town along the Marmara Sea where we had lunch. Along the way we began noticing that there were many unfinished houses. We inquired about that to Incy, our guide. She explained that there is a strange law in Turkey that states that taxes are not assessed on property until it is completed. Therefore, many people build houses that are three or four floors high. However, they will leave one of the floors unfinished and that way they don't have to pay taxes.

We visited the Military Cemetery at Gallipoli where many soldiers from Australia and New Zealand were buried.

At Troy we were able to walk up to the top of the replica of the Trojan (Wooden) Horse. We saw the ruins in Troy who some believe are seven civilizations on top of each other dating back from 2600 BC to 2300 BC.

Next were the ruins of Pergamum, which included the Shrine of Artemis, the Acropolis, and the Asklepieion, which is believed to be the world's first full-service health clinic.

On to Ephesus we saw the famous library, the amphitheater, the gymnasium, the stadium, and the royal baths. We also saw the House of the Virgin Mary. Many believe it to be the place where Saint John took the mother of Jesus after the crucifixion and from which she ascended to heaven. Pope Paul VI visited this site in 1967 and confirmed its authenticity.

In Pamukkale, there is mineral-rich volcanic spring water that cascades over basins and natural terraces, crystallizing into white curtains of solidified water seemingly suspended in air. The hot springs in the area were being used by people who believe that the water can cure rheumatism and other problems. Our hotel had a thermal pool, a Turkish bath, and a whirlpool.

The next day we drove toward Konya. On the way we passed the city of Denezli, visited a rug-making factory, saw a demonstration of silk-making from cocoons, saw typical tents that were home to nomads, and had an unexpected visit to a local school.

In the town of Perge, there were ruins that date back to the third century BC. St. Paul, who sailed here from Cyprus, is said to have preached at the basilica near the end of the street.

Aspendos is a theater that was built during the reign of Emperor Marcus Aurelius (AD 161-180) by a local architect called Xenon. We were able to attend an evening performance there by the Whirling Dervishes under a full moon.

Kaymakli, in the Cappadocia region, was an underground city. From the seventh to the tenth century the Christian Cappadocians were under siege from Arab raiders. They took refuge in about forty underground cities. These cities, some stretching as much as twenty stories below the surface and were able to house as many as twenty thousand people.

Most people associate the Cappadocia region with the "fairy chimney" rock formations. Many of these can be seen near the city of Goreme and Uchisar.

However, in the city of Zelve there is a monastery carved completely out of stone and there is also an open-air museum. The city of Avanos in that same area is well known for its pottery making and carpet weaving.

While our group was being offered a tour of the pottery-making shop, they volunteered for me to be the person from our group to use the turning wheel and make a jar or an item of any sort from mud. I have pictures of that to prove that I was able to make a jar.

Our next major stop was Ankara, the capital city of Turkey. The major attraction in Ankara is the Tomb of Ataturk. He is considered somewhat a God by a lot of the Turkish people. He was the leader of the war of independence, the founder and the first president of the Republic of Turkey.

Our tour ended upon arriving back in Istanbul. I had planned to stay two or three extra days before returning to Washington. I overheard our guide talking to the front-desk clerk. She was speaking in Turkish and I couldn't understand what she was saying. However, I kept hearing my name in the midst of the conversation. I asked her what was happening or if something was wrong. She told me that since I was going to stay a few more days she was bargaining with the gentleman at the front desk in order to get me a good room. I had a suite on the top floor! What a way to end the trip!

Friends of mine from New York and New Jersey came down to Washington in December. We drove to Williamsburg, Virginia, because we wanted to get the feel of how Christmas was many years ago. On our way back to Washington we stayed at the historic Jefferson Hotel in Richmond.

1998

Paris, London, and Eastern Europe

In January of 1998, my travel agent, who is also a longtime friend of mine, was planning to attend another convention with other travel agents in London. He again asked me if I would like to accompany him. Needless to say, I accepted the invitation. Since neither of us had had the experience of traveling through the Chunnel, made a suggestion that we leave a few days earlier than initially planned, spend a few days in Paris, and take the Chunnel from Paris to London and arrive just in time for the beginning of the convention. He liked my idea.

The segment of the Chunnel in which one is under the English Channel is only about twenty minutes. During that part of our crossing we were approximately half way through and were having our nice lunch with wine. I looked out the window atnothing but darkness on the other side and said, "I just saw a fish go by." He had just taken a sip of wine and—oh well, you can guess what happened to the wine!

In March of 1998 I was a "super" in *Dangerous Liaisons* at the Kennedy Center. This just so happened to be the last opera that I would appear in at the Kennedy Center. I had finally come to the realization that since I am retired, I just didn't have the time to continue doing this.

In September of 1998, I took a Cosmos group tour to Eastern Europe. The tour was to begin in Berlin. However, I decided to go a week ahead and see a few other places. I flew into Frankfurt and spent several days there exploring the city and seeing the Old Opera House, the New Opera House, and Römer Square.

I took the train from Frankfurt to Heidelberg. My first visit here was in 1962, thus thirty-seven years before! Needless to say, it had changed. However, I did enjoy taking several pictures of the castle, the river, the old bridge, and the walking street. It had not been a walking street on my previous trip. I wanted to compare the pictures and really be able to see the difference.

Another day, I took a train to Weisbaden. There I saw the Old Town Hall, City Hall, and Kerhaus Exhibition Hall. The exhibition hall had a casino on one side and a theater on the other.

I had enjoyed these few days exploring parts of Germany that I had visited previously and now it was time to join my other traveling partners in Berlin. My last visit here was in 1976 when my friend and I almost missed our stop and ended up back in East Germany.

I felt fortunate to visit where "The Wall" had been and to see what was left of it now. Most of the area had large cranes that were being used in construction of many new buildings. We visited the Kaiser Wilhelm Church and drove by many other places of interest.

We visited Potsdam and saw the building where the principal allies of World War II met for the Potsdam Conference. In attendance were President Truman, Premier Stalin, and Prime Minister Churchill. We also visited the San-lSouci Palace in Potsdam. This was the summer home for Fredrick II. After World War II, it was in East Germany. Since 1990 it has reverted back to just being in Germany.

Warsaw was our next stop and what a change! When I had visited here in 1976 everything was very dark and dreary. At night about the only thing one could see would be one of the illuminated "wedding cake" structures of the communist period. Now, in 1998 there is a new railway station, several large chain hotels, and advertising!

We visited the Chopin Memorial, the Lazienkowski Palace, the Opera House, the Royal Castle, the Monument to the Jewish Ghetto, and the Old Town. I remembered going to a small theater in the corner of the Old Town and being able to see a movie on the destruction of Warsaw during World War II. The Church of the Holy Cross has an urn in which Chopin's heart is encased. He had lived in Paris for many years, but wanted his heart to be in Poland. We visited the Jasna Gora Monastery. This monastery is one of the most famous shrines in Poland and one of its most treasured possessions is the Black Madonna.

We then visited Auschwitz Concentration Camp. Words can't express the feelings that one has in walking through this place. Just seeing the place where there were firing squads and gas chambers brings cold chills.

We visited the Jewish ghetto in Krakow. We also saw the Royal Castle and the factory where employees of Schindler's List worked.

Just outside Krakow we visited the Weiliczka salt mine. It is almost one thousand feet deep and is large enough that there is a huge cathedral inside made completely out of salt. I distinctly remember the large old elevator that was used in bringing us back to the top.

Out next stop was Budapest. We toured Heroes' Square, the Royal Museum, St Matthias Church, Fisherman's Bastion, and the Gellert Baths. While there I was able to see my friend that I had met on my first trip to Budapest.

In Vienna, we toured Belvedere Palace, City Hall, the Hofburg, St. Stephen's Church, the Natural History Museum, and the Parliament. This was my third time to visit Vienna.

In Prague I witnessed almost exactly what I had witnessed in revisiting Warsaw. The city had really come alive. One didn't have to go to the State Tourist office in order to get a hotel reservation. By the way, the hotel in the river where I stayed in 1976 was still in operation. There also were many new buildings, new hotels, and new businesses.

Our hotel in Prague wasn't centrally located. Four of us decided that we would take the tram into the center of the city and return later that evening. We tried to keep an eye on exactly which direction the tram was going so we would hopefully be able to retrace our way while returning that evening.

We got on the tram to return to the hotel. Everything went fine for a while and all of a sudden the tram stopped and everyone began leaving. One lady saw the befuddled looks on our faces and in her broken English told us that this tram had finished for the evening and wouldn't be going any further.

As we began walking in what we thought was the correct direction for our hotel, we saw people sitting in front of their homes. Several times we just mentioned the name of our hotel to them and they would point in a particular direction. We finally breathed a sigh of relief when in the distance we spotted the illuminated light on our hotel.

1999

Florida, Hawaii, and Europe

In 1999, I spent almost an entire month in Florida. It was again great to be away during the cold weather and be able to visit many friends in Florida.

In April, I made another sojourn to Hawaii to visit my friend there. And as usual, I visited friends in Sacramento on my way there and San Francisco on the return.

In August 1999, I was a "super" in *Tosca* at the Lisner Auditorium on the George Washington University campus. I was a priest in the first act with an elaborate costume. In the final act I was one of the members of the firing squad for Tosca.

Also, in August 1999, I was a "super" in *The Magic Flute* at Wolf Trap. I was the back half of a giraffe, and being in the heat of summer with high humidity on an outdoor stage, it was extremely uncomfortable inside that costume to say the least. We had a little rectangular window underneath in what would be the stomach area. This opening allowed us a place to get some air and to see through enough to know where we were walking. They did give us little frozen wands to put around our neck, which did seem to make it a little cooler.

A very good friend of mine in Washington had been stationed at High Wickham outside London during World War II. He had said many times that he would like to return there sometime before he died. Finally, one day I made him an offer. I said, "Why don't we go to England in September and you will be able to return to High Wickham." He was ecstatic.

A few weeks later he indicated that his father was from Ireland and that he would like to go to Ireland for a few days. I told him that you couldn't just go to Ireland for a few days. We would need at least a week. He was pleased with that.

However, a few days later he said to me that he had often heard me exclaim my love for the city of Amsterdam and that he had never been there and would like to go.

Even though he was in his eighties at the time, we began our trip by flying to Dublin. Some of the highlights of Dublin included the Oscar Wilde home and monument, the Guinness factory, and The Book of Kells at Trinity College.

We rented a car and drove all the way up to Northern Ireland and down the west coast to Galway, where we spent the night at the Ardilaun House Hotel. In Galway we joined several other tourists in having a medieval dinner at Dunguaire Castle.

We drove to Kilarney, which was the area where my friend's father was born. Being a small town, there were actually people there who said they remembered some members of his family.

We then drove around the Ring of Kerry and on to Cork. My friend was determined that he wasn't going to visit Ireland and go back home without being able to say that he kissed the Blarney Stone. He made it up all the steps and fulfilled his longtime desire.

We toured the crystal factory in Waterford and continued on to Dublin. Part of this was almost exactly what I had done with another friend in 1989.

We flew from Dublin to London. We spent three or four days seeing the sights of London and had the occasion to visit High Wickham. He finally did get to return there.

From London we took a train to Edinburgh where we spent two nights. We visited the castle and walked the main street. I distinctly remember our dinner at the Dome Restaurant. It was a beautiful building that had been a bank at one time. Yes, we did have haggis. Once is enough.

We returned to London and continued our sightseeing there. We took the subway to Greenwich. There we saw the Cutty Sark and the Millineum Dome, which was just being completed. We toured the Royal Naval Academy. The palace there is where Henry VIII was born.

We took the Chunnel to Brussels and transferred to another train that would take us to Amsterdam. We spent four nights in Amsterdam and he seemed just like a little kid enjoying all the things that I had seen about five times before—the Rijksmuseum, the canals, Volendam, etc.

We were at the airport waiting for our flight home and he took a walk through the terminal to stretch his legs since we had a long flight ahead of us. Upon his return I decided to do the same thing. While I was walking I spotted a person who looked familiar for some reason. Just about that time another person came into the picture. It was then that I realized that these were two ladies that I had previously met on my trip to Iceland! Again—a small world story!

Igauzu Falls, Argentina 2003

Sun City, South Africa 2004

Pyramid, Egypt 2005

The Treasury at Petra, Jordan 2005

Timbuktu, Mali 2006

Agadir, Morocco 2006

Cape Town, South Africa 2006

Entrance to Ming Tombs, Beijing 2007

The Three Gorges, Yangtze River 2007

Potola Palace, Lhasa Tibet 2007

Art Deco Weekend, Napier, New Zealand 2008

Sand Dunes Perth, Australia 2008

Hue, Vietnam 2008

Ho Chi Minh Mausoleum, Hanoi, Vietnam, 2008

2000

California; Cancun

In June of 2000, my friend from Brooklyn flew to San Diego and I flew from Washington to San Diego where we met at the airport. We spent a few days seeing the sights of San Diego and then drove to Palm Springs. It was really hot there!

From there we drove into Los Angeles. While there we went to the tourist places in Hollywood, Venice Beach, the Huntington Museum, and Santa Monica pier. We were able to get tickets and saw a taping of *The Tonight Show with Jay Leno.*

We drove up the coast and spent the night in Morro Bay. The next day we drove to see the Hearst Castle. By the time one finishes the tour you feel a little depressed in that you knew there would never be a way that you would be able to live that way.

Carmel and Monterrey were our next destinations and what places! The mission at Carmel is a marvel. The city of Monterrey has a lot of of history. We enjoyed seeing Cannery Row, Fisherman's Wharf, Doris Day's home, and the golf course at Pebble Beach.

The next day we drove on through San Francisco to Sausalito where we did some shopping and had lunch. We spent the night in Napa Valley amidst all the vineyards. We then spent two or three days in Sacramento visiting my childhood friend who lives there. From Sacramento we headed to San Francisco. This was our last stop for the trip. By the time we were ready to go home, we both felt that we had really been able to see a lot of the state of California on this trip.

2001

Toronto, Chicago, and New York

In 2001, I took a trip to Toronto. It had been a while since I had visited here and felt it was time to come back. My luck had followed me. As we were waiting for the flight we were notified that the flight was overbooked and that they needed volunteers to go on a later flight. I volunteered because I was not restricted to any schedule or timetable. My reward for doing this was that I received a free ticket to be used on that airline to anywhere in the continental United States and Canada within the next year. I used the ticket the next year and returned to Canada and visited Montreal and Quebec.

When I first moved to Washington in 1965, I had a roommate who was from Chicago. During the six years we were roommates we would frequently travel to Chicago. In 2001, I began to realize that it had been at least thirty years since I had been there.

A friend of mine and I flew there and spent a week. It was great to have a week in order to take in all the things we wanted to do. We visited the Navy Pier; we went to the top what was then the Sears Tower, the Hancock building, several museums, theater, etc. We also took the train out one day to Oak Park and saw the Frank Lloyd home.

I, like so many others, have seen New York City and possibly Niagara Falls, but haven't seen any of the remainder of that large state. Because of this I decided that it was time I saw the "other" New York.

The first night was spent at West Point. I had never been there before and really enjoyed seeing the campus, the church, and the setting along the Hudson river.

The next day I drove to Albany and toured the capital city. From there I drove on north to Lake George, Lake Placid, and Saranac Lake. I toured the Olympic stadium where the Olympics had taken place in 1932 and 1980. Of course, we all remember the 1980 hockey game between the United States and Russia. It was a thrill to be able to stand at the top of the high ski jump and look out over the area. It was October and the trees were at their glorious best.

From here I drove to Watertown to see the one thousand islands. I took the boat tour there and it was wonderful to see all the old houses there. From there I continued on to Syracuse, where it did snow that night—in early October!

In Rochester I toured the Eastman mansion, saw the old Kodak factories, and the Susan B. Anthony home.

I was able to drive through the Finger Lakes area. I saw the campus of Cornell at Ithaca. I toured the Corning Glass Museum in Corning.

By the time I arrived back in Washington, I felt that I had finally seen most of New York.

However, I decided to go to New York for Christmas. This was the year of 9/11 and the city was literally begging people to come and visit. I was able to get a nice room just off Broadway for about $70 per night, which was almost unheard-of in this city.

Not only was the hotel a bargain, I was also able to get a ticket for the *Radio City Music Hall Christmas Show* on Christmas eve night in the orchestra in about the fifteenth row for half price!

After I had my dinner that night and was walking to the theater, I decided to call my family in Georgia because I knew at this time they would all be together having their Christmas dinner. While I was talking to a niece of mine she couldn't contain herself without asking me—"Are you wearing your fur coat?" And I said, "Of course I am!"

2002

Cuba, Southern United States, Canada, and Portugal

In January of 2002, I went on a legally sanctioned tour to Cuba. There were sixteen in our group and it was set up as an art and architecture study group. We stayed at the Parque Central Hotel. It was a beautiful hotel and had been built by a Dutch company. It was the near Capitol building and faced the central park. We had a very nice tour of the Capitol Building. We had dinner and a show at the famous Tropicana night club in Havana.

I was thoroughly surprised at the amount of reconstruction that had been completed on so many of the old buildings. The former palace of a count is now a very nice hotel. The Castillo de la Real Fuerza is the oldest of four forts guarding the harbor and it had been redone. The Palacio Del Segundo Cabo that was built in 1772 was used at one time as a post office, housed the Senate at one time, and now it is a bookstore.

Ernest Hemingway lived here off and on throughout the 1930s. We had dinner one night at La Bodeguita where he spent a lot of his time. We also visited The Floridia which was a bar where he would go for his daiquiris.

Our guide gave us a fairly long speech when we were visiting the Palacio de Los Capitanes Generales and explained a lot of the architecture that we would be seeing while in Havana. This palace was home to sixty-five governors between 1791 and 1898. Between 1920 and 1967 it was the City Hall. When we were there in 2002, it was being used as The Museum of the City of Havana.

One can not go to Cuba without looking forward to seeing all the old automobiles from the 50s. Several of our taxi rides were in vehicles like that. It was interesting to be walking and see people making repairs on the cars.

Fortaleza de San Carlos de la Cabana is one of the largest fortresses in the Americas. It was built between 1763 and 1774. From the fort there is an excellent view of the old city of Havana.

The Presidential Palace was opened in 1913 to house the provincial government. Before it could be finished it was earmarked as the Presidential Palace. Batista narrowly escaped with his life here in 1957 from revolutionaries. Some of the interior was actually completed by Tiffany's in New York. Following the revolution it was changed to the Museum of the Revolution.

The Granma Memorial contains an eternal flame. In the glass enclosure is the *granma,* which was the boat that brought Fidel Castro, Che Guevara, and the other revolutionaries from Mexico to Cuba in 1956. Other vehicles used in the revolutionary war are on display around the structure.

We were taken on a tour of the Pargagas Cigar Factory. We were shown the various kinds of tobacco and told of the uses for each. Some leaves are used for the interior of the cigar while the best leaves are kept aside to be used as the wrapper.

Our group was taken to the famous National Hotel where we also received a nice tour of the hotel and its grounds. It seems that every time we turned around in Cuba they were giving us another mojito, their famous cocktail. It is their equivalent of a mint julep. They are made using a half teaspoon of sugar, the juice of a half a lime, a crushed sprig of mint, soda, and, of course, Cuban rum.

We toured the Plaza de la Revolution. There is a huge monument in this plaza for Jose Marti. On the side of the Department of the Interior is the famous silhouette of Che. The National Theater is in the plaza also.

Our group was given a tour and had lunch at the home of Jose Fuster who is a famous artist here in Havana.

We did travel outside Havana. We drove to Cienfuegas where we stayed at the Hotel La Union. Along the way we were given lectures regarding the local architecture. We toured the city seeing its beautiful squares and cathedrals. In the afternoon we sat outside and were entertained with music and a fashion show. While we were involved in watching what was going on, a gentleman did an individual caricature drawing of everyone in our group. They were quite nice and it is still in my phone album.

We had a wonderful lobster dinner at the restaurant section of the Palacio de Valle that was a Moorish style palace built in 1917.

The Tomas Acea Cemetery in Cienfuegas was named after a very rich man who donated a lot of money. Some of the headstones in the cemetery are quite elaborate.

The cemetery has a huge neoclassical pavilion surrounded by sixty-four Doric columns.

Trinidad is the most preserved city in Cuba. Thanks to UNESCO, it was declared to be a World Heritage Site in 1988 and many of the buildings have been preserved. The Historical Museum in Trinidad was the former home of a wealthy Cuban who came from Germany and made his fortune from sugar.

The most spectacular views of the city of Trinidad can be had by walking to the top of the tower of the Saint Francis of Assisi Convent.

In April of 2002, I did another one of my circle tours of the south where I was able to visit a lot of relatives and also be entertained with sightseeing. Again this included North Carolina, Tennessee, Mississippi, Louisiana, and Georgia.

In July, I used my free ticket from the year before and went back to Canada. However, this time it was to Montreal and Quebec.

In September I had decided to take a tour to Portugal. It was interesting to note that any tour before the one I had chosen and any tour after seemed to be sold out. I didn't figure it out until I arrived in Portugal and discovered that we only had nine people on our tour. The reason for this was that it was the first anniversary of 9/11 and people were afraid to fly. Fortunately, we didn't have any problems.

My first visit to Lisbon had been in 1968. One of the things that I remember from that trip was the patterned designs in the street made from different colored stones.

Most of the streets in the downtown area of Lisbon are still highly decorated with these granite stones.

A large statue of The Marques de Pombal is strategically placed in a large plaza in the downtown area. He was instrumental in the rebuilding of Portugal after the 1755 earthquake, which left the city and most of the country in rubble.

Another major square in Lisbon is called Restoration Plaza. This square was named for the men who, in 1640, revolted against the Spanish reign. The event led to the reestablishment of Portugal's independence. An obelisk in the square commemorates the uprising.

An interesting area to walk through is the Bairro Alto or Upper City. This area can be reached by taking a lift or if you are in good shape—walking up. Most of the buildings in this area survived the earthquake and is now home to many small restaurants and bars.

Our group visited the Alfama, an area where the Moors lived in the eighth century. There are many small streets winding through this area where you can see fresh fish for sale and women washing their clothes on rocks since most of the houses don't have hot and cold water.

We toured the Lisbon Cathedral and the Castle of St. George in this area. Many of the residences and other buildings in this area are covered with the beautiful tiles for which Portugal is famous.

The Monastery of St. Jeronimos is a must-see. It was built in 1502 to commemorate Vasco de Gama's voyage to India. The Manueline style of architecture is used in its construction. Vasco de Gama is entombed here.

The Tower of Belem was erected between 1515 and 1520 and is considered to be Portugal's national landmark. It was built to defend the port entrance, but also served as a prison. The map there shows the voyages of Vasco de Gama.

Nearby is the Monument of the Discoveries that was built in 1960 for the five hundredth anniversary of the death of Prince Henry the Navigator and on the spot where Vasco de Gama embarked on many of his trips.

Upon leaving Lisbon, our first stop was in Obidos. It is a walled medieval city that rises above a valley of vineyards and is considered to be one of the most well-preserved cities in Portugal.

Continuing north, we stopped at the St. Mary Monastery in Alcobaca. It was constructed in the twelfth century and has the largest church in Portugal. The nave is 350-feet long. The tombs of Pedro (son of King Alfonso IV) and Ines are here. They are considered to be the Romeo and Juliet of Portuguese history.

Our group stopped in Nazare, a beach town, for our lunch. And as in most group tours, we had time for shopping.

In Batalha, we toured the Monastery of the Virgin Mary. It was built between 1388 and 1533. Some fifteen architects were involved in the building through the years.

This led us to our next stop, which to most of us in the group was the stop that we were anxiously awaiting. Fatima is a world-famous pilgrimage site because of the reported Virgin Mary sightings in the early twentieth century.

We visited the University of Coimbra. It is one of the oldest universities in Europe and is the oldest university in Portugal. There are eight different schools incorporated into the university.

The university library contains more than a million volumes. The interior consists of a triptych of high-ceilinged salons walled by two-story tiers of lacquer-decorated bookshelves. The pale jade and sedate lemon marble inlaid floors complement the baroque decorations of gilded wood. The library tables are built of ebony and rosewood, imported from the former Portuguese colonies in India and Brazil.

Up to this point in all my travels I had only visited one place, Sophia, where I only stayed one night and stayed in two hotels. I guess it was time for the second. Yes, in Porto we had just begun to get settled in when we were informed that there had been a misunderstanding in our reservation and we were moved to another hotel.

In Porto we visited the Stock Exchange, toured a winery, and had a very nice lunch in a restaurant on the walking street.

We had a tour of the Mateus Palace and the vineyards where the famous Mateus wine is made. There are many vineyards in this area and we would see large trucks filled with grapes.

We stayed at the Dom Fernando Hotel in Evora. Here we saw the Roman Temple (Temple of Diana). It was originally built in the second or third century. It was largely destroyed during the invasions in the early fifth century. The Church of St. Francis contains a small chapel called The Chapel of the Bones and this small chapel is one of the most-visited sites in Evora. The chapel is lined with human skulls and other parts of skeletons. Legend has it that the bones came either from soldiers who died in a big battle or from plague victims. A saying across the entrance translates to "our bones that stay here are waiting for yours."

By this time we had made our way to the most southern part of the country and delighted in the beach area of Algarve. Our hotel was in Carvoeiro south of Lagoa.

Considering the fact that winemaking is a big part of Portugal's economy, it is interesting to know that the country also has many cork trees. When the cork is taken from the tree, a number is etched on the tree indicating the year it was taken. This lets them know how long it will be before that particular tree will be ready to produce more cork.

In making our way back to Lisbon we had a stop in Setubal. I indicate the word "stop" in more ways than one! Yes, as we were on our way through the city, our small bus caught a few low-hanging wires. We yelled to our driver to stop. By the time he did we had pulled down several wires that were attached to several houses. We called the police and the cable company and waited for them to arrive. Once we were dislodged from the wires, we were allowed to continue on our way.

We made it back to Lisbon and had a nice farewell dinner. Since our group had only nine members, we sort of felt like family. Some of us are still in contact with each other and continue to share Christmas cards each year and let each other know what our current travels include.

2003

Antarctic, World Tour, and Mediterranean Cruise (All Seven Continents in One Year)

In February I was able to fulfill another longtime wish—I was able to go to the Antarctic. I toured in Buenos Aires for a couple days with two other guys who had signed up for the trip through the same travel company that I had.

The first day there I went to lunch with the guy in our group from New York City. When he found out that I was from Washington, he asked me if I knew two people who were good friends of his. I knew both of them. In fact, we have been members of the same social group for a long time. It is a small world in some ways.

We visited Casa Rosado, the Presidential Palace, on our city tour the first day there. We all know from the movie, *Evita,* the importance of the balcony of this structure and will always associate it with Evita singing "Don't Cry For Me Argentina." Two British ladies appeared and asked our guide if it would be possible for them to ask him a question. Of course, he said that it would be no problem. Their question was "Is that Madonna's balcony?"

The main square in front of the palace is called Plaza de Mayo. It was laid out by Juan de Garay in the 1580s. The square comprises the palace, the metropolitan cathedral, and the state bank. If there is ever a demonstration by the people for any reason it would probably be held in this square.

Based upon my observations, I would assume that the second most-visited site in this city would be the Recoleta Cemetery. It was designed by a Frenchman and opened in 1822. The cemetery contains many elaborate mausoleums built of granite, marble, and bronze. It is this cemetery where the extremely rich and famous would be buried. Hence, the tomb of Evita is one of the most visited.

Avenida 9 de Julio is considered to be the main street in Buenos Aires. It actually is an extremely wide boulevard and stretches almost the entire length of the downtown area. On this street and almost in the center of the city is a giant obelisk, which is a historical monument that was erected to commemorate the fourth centennial of the founding of the city. This obelisk is almost like an icon and serves as a symbol for the city. As soon as one sees it, they associate it with Buenos Aires in much the same way that someone would associate the Washington Monument with Washington.

The Torre Monumental in Buenos Aires looks somewhat like Big Ben and was a gift from the Anglo-Argentinos and was known as the "Torre de los Ingleses." However, since the Falklands War they only refer to it as the Torre Monumental with no mention of the English.

Caminito is an area of the city that receives it name from a 1926 tango and is considered to be the birthplace of the tango where sailors, hustlers, drinkers, etc., would hang out and rub shoulders with the flashy people from Europe.

The corrugated-zinc shacks owe their vivid colors to the imaginative but impoverished locals who would beg incoming ships for their excess tins of paint. They would then use this paint to spruce up the appearance of their home. Some of them might have three or four different colors. It just depends on how much area can be covered with the amount of paint you have.

We flew from Buenos Aires to Ushuaia. Ushuaia is the southernmost city in the world. We spent one night here at the Hotel Del Bosque before boarding the ship the next day for our Antarctic cruise.

Our ship for the nine-day Antarctic cruise was the Professor Molchanov and was built in Finland for Russia in 1982. Its major purpose was to be used for global and oceanographic research. It was later converted to a passenger vessel.

We had been told about the Drake Passage and that it was known as the most turbulent and treacherous passage in the world. Our multi-hour crossing of the passage was extremely calm with no big waves and no rocking of the ship whatsoever. We, of course, just assumed that the crew was "pulling our legs."

As we were approaching the South Shetland Islands we were able to see whales, petrals, albatross, and other sea birds.

Our first sighting was at Penguin Island, which is a one-mile long volcano that lies just off the east coast of King George Island in the South Shetland Islands. We saw whale bones along the shore. The island boasts of approximately 7,500 Chinstrap penguins and about three thousand Adelie penguins.

One of the advantages of being on a small ship such as the one we were cruising is that it can maneuver into some of the small cays, which is impossible for the larger ships. I have talked to people who say they have been to the Antarctic. When I ask them how many times they were able to get off the ship and walk around, the answer is usually none. Fortunately, our's was small and there were days that we got off and back on four times during a single day. We did a lot of boot washing!

Bailey Head is a rock headland making up the southeastern extremity of Deception Island. This island is home to 160,000 pairs of breeding Chinstrap penguins. Cuverville Island is a small, rocky island with a considerable moss cover and has the largest Gentoo penguin colony with about five thousand pairs.

We went through the Errera Channel; saw the Petzval Glacier and Paradise Bay.

The Almirante Brown Station was unoccupied when we were there. It was named after the founder of the Argentine navy. It was here that we had our first steps on the White Continent itself. Our prior visits were on the chain of islands along the Antarctic Peninsula.

When we stopped at Danco Island the weather was such that a couple of us took off our shirts and soaked up the sun for a while!

The Lemaire Channel is a seven-mile long one-mile wide passage that separates Booth Island from the Antarctic Peninsula. This passage offered some of the most spectacular views that we had on the trip. We were able to spot humpback whales at play near the ship.

Pleneau Bay was our southernmost destination. There we took a Zodiac cruise and saw the huge icebergs, some of which had floated from as far as the Ross Ice Shelf.

Another island where we stopped and walked around had been at one time an active research station. However, at the time we were there, it was no longer in use. Port Circumcision was named by Charcot, a Frenchman, when he wintered here in 1909.

At Petermann Island, I still have vivid memories of sitting on a hillside here with an enormous number of Adelie and Gentoo penguins walking in the area at the bottom of the hill. It was so quite and peaceful sitting there and forgetting that there was possibly any problems anywhere in the world.

The Vernadski Station is a Ukrainian base and is dedicated to biological and upper ionospheric studies.

Port Lockroy is part of the British Antarctic Territory. The station here does research. There is a museum and a post office there. We were able to obtain post cards and have them postmarked from the Antarctic.

One of our last stops here was in the Neumeyer Channel. We were to spend about two hours looking at whales. I decided that I didn't want to be hampered by my camera and left it on the ship. I must say that I am glad that I made that decision because it was one of the highlights of the trip. We saw many, many whales coming up out of the water in close proximity to our Zodiac!

Remember at the beginning of this section when I mentioned the calmness of the Drake Passage on our southbound crossing? Well, they weren't kidding! On the northern crossing at the end of our cruise, there were big waves and the boat rocked excessively for many, many hours! My cabin was directly under the captain's cabin. It was a corner room at the front of the ship with a window in front and another window on the side. There were times that both windows would be completely covered with water. We had two straps for strapping ourselves to the bed when we retired for the evening.

Looking out from the bridge, it was possible to see a large wave coming in front of the ship and as it approached it wasn't unusual for the water to come all the way over the ship!

Needless to say I have never been so happy to see anything as I was when Cape Horn became visible and I knew we were approaching the Beagle Channel and things would calm down.

We flew back to Buenos Aires where we spent one night before flying to Iguazu Falls the next morning. We were able to see the falls from the Argentinian and the Brazilian sides.

A little advice to future travelers who want to do this day trip to Brazil is to make sure that you obtain a stamp for your passport. If you do not and return to Brazil on a future trip, you must obtain another visa. I learned this the hard way. Since my visa had not been stamped within a certain period it was no longer valid.

We flew then back to Buenos Aires to connect with our flights home. Upon arriving at the counter to check-in, I was told that my flight had been cancelled. It seems that there had been a huge snow storm in Washington, D. C, and the airport was closed.

I was instructed to proceed to an office in the airport that would assist in getting an overnight accommodation. I was told that I could have a suite in a hotel in the downtown area that would include a bedroom, a living room, a bath, and a small kitchenette. Breakfast would be included, as well as the transportation to from the airport. By this time I was beginning to wonder how much all of this would cost. The response to my question was that it would amount to approximately $35! For that price I was tempted to stay another week!

The prices changed somewhat upon my arrival back at Dulles airport. The regular buses were not operating because of the snow. And because of the inclement weather, the taxis were able to charge double fees. I had paid $35 for transportation, accommodation, and breakfast in Buenos Aires and the taxi ride here cost me $60!

When I arrived at my house I couldn't resist the temptation of taking a picture of my patio. There was about two feet of snow! It looked like the Antarctic of the north.

The tenth anniversary of my retirement was fast approaching. I reminisced as to how I celebrated that joyous occasion by taking my first trip around the world. Now it was time to take another one to celebrate ten years of retirement.

I flew from Washington to San Francisco where I stayed at the Cosmos Hotel. While there I was able to get a ticket to see the play, *Urinetown: the Musical.* Frankly, I didn't really expect very much from seeing it. However, I was pleasantly surprised and really enjoyed it.

At that time I had been ushering at two local theaters in Washington, D. C, for several years since my retirement. During the intermission I struck up a conversation with the lady who was ushering in the section where I was sitting. We shared several strange and funny experiences that we had encountered during the time that we had been ushering.

My friends from Sacramento came down and spent a day while I was here. Then it was time to continue on to the next stop, Honolulu.

Of course, it is always a pleasure to be back in Hawaii and spend some time with my longtime friends there. We always try to choose something to do that I haven't done before. This time I actually had a tour of the University there. We revisited Punchbowl, the military cemetery that I had visited almost thirty years prior.

Sydney, Australia, was my next stop. Sydney, like Hawaii, had been visited several times and I try to find places to visit that I didn't have time for on a previous trip. This year I went to Hyde Park, the Anzac War Memorial, the Sydney Aquarium in Darling Harbor, the Chinese Garden of Friendship, and a night cruise from the harbor quay. I also went back to the top of the tower. On the previous visit I had toured the tower in the evening before dinner and had seen the city at night. This time I visited in the daytime and was able to see a completely different Sydney.

The walk on the Sydney Harbor Bridge was another thing that I wanted to do. However, when I called to find out if it was possible, I was told that I could do it the following morning at 6:00 a.m.! It was their wintertime and I decided that there would be another time to do that.

I flew from Sydney to Perth, which is a five-hour flight, similar to flying from Washington, D. C to California. I stayed at the Perth Ambassador Hotel.

There is a building with a bell tower in Perth that is supposed to represent a "Black Swan," which is the symbol of the city. I was able to see several black swans in the pond of a city park here.

Also in the city of Perth I saw the Parliament Building, the Opera House, and several classy new apartment buildings. The architecture of many buildings in Perth have an English flair to them. Then, on the next corner there would be a building that looked as if it had been picked up from the outback and brought here as a museum.

There were two ways of approaching the City Park and the Botanical Gardens. The long way was by using the street by Parliament and the short way was by using the steps! There must have been three hundred or more steps, and there were actually people going up and down them as part of their exercise routine. I chose the street to get there and the steps in my departure.

Freemantle, the port city, is only a thirty-minute train ride from Perth. It was a real treat to see this city. I visited the railway station (of course), the Maritime Museum, the harbor, the prison, and had time to leisurely walk around the city.

On my last day in Perth I went to an Internet café. This is such an easy way to keep in contact with those back home. I had sent several e-mails to my friends and family when I was in Sydney the week before. In those e-mails I had specifically mentioned that it was 9:00 a.m. on Friday. When I opened my e-mails in Perth, I had several e-mails from those friends, and they were surprised that I had sent the e-mail from Sydney at 9:00 a.m. on Friday and they received it on Thursday! I had planned that one!

I flew from Perth to Kuala Lumpur, Malaysia, where I stayed at the Hotel Equatorial. From the window in my room I could see the Petronas Towers in the reflection of the glass building across the street. If I looked to the right from my room, I had an excellent view of the tall television tower. This tower is used mainly as a communications tower. It also comprises a revolving restaurant.

My first visit to Kuala Lumpur had been on a day trip in 1974 from Singapore. At that time there weren't any high-rise buildings. Now, on this visit in 2003, the

Petronas Towers are the tallest buildings in the world. I took the tour of the towers where one is allowed to go up as far as the bridge, which is located on the forty-first and forty-second floors of the building.

There is a large shopping center adjacent to the towers with many high-end shops and a lot of excellent restaurants.

The architecture of the buildings surrounding the Independence Square is quite varied. The Supreme Court building is of Indian Moghul architecture. The Selangor Club is very British. Near this square is the railway station and the architecture of that building is noteworthy also. Across the street from the railway station is the largest mosque here, The Masjid Jamek Temple.

I was waiting to cross an extremely wide boulevard here one day. When the green light indicating that you were allowed to walk was illuminated, I saw an outline of a human body walking. The figure maintained a somewhat slow pace until you are about halfway across the street and then the legs began moving very rapidly, indicating that you had better hurry!

My arranged tour here included a nice drive around the city. By the time we reached our first stop the tour company had discovered that they had me on a tour by myself and had another tour with only three Japanese boys in it. They combined us into one group.

One of the stops on that tour was the Presidential Palace. While we were standing there to get a good picture through the gates, we were told to move back. Just about that time the presidential limousine exited the palace grounds.

We had a tour of a typical Malaysian home that was built on stilts in order to allow the flow of air under the house. This architectural feature helps to keep the house cool. One room of the house was set aside to be used for weddings.

Also included on the tour were the Thean Hou Temple, a pewter factory, a batik factory, and the Batu Caves. To reach the entrance to the caves one has to walk up a series of approximately three hundred steps! There were workers doing some work there and we were asked if we would volunteer to carry a bucket of cement up the steps as we ascended. The three young Japanese guys were impressed that I made it up the steps without any difficulty as I was almost sixty-five years old.

On my own I went to the bird park, which was considered at that time to be the world's largest. Nearby were the Butterfly Gardens. And within walking distance of that, was the Orchid Garden.

The next stop of my tour was to be Tunisia. To get there I had to fly from Kuala Lumpur, Malaysia, to Amman, Jordan. Since we were to have a long layover in Amman after our overnight flight, we were transported to a hotel near the airport where we were able to get a little sleep, freshen up, and then be brought back to the airport for our flight to Tunis. I saw a bulletin board in the lobby of the hotel advertising various day tours that could be taken. If I had known this before I left home, I would have planned the trip so that I would have stayed here a few extra days.

When I arrived at the airport in Tunis, the temperature was about 45 Celsius, which was about 114 degrees! I stayed at the El Hana International Hotel. The hotel was centrally located in the downtown area which made walking around convenient.

Just across the street from my hotel was what looked like a huge old theater. I kept seeing people walk in and out from the corner and wondered exactly what was located inside. To soothe my curiosity I decided to take a walk over and find out. It was a multilevel shopping center.

Near the hotel was the Independence Tower. With what has just happened there this year (2010) it will be interesting to see if that Independence Tower is replaced by yet another one! I remember seeing the Victory Monument when I was there. This was another structure that was always shown in the news of the demonstrations of 2010.

Not far to the right from my hotel was the Medina. In this old shopping area there were many shops selling fruits and vegetables, gold, and silver, carpets, etc.

My guide in Tunis explained that during the months of July and August the workers work only four hours a day because of the heat. Consequently, they seem to have rush hour all day.

The highlight of visiting Tunis was The Bardo Museum. The museum contains a magnificent display of Roman mosaics. Also in the museum there are artifacts from Greece and exhibits of antique jewelry.

The only part of Tunisia I saw other than the capital city of Tunis was Carthage. During the drive to Carthage there was a section of large new houses, which were built on landfill alongside Lake Tunis.

My tour in Carthage included the ruins of Mt. Byrsa. The view from here was spectacular. The Cathedral in Carthage was built under French Protectorate for Carmelite priests. The Seminary was being used as a museum. I was able to tour the Roman Baths and the ruins of the Amphitheatre.

The American Cemetery and Memorial here comprises the burial place of some three thousand people who were killed during World War II.

My next stop was the island of Malta. I stayed at the Hotel Phoenix in the capital city of Valletta. This hotel was located just outside the gates to the old city. The beautifully landscaped gardens in the back of the hotel created a nice place to take a stroll in the evening. The pool that was located at the end of the property had a fantastic view of the old section.

Valetta sightseeing included walking the entire length of Republic Street, which is the main street in the old section. Many buildings in the old section of town have what is called a Maltese Window that is usually on the second or third floor and is made of wood and extends out over the street like a bay window.

Also saw the Presidential Palace, The War Memorial, and the Lower and Upper Barrakka Gardens. The *Malta Experience* is an audiovisual spectacular and is offered in twelve different languages!

The Lascaris War Rooms are located in a tunnel under the Upper Barrakka Gardens and were used during World War II by the military as a communications center, and a place where they could track enemy aircraft. There were large maps that were used for plotting the locations of these attacks. One of the offices had been used by General Eisenhower.

St. John's Co-Cathedral and Museum in Valletta could take more than a day to see just the major things. The Cathedral has an elaborate main altar and several other chapels on either side. The floors of the cathedral consisted of panels and marble inlay. The museum contained a famous painting, *the Beheading of John the Baptist*, by Caravaggio. There were several other paintings of his in one gallery. The museum also had exhibits of elaborately colored and illustrated music books from the fifth century. Another section of the museum contained several capes and priestly garb.

While touring the island I was able to do a walking tour of Floriana, and saw Mosta, Naxxar, Gharghur, Mdina, and Rabat. The Parish Church of Assumption of Our Lady in Mosta has an interesting story. A bomb hit the dome of the church during World War II and it didn't explode. They consider it a miracle and a replica of the bomb is still on display in the church.

It was necessary to rise very early in order to take the high-speed hydrofoil ferry on a day trip to Sicily. While on the island we were able to visit Mt. Etnathat had just recently had an eruption. I remember seeing one house that was almost completely covered in lava. We had some time to sightsee and have dinner in the beautiful and hilly city of Taormina.

There is another small world story that happened on this trip. In the early morning crossing on the hydrofoil, I caught myself looking at this particular person and saying to myself that that person looks a lot like me—red hair, ruddy complexion, and about the same height and weight. I didn't think too much about it until we were preparing for our return trip to Valletta. The boat was slowly filling up with people and there weren't many seats available. This gentleman came aboard and asked if the seat next to me was taken. I said no and he occupied the seat. A few minutes later we were chatting and decided to look at our passports to determine if we had received a stamp showing that we had been to Sicily. We discovered that not only had we had both been born on the same day but also the same year.

This world trip was slowly coming to a close. I flew from Malta to London where I was able to stay a few days. One of the things I did there that I had not been able to do previously was to ride the new London Eye. I arrived early in the morning and was able to be on the first ride of the day. It was great to see the city from this viewpoint and take lots of pictures.

One thing I had done once on a previous visit to London was to take a tour of the Parliament. I decided that after forty-one years it was time to do it again.

My longtime friend and I met at my hotel and went to a nearby exhibit of Ossie Clark's dresses from the 1960s at the Victoria and Albert Museum.

Now, it was time to head to the airport and get my flight from London back to Washington, D. C and complete another circumnavigation of the globe.

You would think that by this time the travel bug would have been satisfied for the year. However, in September I took a Mediterranean cruise with a friend of mine.

The cruise started in Barcelona and proceeded to Cannes, Monte Carlo, Rome, Naples, Mallorca, and back to Barcelona.

The year 2003 turned out to be an historic one for me! Most people are never able to say that they have been in all seven continents. In the year 2003 I had traveled in all seven continents within the same year!

2004

South Africa, Swaziland, Lesotho, and Mozambique

In 2004, I took a Globus tour to South Africa. The tour began in Cape Town where I stayed at the Cullinan Hotel. One of the things I remember about staying there was the harpist playing outside the restaurant while we had breakfast. It was a very pleasing way to begin the day.

The hotel was centrally located near the famous waterfront and there was also a nice view of Table Mountain from here.

Another member of our tour and I took a taxi to Table Mountain. The views from there are wonderful if you can plan to be there before the fog comes and covers the Table. We were fortunate. However, on our way back to the hotel from Table Mountain my camera inadvertently fell from my pants pocket. It wasn't until we had left the taxi and was in the hotel that I discovered that it was missing. By not having the name or the number of the taxi, it was impossible to retrieve it. I walked to the shopping area at the waterfront and purchased a new camera for the trip.

Near our hotel was a statue of Dias, a Portuguese navigator who came to Cape Town in 1652. There was also a statue of General Smuts who was active during both World Wars and helped to draft the United Nations Charter. He was also elected twice as prime minister. In that area there was the Parliament building, the National Library, and a Planetarium.

As soon as one leaves the downtown area, the city changes completely as you begin to see shanties for what seems to be miles and miles where hundreds of thousands of people live. South Africa gets a lot of immigrants from other African countries.

Our group was able to see several suburban areas around Cape Town. We also drove to the Cape of Good Hope. On another day we went to Robben Island, where Nelson Mandela was imprisoned. We had a day also to visit the wine country. It was interesting to see the Dutch influence in the architectural style of the dwellings there. We were able to participate in a wine tasting and spend some time in the town of Stellenbosch.

We began our tour of the Garden Route. Our first stop was at Cape Agulhas, which is the southernmost point of the African continent and where the Indian Ocean and the Atlantic Ocean meet. It is possible here to have your picture taken with one foot in the Indian Ocean and the other in the Atlantic.

We stayed in Arniston, which is a small fishing village. There are stories about how navigators many, many years ago, without the use of modern day instruments, would get lost or think that they were at the Cape of Good Hope and later realize that they hadn't reached that point yet.

In Mossel Bay there was a tree called The Post Office Tree. Local residents would go there and place a message on the tree as a way of communicating. In the sixteenth century wayfarers would leave messages for each other in a shoe on the tree.

One of the highlights of any trip is to find just the perfect gift to bring back home. In Cape Town I had seen a lamp that was made from an ostrich egg and had been etched so that it resembled the globe of the earth with perforations indicating major cities. I didn't buy it there in the hope that I would find one later and not have to carry it around for the entire trip.

We stopped at an ostrich farm on our Garden Route. I saw the lamp again in their gift shop and decided that I had better get it here in case I didn't see another one. I was glad I did. A couple other tourists had decided to wait until they arrived in Johannesburg and couldn't find one anywhere!

Oudtshoorn was a town established in 1847 for farming. The demand for ostrich feathers to support Victorian and later Edwardian fashion trends, created a sharp rise in the industry in 1870-80. During that time the farmers built extravagant homes. Since they had been financed on ostrich feathers, they were known as "Feather Palaces." However, several factors caused their demise—World War I, changes in fashion, and the fact that with enclosed automobiles the ladies didn't have the space for the feathers in their hats as they had in the open carriages.

We visited the city of Knysna where we saw the harbor and took a boat ride. This led us then to Plettenberg Bay where many rich South Africans have homes. Our guide told us a funny story about this place. On the first day of school a student would ask a classmate if they went to Plet for the summer. The classmate would reply that they didn't go there anymore because there is no place to park the plane.

We flew to Durban where we stayed at the Holiday Inn. There we did a city tour and saw the botanical gardens. There was a large park across the street from the hotel and in it was a big outdoor market.

Outside Durban we visited Shakaland. This is where the film *Shaka Zulu* was filmed. Our rooms here were individual round structures. We were given a tour of the area, and in the evening we were entertained by the residents of this enclave.

We drove through Swaziland and spent the night at Piggs Peak Lodge and Casino. The views here are spectacular. This place became popular in the late 1800s when people came here in hopes of finding gold. However, their main industry today is forestry.

Our next stop was the Protea Hotel located just outside the gate at Kruger National Park. There we saw elephants, impalas, rhinoceros, zebras, wildebeest, alligators, lions, and many birds. We were driving along early in the morning when we approached several lions. We drove very slow and were told to make sure that we kept our hands and arms inside the vehicle. A lion walked right past the vehicle!

From Kruger Park we drove through the mountains and saw Blyde River Canyon where we saw the Bourkes Luck Potholes caused by erosion through the years. We had lunch in Pilgrim's Rest, an old mining town.

We stayed at Critchley Hackle located in the small fishing town of Dullstroom. The accommodations here are wonderful! Each person or family has their own house to live in complete with fireplace. It was so "upscale" that I decided to dress for dinner and wear the only coat and tie that I had packed for the trip. The tie that I wore is a nautical map of Portugal from 1559.

From here we drove to Pretoria, the capital city of South Africa where we saw the Palace of Justice, the Paul Kruger statue in Church Square, the Union Building, and the Natural History Museum.

We ended our trip in Johannesburg and stayed at the InterContinental in Sandton. My room number here was 1559, which just so happened to be the same number as the year on the tie I wore the night before! Another small world happening!

In Johannesburg we toured the Museum Africa. The offices of a large diamond company there were built in the shape of a faceted diamond. We also took the tour of Soweto and its museum where Nelson Mandela had lived.

The members of our group were on their way home. I stayed so that I would be able to go to Sun City, Lesotho, and Mozambique.

The guide that we had in South Africa was by far one of the best guides that I had ever had in all my travels. He gave me some excellent information for my extended trip where I was going to be traveling alone.

I flew to Sun City from Johannesburg on a small plane. There were only five or six of us on the flight. Sun City was the inspiration of a self-made millionaire hotelier. The complex was built in the 1970s on a land where gambling was legal although gambling for South Africa was illegal. The casino was a key element in the initial success. It then included only one luxury hotel, a man-made lake, and a challenging eighteen-hole golf course designed by the former South African golfing champion, Gary Player.

Two more hotels had been built since last when I visited. Las Vegas style shows are performed nightly in the Cascades complex. The Miss World contest was held here one year.

The Palace of the Lost City is a magnificent building. It is a five-star hotel and the architecture is a photographer's paradise! I was able to have afternoon tea here.

The time came for me to fly back to Johannesburg. I was waiting in the lobby of the hotel and was beginning to think that I had been forgotten. The person at the front desk assured me that the van would be there soon. I arrived at the small airport and there was almost no one there. I asked where I was to go to get my boarding pass. The gentleman said to follow him. He turned on the computer, printed out my boarding pass, and proceeded to turn off the computer. I looked around the terminal and didn't see any aircraft there. A few minutes later a small plane arrived. I assumed as soon as the people from that flight deplaned, I would probably take the same plane for my flight. No one got off the plane! The company had sent a plane just for me since I was the only one flying from Sun City back to Johannesburg that day.

When I got on the plane the flight attendant said that I could sit anywhere I pleased since I was the only person! When we arrived at the airport in Johannesburg I got the flight attendant to take a picture of me getting off my private jet!

In some air terminals the plane doesn't pull into the terminal. The passengers are then transported from the plane to the terminal by a long bus. That day I was the only person on the bus.

I spent the night in Johannesburg and flew the next day to Lesotho. While in Lesotho I was able to tour the downtown area of Maseru, the capital. My English-speaking driver then took me around the country. It was interesting to see how the people in the rural areas live. The amount of income per year is quite low and that is reflected in their daily lives. Some of the houses are made of clay and not everyone has electricity.

We picked up a female hitchhiker who happened to be an American who was there as a volunteer worker. We both agreed that she wouldn't be able to hitchhike in the states in that it would be too dangerous. She indicated that it didn't seem to be a problem there. She said that AIDS was a big problem at that time in Lesotho.

My last stop on this trip was to Mozambique. I stayed at the Ibis Hotel in Maputo, the capital city.

A large athletic competition for all of Africa was being held in Maputo at the same time I was there. Enough of the athletic teams were staying at my hotel that they were having their meals in the main dining room and it was closed to the others who were not there for the competition. There was a buffet set up in another room where we took our meals.

My driver for the day took me sightseeing around the city. We first went to the Museum for Money. We saw the local television studios, the major government buildings, and the train station. We visited an old fort that was built in 1795.

Driving along the road there would be all kinds of businesses, selling everything from vegetables to furniture in the open air. Ladies would be carrying large loads of goods on their head. Other goods were being transported with large carts being pushed by hand.

Being a former teacher, I noticed that there were school kids on the street at noon. My guide told me that most of the schools begin classes as early as 6:00 a.m. and finish at noon because of the severe heat. Most of the classrooms are in tents.

One section of the city along the seaside had some really large upscale homes. These homes all had walls around them and most of them had razor wire or electric wire at the top of that.

There was a huge May Day Parade on the last day of my visit. The parade lasted for about two hours or more. There were groups promoting equality in the work place, AIDS (known here as SIDA), and nondiscrimination. People from these various groups were allowed at the end of the parade route to talk to the President regarding their concerns.

2005

World Cruise

One day, while I was looking through a travel magazine, I suddenly realized that I was looking at an ad for a world cruise. For some reason I had never even thought of such a thing. I started reading the itinerary and as I continued through the list of ports to visit, the excitement began to grow. By the time I had finished the itinerary, I noticed at the bottom of the ad that it was to be on the *Queen Elizabeth 2*! I had heard so much through the years of this ocean liner and had thought of the possibility of taking it for a transatlantic crossing. Gee! My next thought was why shouldn't I just go across the ocean when I can go around the world! It wasn't long after that until my reservation had been finalized.

The next major decision to make in regard to the journey was what to pack. The cruise would be going to places where I would need clothes for hot weather and cold weather. It would be necessary to take casual clothes for ship excursions and also formal clothes for the formal evenings.

I began my circumnavigation by taking the train from Washington, D. C to New York where I stayed in a hotel for a couple days and had some time to visit some friends before departing.

A gentleman who was working at the hotel where I was staying commented about the excessive amount of luggage I had. I told him I was leaving to go on a cruise on the *Queen Elizabeth 2.* He then asked me where I would be going on the cruise. I said, "To New York." He looked at me with his head turned to one side similar to that of a dog wanting to know what his master wants and said, "You're already there."

The cruise started from New York City on January 2, 2005. As the ship slowly left the harbor and passed the Statue of Liberty I almost had to pinch myself to realize that this was really happening!

The first stop was in Fort Lauderdale where we had most of the day to do whatever we wanted. There were several excursions offered but since I had been in this area many times I declined. Instead I had made plans to have lunch with several friends. Two of them were friends that I had just met the year before on my trip to

South Africa. The others had lived in Washington, D. C previously, but were now living in Florida.

In the gift shop of the *Queen Elizabeth 2* I had discovered a small cuddly bear. I purchased several of these and named them after friends back home. I displayed them on the additional bed in my cabin. When I arrived back home from the cruise, I gave the bears to their namesakes and told them that they had gone around the world with me.

By evening the ship was on its way to Curacao. While making my rounds on the ship, I discovered that two people that I had worked with during my teaching career had joined the ship in Fort Lauderdale.

Being the person who is really big on Christmas, you might know that one of the first things I saw when I began my exploration of Willemstad. Yes, it was a giant Santa Claus standing outside an eating establishment.

It was nice to be back in this city again and see the houses with their brightly colored walls. Fort Amsterdam here was built in 1635 and is now used as the Governor's Palace and for other government offices.

We transited the Panama Canal the next day, which took most of the day. Some of the locks the ship went through didn't have much space on either side. The new *Queen Mary 2* is so wide that it can't go through the canal. They are in the process of widening the canal today. During our transit we saw many freighters from the Far East filled with large containers.

On approaching Panama City we had to go under the Bridge of the Americas. From the top deck it looked as if we were going to hit. There wasn't much space between the top of the ship and the bridge.

The Plaza de Franzia (or The French Plaza) in Panama City contained a monument to those who had died while building of the canal. There was a statue of Ferdinand de Lesseps, who was the architect of the Panama Canal.

I was surprised at the skyline of the city. There were many new apartment buildings.

We visited the Church with the Golden Altar, the Cathedral, the Opera House, and the State Theater. We drove through an area that was being completely reconstructed.

There were two days at sea before reaching Acapulco. Some people think that those would be the days when you would be bored—wrong! There are so many options to keep you busy. However, it seems that you can always find the time to eat!

Two acquaintances from the ship and I spent a lot of our time in Acapulco at the market. We knew that the next day on the ship was to be a big Mexican Fiesta Ball. This was one of several balls during the cruise. The Queen's Room would be lavishly decorated for the ball and most of those in attendance would be dressed for the occasion. My two friends and I were ready with our panchos and large Mexican hats that we had purchased at the market. We went as "Los Tres Amigos."

During our stop in Los Angeles another friend of mine met me at the ship and we spent the day together.

Now it was time to head to Hawaii. That meant that we had a few days at sea. In Hawaii, I was able to spend the day with my friends there. They took me to a restaurant for lunch that Bill Clinton had gone to on his last visit to Honolulu.

The planned stop for Kona had to be canceled because the waters were too rough to accommodate the tenders that were needed in transferring from the ship to the shore.

A dancing group came aboard in Hawaii and performed for us prior to our departure for Tahiti. A similar group had been on board as we were leaving Acapulco.

On our way to Tahiti we crossed the equator. This allows everyone the opportunity to participate in the King Neptune Crossing the Equator Ceremony. This historic tradition dates back to the thirteenth century. Pollywogs would be covered with various nasty liquids found in the bilge of the ship. However we had spaghetti, catsup, mustard, jello, and anything they could find from the kitchen. As soon as you are covered, you are then pushed into the pool. I'm sure they had fun draining and cleaning the pool after this ceremony.

We arrived in Tahiti early in the morning. This was my revisit after thirty-one years! Needless to say there was quite a change.

We toured the home of James Norman Hall who was the author of *Mutiny on the Bounty*. We toured the Museum of Tahiti and the Islands where there were many exhibits regarding the history of the area. Also on our island tour we saw the Arahoho Blowhole, the Old Lighthouse, and the One Tree Hill lookout.

The island of Moorea had not changed as much as Tahiti. This island was used in the filming of South Pacific. From the spectacular Belvedere Lookout you can see the spires of Mt. Rotuii, Mt. Tahiea, and Mt. Mouaputa.

Continuing south we reached Auckland, New Zealand. The one thing that was here on this visit and had not been on my previous visits was the Sky Tower. This tower is 1,072-feet tall and with two observation decks. The floor of the observation deck is plexiglass and you can see right through to the ground below. It is possible to make a bungy-type jump from the top—maybe next time—or not!

As in so many of the ports we visited there would be a band and or dancers on the dock to welcome us. We also, as in Mexico and Hawaii, had a group to come on board in Auckland who presented us with a Maori Folklore show just before we left for Christchurch.

The city of Christchurch is on the south island. It was nice to be able to see this beautiful city once again. The park along the Avon river there is so peaceful. I just hope that the latest earthquakes there have not destroyed too much of the city.

The members of the crew never let one holiday pass by without having several activities planned for that day. For Valentine's Day the ship had many floral arrangements throughout the ship some of which were about ten-feet tall.

Our next ball was the Mardi Gras ball. I had planned for this one. I had taken a whole bag of beads and a couple masks from New Orleans. It turned out to be a very festive gala affair.

A world cruise is usually divided into segments. This means that there were some passengers who traveled from New York to California, some traveled from California to Australia, etc. Usually on the last night of a segment, there would be the "Baked Alaska" night in the dining room. The waiters would walk through carrying the flaming desserts and sparklers. The dining room would be decorated with flags from various countries.

There were over seven hundred passengers on this world cruise for the entire journey. We were told that the number was more than in any other year.

Our ship docked near the Opera House in Sydney. If you remember, on my previous visit here, I had wanted to climb the bridge, but didn't want to do it in the middle of winter and very early in the morning. I had said then that there would be another time. Well, that time came!

When I told my tablemates that I was doing the climb the next day, they couldn't understand why I would pay that much money for torture. I told them that it wasn't going to be torture for me. It did seem like a lot of money to pay for it. However, by the time I finished, I felt it was worth every penny that I had paid. Fortunately, I was able climb late in the afternoon. That way I was able to see the city in the daylight on my way up and was able to see the city lights on my way down.

While on this visit I went with two friends from the ship to Manly Beach for a day.

Our next stop was Melbourne. The one thing that I did on this trip that I had not done on any previous trip was to take the Colonial Tramcar Restaurant tour. The tram operates similar to a city tour. However, you actually feel like you are riding on a train. It was elaborately decorated and the food and service were impeccable. All waiters should wear white gloves!

In Adelaide I took the tour to the Mt. Lofty lookout and lighthouse. From there you had an excellent landscape view looking back at the city of Adelaide. There was just enough time to also take in the Cleland Wildlife Park.

In Freemantle I did something that I had never done before—sandboarding! There were about fifteen of us in a small bus. We arrived at the edge of a large sand dune and stopped. The bus started easing forward slowly, and yes, we were on our way down the dune! Of course, we were startled so say the least. When we stopped and the bottom our driver asked if we wanted to do it again we all said yes. So we did. The next time we were asked to get out of the bus and pick up our boards and go down the dune on the small board. It was a day that I will never forget!

As the ship was leaving Freemantle, there were hundreds of people standing along the sides waving us good-bye. We were to have a stopover in Exmouth, however, just as the day in Hawaii, the waters were not cooperative, and the stop was cancelled.

So our next stop was Subic Bay in the Philippines. The excursion that I took at that stop took me to Corregidor Island. We saw the statue of General Douglas MacArthur at the Lorca Dock where he departed for Darwin, Australia, and while there uttered the words, "I shall return."

The Malinta Tunnel there was constructed from 1922 to 1932. Being bomb proof, it was used as an undergrouned hospital and served as the seat of Philippine Government. We saw the ruins of the Mile Long Barracks, which at the time was supposedly the longest military barracks.

The Battery Way was completed in 1913 and was armed with four twelve-inch mortars capable of firing up to 14,610 yards in any direction at the rate of one round per minute per mortar. Three of the mortars opened fire on April 28, 1942. On May 2, two of these were hit. After more than twelve hours of continuous firing, the remaining mortar finally froze tight on May 6. It was the last of Corregidor's "concrete artillery" to cease firing before the surrender.

The Pacific War Memorial was built in 1968 by the U. S. government and is dedicated to the Filipino and American soldiers who shed their blood in Corregidor. The museum here has been visited by several U. S. presidents.

The Pacific leg of our journey brought us to Nagasaki. We visited the Peace Park, which was the site of the atomic bomb explosion on August 9, 1945. Several countries from around the world have placed statues in this park. We also visited the Nagasaki Atomic Bomb Museum. The one thing I remember in this museum is the clock that indicates the time the bomb struck at 11:02 a.m.

In Nagasaki, we also visited the Dejima Museum of History. This is a nationally designated historic site for the former Dutch East India Company factory. Although Dejima was originally an artificial island, it has now been joined to the mainland by land reclamation. This Dutch outpost was Japan's only contact with the western world for over two hundred years. The exhibits are contained within several structures and portray how the trading system worked between Japan and The Netherlands.

In Japan, we also had a stop in Osaka. There we visited the Osaka Castle Museum that was first built in 1583. It was destroyed in the early seventeenth century and rebuilt. Then it was struck by lightning and burned. Built again in 1931 and survived the air raids. The park and gardens surrounding the Osaka Castle contains many cherry trees and they were in bloom during our visit.

After having lived in Washington, D. C for so many years one can not see cherry trees without thinking of the ones we have that were a gift of the Japanese in 1912.

Next to the ship where we docked in Osaka was a giant ferris wheel that had been erected in 1997. It is over three hundred-feet tall and at night there are various colors that are used to tell what the weather will be the following day.

The ship arrived in Hong Kong. It was good to be back in this city again. It was beginning to feel a little like home. The first night there I went with three friends from the ship to the Peninsula Hotel where we had dinner in the restaurant at the top of the hotel. We were sitting next to the window wall, which was convenient at 9:00 p.m. for watching the nightly laser show. Laser lights are directed from the tops of other buildings across the harbor.

The next day I had to make my pilgrimage to the top of Victoria Peak. While there I saw a handsome silk brocade jacket that I felt would be perfect for the Asian

Festival Ball that would occur on the ship as we left Hong Kong. Another strong point in purchasing the jacket was that it was reversible. I could wear it again later and it would be as though I had a new jacket.

We sailed away from Hong Kong and headed toward Bangkok, Thailand. I couldn't believe that it had been fourteen years since my previous trip here—the one that included Burma, Laos, Cambodia, and Vietnam.

The ship offered an excursion that one could take, whereby you would leave the ship and be taken into Bangkok, do sightseeing, spend the night, and return to the ship the next day. I felt the cost of the trip was too expensive. So before I left for the world cruise, I had my travel agent book me a room at the Peninsula Hotel, the same hotel that the ship-sponsored tour was using.

I asked a fellow passenger on the ship if he had planned to go into the city. When he said that he would like to but he hadn't made any arrangements, I explained to him that I had a reservation at the hotel. So we signed up just for the transportation to and from the city.

Upon arriving at the hotel we were told that our room wasn't ready. We were told to go into the bar area where we could have a complimentary drink and some hors d'ouvres while we waited. A few minutes later the gentleman came and informed us that our suite was ready. It was on the thirty-fourth floor and was enormous. We were given a tour of our accommodations. Even the curtains in the bedroom were on a remote control. The bathroom was in four separate areas with his and hers basins and two television sets. When the tour was over, we pulled out our cameras and began taking pictures.

We had booked a tour for the next morning. We were picked up at the hotel and began our "long boat" tour of the canals. It was interesting going by the many temples, feeding bread to the fish, etc. However, at one point our guide mentioned what we were going to do next and we had a confused look on our faces. She asked what was wrong and we explained to her what tour we had signed up for. It was then that she realized that the tour company had made a mistake. We had actually been doing a completely different tour than the one we had signed up for. So we shifted gears and began in a different direction. We actually got two tours for the price of one.

By the time we finished our sightseeing it was time to be dropped off at the location for us to catch the bus back to the ship. We had had a wonderful experience and it had cost us about one-half as compared to the cost if we had booked through the ship.

When we arrived in Singapore, the first thing we decided to do was to go to Raffles and have a Singapore sling. In the initial phase of our cruise, we had met an interesting person and became good friends. Unfortunately, he left the cruise at the end of one of the earlier segments. He had to return home. When we were in Freemantle he showed up to have dinner with us. And now in Singapore he showed up again to have drinks with us.

The next day I took the tour that went to the National Orchid Gardens and the Singapore Botanical Gardens.

For our next stop of Kuala Lumpur, it was necessary to take an hour bus ride from the ship into town. It was good to have a few hours here and retrace some of the places I had seen when I was here just two years prior.

Then it was off to Colombo, Sri Lanka (again). The one place I remember seeing that I had not seen on the first trip was the Gangaram Temple. Our group went to the Galle Face Hotel for noon tea. It was located along the Indian Ocean with nice views of the city in the background.

We sailed around the southern part of India and were in Mumbai the next day. There we visited the National Art Gallery, The Prince of Wales Museum, The Gandhi Museum, and the very ornate railway station. We had a nice drive along the Marine Drive and saw some of the more expensive apartment buildings.

We drove by the Dhobi Ghat, a vast outdoor laundry, where you could see many people working there. If you saw the movie, Slumdog Millionaire, you saw this area. As we were getting back on the bus from taking our photos, there were many street sales people there vending their wares.

Our next scheduled stop was Dubai. However, again we were out of luck in being able to get into the port because of the high winds that was causing big waves, etc. So the ship circled all night and was able to go in the next morning. It didn't hamper some of us as much as others. There was a large group of people who were supposed to disembark the day before to return home. Needless to say, they didn't make it and had to make other arrangements for the following day.

We were able to go to the beach area near the world famous Burj Al Arab Hotel where we took pictures of a guy walking his camel down the beach. Our guide told us that she could leave Dubai for a week or so and when she returned she would see new buildings that weren't there when she left.

The streets in the new section of town were filled with beautiful flowers and the grassy areas were meticulously manicured. Being that it is in a desert-like setting I can imagine the expense of their sprinkling systems in order to keep things alive. The extremely-large Jumeira Mosque was located in this area.

We visited the Dubai Museum where there were exhibits showing the way of life for the people in yesteryear. There is a creek connecting this area with the shopping area where the gold souks are located. It is possible to go from one side to the other by using the water taxi.

South of here we stopped at our next port of Muscat, Oman. The city of Muscat lies on the waterfront with many, many high mountains in the background.

Our tour here started with a visit to the Seeb Beach Fish Market. Several varieties of fish are brought here in an open air market. The fish were just caught the same morning.

Outside the city we visited the Nakhal Fort. This fort was built approximately 350 years ago. It was built to protect the trade route. Its military-like architecture has several towers, which were used as lookout towers in case the enemy would be approaching. Nearby this fort was an oasis with hot springs and the water was said to be able to cure certain ailments.

On our way back to the ship we saw the large Zawawi Mosque with its twenty-two-carat gold-leaf dome.

Our other stop in Oman was on the southern part of the country in the city of Salalah. We saw various blooms on desert bushes and had the experience of tapping an aromatic frankincense tree. The countryside had many camels. We were able to see the imposing cliffs near Mughsail Beach.

The highlight of the stop here was the visit to Job's Tomb. This sacred sight draws pilgrims from the Christian, Jewish, and Moslem faiths. Legend tells us that it contains the remains of this much-revered Moslem and Old Testament prophet.

We saw the Al Husn Palace, the Salalah residence of the sultan of Oman, His Majesty Sultan Qaboos.

Upon our return to our cabins on the ship, we were pleasantly surprised that an Easter basket with eggs and chocolate had been placed there (I'm sure) by the Easter Bunny!

Our next stop was in Aquba, Jordan. We took a bus from the ship and saw the sights in Petra. The Treasury is the most sought after thing to see here. We also saw the Royal Tombs carved into the hills.

After a lunch at a local hotel we returned to the ship and were on our way up the Red Sea to Sokhna, the port city of Cairo. There was a caravan of about eighteen buses in order to accommodate all the passengers who had signed up for the excursion in Cairo. There was a police escort in front of the caravan, one at the back of the caravan, and an individual police on each bus. We were escorted through all the intersections without stopping.

We visited the step pyramids of King Zoser in Sakkara and had lunch at the Mena House Hotel. We were taken to a gift shop where I found a nice gold cartouche ring that I couldn't resist. I own a cartouche for a chain that I had purchased on a previous trip, but I had never seen a cartouche ring. The lady assured me that my name would be on it and they would deliver it to our bus before we returned to the ship.

We had our photo ops at the pyramids with each of us taking pictures while on a camel.

We continued from the port at Sokhna to the Suez Canal where we could see Egypt on one side and the Sinai Peninsula on the other. We went under a huge modern bridge connecting the two sides not far from the Mediterranean Sea.

After crossing the Mediterranean we made a stop in Marmaris, Turkey. This scenic seaside city has a large yacht basin.

The tour that I took started in Dalyan. We took a local boat along the river to see the rock tombs carved into the hillside. Our boat also took us to the ancient city of Caunos where during the sixth century BC; the people resisted the attempted Persian conquest. During the second century BC, this city was sold to Rhodes by

Egyptian generals before it suffered defeat in the first century BC. Here we saw ruins of the market place, a bath, a theater, a Byzantine church, and a terraced temple.

I remember telling the lady who was our guide for that day that I had had a fantastic journey in Turkey a few years before and that I had a wonderful guide for that trip. She asked me if I remembered the name of the guide. I said, "Yes, her name was Incy." Her response was "I don't believe this! She and I were roommates at one time." I asked her to tell Incy hello for me—another small world story!

In Naples, three of us took the boat to Capri where we roamed and had lunch. Upon our return to Naples, we went to the Opera House, the Castel Nuovo, San Francesco di Paola cathedral, and the Royal Palace.

The crew of the *Queen Elizabeth 2* had arranged several fundraisers during the world trip. All of the monies raised were to be given to the children affected by the tsunami in Thailand that had just happened a few months before the beginning of our trip.

In one of the fundraisers, I gave a donation and was allowed to go on a private tour of the bridge. It was interesting to have an explanation of all the equipment used in assuring our safety and to have a picture of me sitting in the captain's chair wearing his cap.

From Naples our next stop was Barcelona. I took advantage of the "free" day to enjoy the city on my own. I chose first to visit The Sagrada Familia. On my previous visit the lines were so long I decided against the wait. This time I was not only able to enter, but I walked to the top of the towers! Gaudi started work on this Roman Catholic Cathedral in the late 1800s. And they are still working on it!

In the afternoon while walking on the main street, Ramblas, I encountered several of my fellow passengers. We sat and had a beer and enjoyed watching people. One of those passengers took a picture of me later eating a large cone of ice cream. You'll understand why I mention the ice cream in a later story.

At some time during the world cruise, those passengers who are going on the entire journey are treated to a World Cruise Dinner. For the world cruise in 2005, this dinner was held at the National Palace in Barcelona.

I will never forget arriving at the palace. There was a band playing on the outside of the Palace as all nine hundred of us arrived, dressed to the nines, in our formal attire. Tourists across the way were in awe wondering where all these people were coming from. As we entered the Palace the pleasant sounds from a string quartet welcomed us. Further along, we entered the large room where the dinner would take place. An area in that room was also set aside for dancing with a large orchestra playing.

From our stop in Malaga, Spain I participated in an excursion to visit The Alhambra in Grenada. I had read so much about this place and had seen so many pictures, I felt like I had already seen it. However, there is nothing like seeing it first hand.

On arriving in Southampton, we had to say good-bye to our lovely *Queen Elizabeth 2* and transfer to the new *Queen Mary 2*. This was the first world cruise that included the new *Queen Mary 2* for the Atlantic crossing.

We then spent six nights on this vessel, which took us back to New York. We arrived in New York in mid-April. When we had left here in January it was the middle of winter. As we passed the Statue of Liberty on our return we could see the greenness of spring coming alive.

2006

Mali, Burkina Faso, & England Cruise from Lisbon to Fort Lauderdale via Cape Town, South Africa

I had always heard the expression—been to Timbuktu and back—referring to a person who had been everywhere or to "the end of the earth." Someone asked me why I was going there and I told to them that I had been in over one hundred countries and that I still couldn't say that I had been to Timbuktu and back. So by taking this trip, at the end of that month I would be able to finally say that I had been to Timbuktu and back.

I had planned to visit Libya on this excursion and be in the desert for a total eclipse of the sun. However, just at that time, Libya stopped issuing visas to Americans. So that part of the trip had to be put on hold until some other time. Based upon what is happening there now—who knows when it will be possible.

Ironically enough my itinerary in Mali and Burkina Faso had to be reversed. It just so happened that Muammar Gaddafi was scheduled to meet with several other heads of state in Timbuktu in the same hotel and on the same dates as my reservation.

My tour began in Bamako, the capital city of Mali. I was again a "group of one" whereby I had my own English-speaking guide and a driver. I stayed at the Mande Hotel in Bamako. There was a lagoon on one side of the hotel property and some of the local fishermen would be out there in their small boats minding their large fishing nets. The rooms for the hotel were made of adobe and were round in shape. Each room was equipped with the ever popular net over the bed.

On the city tour we saw the Independence Monument, the local market, and the shops which sold handmade objects. It was obvious that most of the houses here are built of mud.

We drove to Sikasso where I stayed at the Hotel Ikhlas. Just across the street from the hotel was an enclosed lot with several goats and sheep. Also in proximity of the hotel was a water supply where ladies would come to do their laundry.

The hotel didn't have a restaurant. My driver took me to another place where I had my lunch. I remembered later that he had asked me at lunchtime what I would prefer for dinner and I told him that I was very flexible with food—anything. I later found out why he had asked me. Upon arriving at the same place for dinner I was asked what I would like. I chose chicken. I was the only person sitting in the restaurant. Finally, someone came through and turned on the small television with some program that was being transmitted in French.

I waited for almost an hour it seems. Once I got it, it was fine. I asked my guide why it took so long. Then is when he reminded me that he had asked me a lunchtime what I would prefer. That way they would have had it ready when I arrived. Consequently, I had to wait while they went to the market and got the chicken and prepared it.

We visited a local market in Sikasso where they were selling vegetables, meats, and clothing. I distinctly remember meat being unload from carts or trucks. The person would be carrying it on their head with no wrapping. Then, the meat would be displayed for sale while it was covered with flies. And it seemed that in all the markets all the kids were busy with playing what I call table football.

In the late 1890s Mali was being invaded by the French Colonial Army. Huge walls were built around the city of Sikasso in order to deter the French. My guide took me to a section of the remaining wall on our sightseeing tour.

At Mamelon Hill, we visited the cave and escarpment that were used as the residence of the kings of Sikasso and is considered a sacred site that housed the city's protector spirits.

The next stop on the tour was the Hotel Auberge in Bobo Dioulasso, which was our first stop in the country of Burkina Faso. This was a nice hotel and had a large swimming pool that was not only used by hotel guests but could be used by the local population with a small fee. There was also an Internet café located in the complex, which made it convenient in keeping touch with friends and relatives back home.

We visited the usual places, which included the City Hall, the railway station, and the Soccer Stadium. There was a huge mosque here and through the contacts of guide, we were able to go inside. This mosque as all the others was built from mud. Each year after the heavy rains, certain sections have to be replaced.

One of the highlights in Bobo Dioulasso was the Music Museum. In the museum there were displays of various instruments that had been popular through the years. It was almost like a "history of music" museum.

The Deux Bales National Park is just outside Bobo Dioulasso. There I was able to see a large group of elephants arrive to have their morning bath. Near the park was a Sabou Village with its totem crocodiles.

Ouagadougou is the capital city of Burkina Faso. There I was able to visit the Artisans Center where ladies were weaving fabric, bronze figures were being cast, and a lot of art work. I also visited an animal park outside the city where I was able to see ostrich, deer, peacocks, elands, lions, zebras, hippos, and turtles.

I think I was the only person staying in the Amitie Hotel in Ouahigouya. My guide took me to visit the historic Yatenga Naba Compound, where the king lives. Upon asking the guard if it would be possible to see the "king" we were told that he was sleeping at the time. The King supposedly has forty wives and not even children are allowed there. I suppose they have a separate compound for them.

The mosque and the homes in Ouahigouya, the most important town in all of northern Burkino Faso, are also built of mud. The street market there was similar to others in that most of it operated from tents on either side of the street. I remember seeing a large truck pull up loaded with sheep, chicken, and goats. Some of them were actually on top of the truck—some tied and some in handmade crates.

The drive from Ouahigouya brought me back into Mali. On the way we saw people panning for gold. Gold may be a vital part of Mali's economy at the time I was there in 2006, but individual prospectors have mined gold in Mali for at least 1,500 years.

In the twentieth century there was little commercial mining. However, economic and political liberalization in the 1990s, and a revision of the mining code, has attracted a host of multinational mining companies in recent years.

Gold mining in Mali is no longer a matter of looking for nuggets. It seems that in 2006 all mines are open-cast operations where gold particles are obtained from crushed rock using cyanide. But some things stay the same in that locals still dig for gold using picks and shovels.

This is the segment of the trip where we were approaching the Dogon Country of Mali. There is an escarpment that is almost 150 miles long. Many Dogon villages are along this escarpment. Some of the homes are dug out into the hillside. However, some of the holes are tombs. The drive across the escarpment presented exciting views of the countryside.

I stayed at the Hotel Campement Ginna. The rooms were quite basic and were situated in a dormitory-like setting with rooms on either side. The room did include a nice ceiling fan and a net over the bed. Between the building for the rooms and the main building for the restaurant and registration was a nice garden. Surrounding the hotel grounds were several large baobob trees.

While in residence there I was able to witness a funeral. All of the people in the community gather. The men carry guns and do a dance and fire the guns (with blanks I was told). They dance and go to the entrance of the home of the person who died and continue their ritual.

They usually will not bury the person immediately upon dying because it is expensive, and the family saves up until they can afford all the things that go along with the ceremony.

At one point of this trip I began to notice that I didn't see many old people. My guide told me that if there is an old person in the family, they usually stay inside the home and are taken care of by members of the family. I was told that the average life expectancy in Mali is about forty-five years. I probably looked like a relic!

My guide took me to see the home of the Hogon, the Spiritual Leader, of the village. Across from the entrance to his house, one could see white markings on the wall which is where people had sacrificed animals.

I visited Songo, another Dogon village. Here I witnessed residents rebuilding structures that had been damaged by the monsoon rains with mud mixed with straw. Sometimes it was evident that an entire family would be working together. For example, the children would make the mud and carry it to their father who would use it in the rebuilding. The roofs were usually made of straw.

In this village there were open-air structures with very thick roofs. It seems that each generation would add another layer. This thick roof over the open-air area was sensible in that it made the area much cooler and blocked out the extreme heat from the sun. These structures were used for ceremonial purposes.

Gourds are made into musical instruments and are used in the burial ceremonies. One of the local residents gave me a demonstration of the different kinds.

Just outside the actual village was an area called the Circumcision Grotto. Here boys are brought at the age of ten or eleven for circumcision. They are told that they must not scream or make a noise during the procedure.

The walls of the grotto are practically covered with artwork. It was amazing how the colors had remained brilliant through the years.

Driving from the escarpment in the Dogon Country to Bandiagara I saw groups of young boys walking along the road. They were all wearing long white robes. I was told by my guide that these boys were on their way to their Koran classes.

The mode of travel it seems in this area was bicycles, donkey or hand-pulled carts, and a few automobiles. The local gasoline station had pumps that were similar to the ones we would see in the United States in the 30s with a hand pump and the round glass part on top.

I stayed at Le Kambary Hotel in Bandiagara. The individual rooms again were round structures made of mud. The base of the bed was large stones and the ever present net above. There was a small bath adjacent to this room. The restaurant was in a separate building and also continued the architectural design of the remainder of the entire complex.

We left early the next morning for our drive to Timbuktu. It was an eight-hour drive on a washboard-like dirt road through the desert. The driver must have been in a hurry to get there. His speed of driving made me so nervous to the point that I asked my guide to please ask him to slow down.

I guess he didn't slow down enough. In the early afternoon he hit a ditch that made the 4×4 stop. Fortunately nothing was damaged—but the air conditioner! We drove about twenty-five miles at the end of the journey without any air conditioning. A couple of the windows had been opened to get in some air. However, that also let in a lot of dust!

We had to cross the river just before Timbuktu on a ferry. While we were on the ferry I took pictures of the 4×4. It was completely covered with dust and dirt to the point where you couldn't even tell what was the original color.

When I arrived to the Hotel Hendrina Khan in Timbuktu, it was impossible also to determine the color of my luggage. It was supposed to be dark purple. However, now it was tan.

On the walls of the entrance to the hotel were pictures of Muammar Gaddafi and the other heads of state who had visited the week before.

My local guide there took me on a tour of the city. One of the first things he showed me was the doors on the residences. The door knocker was used by the husband after he had been away. He knew the code to use. If anyone else tried to come in, the wife knew that it wasn't her husband.

I was shown the typical dwellings of the Tuareg tribe and their methods of cooking, especially the ovens used for making bread. The Old Mosque in Timbuktu was built in the fourteenth century.

I was taken to see the Archives of Scholarly Islamic Manuscripts. Some date back to the sixteenth century. There are about five thousand items in the collection. If these items were in Washington, D. C they would probably be covered with glass and stored in a room where the temperature and humidity would be controlled at all times. However, here the items were on display in a building without air conditioning.

It is preferable to do most sightseeing in Timbuktu early in the morning and late in the afternoon because of the extreme heat. On this particular day my guide was to pick me up at the hotel around 5:00 p.m. for our camel ride out into the desert.

My guide took me to an Internet café in Timbuktu. Once the computer was turned on, it took about thirty minutes for it to be ready for me to sign on to my Internet service provider where I would be able to enter information for sending e-mails.

The next hurdle was contending with the French keyboard as opposed to the querty one. Thus, the input was difficult and time consuming. Making the input even more difficult was the fact that the computer did not offer a drop-down with e-mail addresses. If you didn't know the address, you couldn't send an e-mail to that person. I struggled through and finally was ready to send the e-mail and just at that time, the electricity in the establishment went out!

After my afternoon ride in the desert we came back to the Internet café and tried again. The exact same thing happened again! And the person in charge wanted to charge me for the time I used the computer and was able to do nothing! I did refuse to pay.

It was then that I decided that my friends and relatives would not be receiving any e-mails from Timbuktu.

The first step was to learn the proper procedure for mounting the camel and the position in which the feet are supposed to be. My guide was somewhat impressed at how quickly I followed his directions. He let me know that he could decipher that this was not the first time that I had done this.

We proceeded out into the desert for a while and stopped at a place where we sat down and prepared a special pot of tea. There is a special feeling one has when you look around you and in a 360 degree turn you see absolutely nothing but sand. That memory never leaves you.

Just about the time we were readying ourselves for the return, we spotted two different caravans with about twenty camels in each entering the desert. I asked my guide where they would be going. He told me that they were probably going to the salt mines.

He then told me that he was born in the desert where the salt mines are located. I asked him how long it takes to get there and he said that by camel it takes about four days.

The visit to Timbuktu comes to a close and it is time again to make our eight-hour sojourn back. We lost our air conditioning on the way in. We had a flat tire on our way back. There was a group of tourists from Germany in a vehicle following us. When they saw that we had a problem, they stopped to find out if they could be of assistance. Even a couple members of that group commented that our driver seem to like to drive fast!

We arrived in Mopti where I stayed at the Hotel Kanaga. It was a real treat to be able to hop into their swimming pool surrounded by beautifully landscaped gardens and palm trees after the dusty memories of Timbuktu.

One of the things that I remember in walking around the grounds of the hotel was the many lizards and their vibrant colors. I suppose I had never seen a lizard that was blue and orange. My camera couldn't resist snapping.

Across the street from the hotel was the Bani river. Some of this area floods during the monsoon season. When the floods have subsided the same area is used for growing rice.

The Bani river is the major asset for this city. It is used to transport everything! Just by sitting at a local restaurant to have a coffee, you can see different boats arriving and immediately the items are unloaded. Some of the boats are hauling meat, live chickens, clothes, firewood, salt, vegetables, and other animals.

Adjacent to the river is a large market. There the local people can come and buy almost anything. There was even a section in the market where they were actually making nails to be used in the construction of boats. I remember a situation—as they were unloading a load of chickens when one of them got loose. I got a chuckle just observing them trying to catch it.

Many of the ladies will have wraps with a small child on the back. It must be a very comfortable way of transporting them as most of the children are sound asleep.

In the latter part of the afternoon, I was taken on a boat ride down the river. I noticed that I was drawing some attention. It could be that I was the only white person I had seen all day. And while the other boats we were passing by would have sometimes as many as twenty people on board and here was my boat with one person.

Along the banks of the river, I could see people using the river to wash their cars, to take baths, and to wash clothes.

Our next stop on the way back to Bamako was Djenne. The major attraction here is the Great Mosque. It is the world's largest mud brick building and is listed as one of UNESCO's World Heritage sites.

We were at a point now where the Bani river and the Niger river had merged and is now just called the Niger river. In Old Segou we visited the Tomb of King Biton Coulibaly. He lived during the late seventeenth and mid-eighteenth century. He was a leader and this area was the capital of the Bambara Empire. Later, he dealt in trading slaves that had been captured in the many wars.

A lot of pottery is made in this area, and along the river there were large markets selling nothing but pottery. It was no surprise also to see many gardens alongside the river because of the availability of water for the plants.

Back in the capital city of Bamako where we had begun our circle tour two weeks prior, we had time to visit the National Museum of Mali and had nice views of the Presidential Palace on the hill overlooking the city.

On my way back to Washington from Africa, I made a stop in England. I visited a friend in London and was able to go to the theater and see the musical, *Billy Elliot*.

I then took the train to Bath where I spent the weekend with two ladies that I had met on the *Queen Elizabeth 2* the year before. We took a tour of the city that included Queen Square, Pulteney Bridge, the Royal Crescent, the botanical gardens, Bath Abbey, the Costume Museum, and the Roman Baths. We attended a performance of *Present Laughter* by Noel Coward at the New Royal Theater. We had brunch on Sunday at the Royal Crescent, which is one of the top hotels in Bath.

Sometimes in traveling you don't realize what an influence you make. One night on the *Queen Elizabeth 2* around-the-world cruise, I decided to go to the bar for a nightcap with these same two ladies I was visiting in Bath. I ordered a Manhattan. One of the ladies asked me what was in the drink. She decided to have one for the first time and she liked it. When we were at the brunch in Bath a gentleman came out with his white gloves on and asked if we would like to have a drink before the brunch. The lady looked at me and said, "I'll have a Manhattan."

My next stop was in Ayr, Scotland, where I also was able to visit a couple that I had met on the *Queen Elizabeth 2* in 2005. They have a lovely home there in a beautiful setting. They have several horses and have won many titles in shows in Scotland.

They showed me the area including the Burns National Heritage Park, the Robert Burns birthplace, Culzean Castle, and the Turnberry Golf Course where the British Open sometimes takes place.

In the fall of 2006, I took a cruise from Lisbon, Portugal via Cape Town, South Africa to Fort Lauderdale, Florida on the Holland America ship, The Prinsendam. It was called The Taste of Four Continents Cruise since it included Europe, Africa, South America, and North America.

I must say that I really had fun going to all the embassies in Washington in order to obtain my visas for this trip. There was an interesting story in obtaining one of them. I had the address and telephone number. However, when I arrived at the address listed there wasn't any name on any door to indicate that they were there. A gentleman came out of another office and I asked him about the embassy and he told me that he thought they had moved. I used my cell phone and called the number that I had and was told that they are now located in the building across the street. I proceeded there and found them. I gave the lady my passport, the application, the money order, and pictures and asked how long it would take for them to process it. She said that it usually takes two or three days, or they could do it now. I indicated that I could wait. Five minutes later it was over!

I spent a couple days in Lisbon before the beginning of the cruise. The one thing in Lisbon that I had not been able to do previously was to visit the Gulbenkian Museum. This is a fantastic museum and I would recommend it as a "must do" on a visit to Lisbon. As the ship departed Lisbon we passed the Monument of the Discoveries and the Tower of Belem.

Out first port of call was the city of Cadiz, Spain. There we saw the Town Hall, the Cathedral of Cadiz, government buildings, the Old Wall of the City, and the Independence Monument.

Time to change continents—we sailed to Casablanca, Morocco. Here we visited the Presidential Palace, a Mosque in the Old Medina, and the Sacred Heart Cathedral. This cathedral was built by the French in 1930 and had some of the most beautiful stained glass windows I had ever seen.

We visited the usual markets that have meats, vegetables, and flowers. However, I also remember going to a market that had nothing but olives. I never realized that there were so many kinds of olives and the scent as you entered was blissful.

The Hassan II Mosque was built in 1989 and is the largest in the world. It took thirty thousand workers and six years to build. The roof is retractable and the minaret is 574-feet tall. Having been a teacher for so many years it was interesting to see large groups of small children having a "field trip" and being controlled by their teachers.

Proceeding south, our next stop was in Agadir, Morocco. Immediately upon arriving here we were taken up a large hill to a fort and a Kasbah. From this venue one has a great view of the city. Agadir is situated within a mining region. Lead, manganese, and zinc are shipped by way of the excellent natural harbor. The chief industries in Agadir are fishing, fish canning, and the manufacture of light metal products. This city was devastated in 1960 by two earthquakes and about fifteen thousand people died.

Dakar, Senegal, was our next port of call. As a part of our city excursion we were taken to an artist center. There were many handmade items available for sale. The most memorable section of this center was seeing an artist complete a painting in nothing but different colors of sand. I couldn't resist one of them and it remains one of the memorable collectibles from traveling.

In Banjul, the capital city of The Gambia, we visited the Kachikally Crocodile Pool and Museum where we were able to get up as close as I felt comfortable to several crocodiles. In this area we saw a three hundred-year-old Banyan tree. As we were walking along the path there would be large armies of ants making their way across. All of us made sure our pants were shaken before returning to the ship.

The Gambia National Museum contains displays where one can learn the culture of the country. Also displayed are many historical documents.

In order to motivate the passengers on this Holland America cruise aboard the Prinsendam, to mix and mingle they ask someone to be Mr. Prinsendam and Miss Prinsendam. Everyone is supposed to ask as many people as possible if they have been chosen. By doing this you meet a lot of people on the cruise. I was asked to be the Mr. Prinsendam for this cruise.

While we were on our way to the National Museum, a lady asked me if I was Mr. Prinsendam. I said no because there were other people around and I didn't want them to know that I had been discovered. While we were in the museum, however, and I was alone in a gallery with the lady who had asked me, I informed her that I was Mr. Prinsendam, but I couldn't reveal it to her earlier in front of other passengers. Both of us later in a ceremony on the ship received several nice gifts.

The local dancers from Takoradi, Ghana, performed for us as we arrived. We were presented to the King of the Village. In the village we were given demonstrations as to how they prepare certain foods. We saw large but flat containers where fish were being dried. They also use special ovens for this. Along the coast there were a lot of people casting large nets for catching fish.

We visited the Cape Coast Castle. Ironically, slaves built the castle and then it was later used to contain the slaves awaiting shipment to another country. It was very dark in some of the large rooms in the lower level. The exit from this dungeon was referred to as the place of no return.

Arriving in Lome, Togo, we were again serenaded with music and dance. Several of them were in brightly colored costumes and were performing on stilts. Again here we were presented to the King. Many of the houses here are made from palm fronds. The highlight of our visit here was to the Fetish Market. The strange offerings, used in traditional medicine and popular culture, offer an unparalleled glimpse into the local life and society. The array of bones and teeth include monkey and bird skulls. The selection of strange charms and amulets is mind-boggling. Each item is believed to cure a particular illness if used by a trained traditional medical practitioner. Some of the talismans induce fertility while others are meant to fend off or attract different spirits.

It was interesting to arrive in a new port of a new country and realize the differences in their native costumes. No stilts here as we arrived in Cotonou, Benin. However, some of the ladies were wearing skirts made of straw and interesting headdresses.

Ganvie Village is a stilted village and is in the middle of Lake Nokoué. It was formed in the eighteenth century when the people were forced to flee in the face of tribal wars. The area was not arable, but offered natural protection from the warriors.

Outside the Palace of Justice in Douala, Cameroon, it was interesting to see that there were reserved parking spaces for officials. I took a picture of one of them that was for vice president No. 8! I don't know how many vice presidents they had!

We walked by a large structure that was the former Presidential Palace and nearby was the burial ground with a monument to the former rulers.

Here in Douala we were given another dance performance that was supposedly the typical dance for their country.

We toured the National Museum in Libreville, Gabon, where they had several displays of their traditional masks. We also saw a large open-air structure that was serving as the local Catholic Church.

While walking around the small town of Walvis Bay, Namibia, I went into a small grocery store and was looking at the various items for sale. I couldn't believe my eyes when I spotted a table with Christmas items on it. I bought several of the little doll-like items and use them every year in my Christmas decorations. Here the musicians came aboard the ship to perform just before we were to leave.

It was nice to see Cape Town, South Africa, again. The view of the Table Mountain is even more spectacular as seen from the ship as we entered to city. We did some sightseeing in Cape Town and had an unexpected layover for an extra day because of high winds and the ship was unable to leave the dock. If one has to stay another day anywhere, this is a good place for it to happen.

Our last port of call in Africa was at Luderitz, Namibia. There we toured Kolmanskop, which was an old mining ghost town. There was a small museum here and one could see where they were able to bowl and had their own doctor's office.

A couple from the ship and I hired an English-speaking driver to take us our into the Namibian Desert. We were able to get some fantastic pictures of the sand dunes.

We were to have two stops in the Atlantic Ocean before reaching South America. The first of the two was the island of St. Helena. Yes, this is the island where Napoleon was exiled. We were able to go through the home where he lived here. We also visited the Tomb of Napoleon even though it has been moved to Paris.

The Plantation House of the island was the official residence of the Governor. In the yard of the house was a giant tortoise that was 170 years old.

The city of Jamestown on the island of Helena is divided into a lower level and an upper level. One can drive to the upper level; however, there is a series of steps where one can walk from the lower level to the upper level. It is called Jacob's Ladder and has seven hundred steps! Upon completion of walking up and down, you are given a certificate.

The second stop in the Atlantic Ocean was Ascension Island. The weather wasn't cooperative, and we were not able to dock. However, we did do a circumnavigation of the island. I think we probably saw more this way than if we had just seen one section.

Fortaleza, Brazil, was our introduction to South America, which was our third continent for the cruise. I was astonished at the number of large buildings along the coast. It reminded me a little of Miami Beach. On the city tour, we saw the Metropolitan Cathedral, the large José de Alencar Theater, the Branco Museum, and the fish market on the waterfront.

The Ver-o-peso Market in Belem, Brazil, covers about four city blocks, probably the largest in Brazil. The Forte do Castelo was built by the Portuguese in the seventeenth century. We also saw the Museum of Sacred Art, the Basilica of Our Lady of Nazareth, the botanical/zoological Gardens, and the Church of St. Alexander.

We traveled almost seven hundred miles down the Amazon river. Santarem was our first stop. Further along, we stopped at Alter Do Chão, which is a popular choice for vacationers. The large cathedral in Alter Do Chão is Our Lady of Conceicao. The Amazon river in front of the church is where the muddy water from one part meets the clear water of another part and you can see the separation point.

About 160 miles downstream from Alter Do Chão we had our last stop in Parintins. The large boats reminded me of what one would see on the Mississippi; however, they were being used as hotels. For the locals who needed to get away for three or fours days, they would go on the boat and for sleeping they brought their own hammock. Upon embarking you could see the people hanging up their "bed" for the trip adjacent to another person.

After we arrived back in the Atlantic Ocean, we headed north to Bridgetown, Barbados. Driving around the island, we saw St. John's Parish Church, which was built in 1836.

From Barbados we were approaching our final port of Half Moon Cay, Bahamas. This was a day to relax, enjoy the sun, and reflect on what had been a wonderful journey filled with lots of memories since we departed in Lisbon almost seven weeks ago and knowing that tomorrow we will be in Fort Lauderdale and completing the cruise in North America, our fourth continent of the cruise.

2007

Palm Springs, *Queen Mary 2*, and China

The year 2007 began with a visit to see friends in Palm Springs, California. It was nice to reminisce about all the good times that we had had on the *Queen Elizabeth 2* world cruise in 2005.

A few months later I took the *Queen Mary 2* on a transatlantic crossing from New York to Southampton. Our group was composed of six longtime friends. We didn't spend any time in London since we had all been there several times. So we flew back to the United States the same day we arrived in England.

In August, I took a tour of China and Tibet with Pacific Delight Tours, the same company I had used in 1986 when I visited China.

Our tour began in Beijing where we visited Tiananmen Square and the major buildings surrounding it including the Forbidden City. Our tour included a visit to the Drum and Bell Towers. We were given a performance called *The Legend of Kung Fu*, which is purported to be the most exciting Kung Fu show in the world.

On our visit to the Hutong, we were driven through the area in a rickshaw. During the visit we were invited inside a family dwelling to further see how they lived. The particular home we visited had a room where they had a wall display of pictures of former visitors to their home. One of the tourists in our group was looking at the pictures and realized that not only had he been in the same house before on a previous trip, but that he was wearing the same shirt that he was wearing on his previous trip!

Not much had changed here in Beijing since my last visit except that on my last visit they had just thought about adding a fourth ring to their highway system. Now, in 2007, they were contemplating about adding the sixth.

The city was preparing for the Olympics that was to be held here the following year and trying to control the pollution. While in China we were able to see on television the celebratory presentation recognizing the fact that it was exactly one year until the opening day. We drove passed the "Bird's Nest Stadium."

Outside the city we also visited the Ming Tombs, the Great Wall, and Summer Palace.

We flew to from Beijing to Xian for our next adventure. The one reason that most people come to this city, of course, is to see the Terracotta Army Soldiers. I had seen them on my previous visit. However, on that visit, only one building was open and no photos were allowed. Now, much more has been excavated, other buildings have been added, and photography is allowed.

We visited the Exhibition Hall, the Shaanxi History Museum, and a Jade factory. Our last evening there we enjoyed The Tang Dynasty Theater's Dinner Show.

We flew from Xian to Lhasa, Tibet. In order to adjust to the extreme change in elevation, we had the afternoon free so that our bodies could acclimate to the change. It worked for most of us, but we did have a few who had a problem with it and missed the sightseeing the next day.

The first stop on our sightseeing tour in Lhasa was to Norbulingka, the summer palace of the Dalai Lamas. The grounds were landscaped using hundreds of beautiful flowers.

We had time to shop in the stalls in the Barkhor section of Lhasa.

Then, we traveled to The Sera Monastery, which is famous for its warrior monks. One of the three colleges in Lhasa that the monks can choose is the one where they enhance their printing skills. It was almost amusing to visit the large outdoor courtyard. The monks divide into groups so that they can discuss the lessons they have just finished. You get the feeling that they were all trying to talk at the same time, thus making very, very loud noises.

As most tours go—they usually save the best till last. We were all anxious to be able to see and visit the Potola Palace. This palace was built by the king in the mid-seventh century as a gift for his bride. It has long been the residence of the Dalai Lama. Chinese invasions in 1959 and 1966 caused the Dalai Lama to flee to India. During these invasions many items were destroyed.

On visiting the palace there are many, many steps to conquer. With an elevation of over thirteen thousand feet, it requires a little extra stamina. There are over one thousand rooms, shrines, and statues distributed over several different levels.

Upon completing our visit in Xian we flew to Chengdu. Here we visited the Wangjiang Lou Park where we were able to see beautiful pagodas, the statue of the poetess Xue Tao, and the Quingyang Gong, which is the main Daoist temple founded in the ninth century.

We traveled outside the city to the Chengdu Research Base of Giant Panda Breeding. I was a little disappointed that we didn't see as many pandas as I had assumed we would. We were told that to see more of them we would have to arrive very early in the morning.

It was a real treat to be able to see several baby pandas in incubators. There was an also excellent movie showing small pandas just after their birth. In one scene of the movie it shows a baby panda making a very loud noise and the mother was kicking it around. Those of us watching the film couldn't decide whether it was funny or sad.

The one thing here that I had not planned for was to see red pandas. I had never even heard of red pandas and now I have a picture of me holding one!

The Sanxingdui Museum contains an enormous amount of exhibits of bronze, gold, jade, and ceramics. The items were found while excavating in 1986, and date back some three thousand years.

On our way back to the city of Chengdu, we stopped at a local farm home. It seems that there was more than one family living in a commune-like setting. It was obvious that most of the men in their spare time love to play mahjong. The children were adorable in their finest clothing thrilling in having their photos taken especially when they could see the photo on the digital camera.

Our group was treated to a performance by the Sichuan Opera. It was a wonderful show. The one entry that I found astonishing was the Changing Faces. It was uncanny how a person could just make a quick nod of the head and the mask on the face would change to something completely different.

We flew from Chengdu to Chongqing. The boundaries of this city had been expanded to include some of its suburbs. At the time of our visit, it was considered to be the world's most populated city with over thirty-one million people!

We had a ride here on an elevated rail line that reminded me a little of the one in Seattle, Washington. The city contains many, many skyscrapers.

We visited what is called the mountainside city where neighborhoods rise in tiers along the steep river embankments. As you meander down you see a fortune teller, many on-street vendors, herbal medical supplies, and all kinds of condiments. For your dinner you could choose from eels, ducks, chicken, etc.

There would be people sitting at sewing machines waiting to repair any item that you might need fixing. During the time they didn't have a person waiting for an item, they would be utilizing that time to make additional clothes to be sold.

We visited the Stillwell Museum that is dedicated to the American General who was stationed here during World War II and did a lot for the Chinese. He was instrumental in aiding the completion of a highway between India and China, which eased the ability to transport ammunitions and weapons.

The Great Hall of the People in Chengdu contains a large rotunda which will seat 4,200 people. It was built in 1954 as a conference hall and is now part of the Renmin Hotel and is sometimes used for concerts.

Near the end of our visit to the Great Hall, I saw several males in the museum shop who appeared to be friends and was using sign language to communicate. I had taken sign language myself and this intrigued me. Even though I was aware that English sign language and the sign language of other countries are not the same, I decided to give it a try. Fortunately, one of the group member was able to communicate a little in English—enough to understand that I had a friend in the United States who couldn't hear and I communicated with him in sign language.

Now it was time to leave Chengdu and begin our Yangtze river cruise. Along the river we saw markings that were indications as to where the level of the river would be at the completion of the dam. Many families, even small towns, had to be moved to higher ground. We were told that these families were supplied with another place to live and were given subsidies. Even with this situation many of them didn't want to move.

Our stop in Fengdu offered the opportunity to take the chairlift to the "City of Ghosts." The temple area at the top of the King Mountain pays tribute to the King of the Underworld.

The second day of our trip had us going through the Qutang Gorge, the first of the three fabled "Three Gorges." We saw where new bridges were being built and one of the old bridges had been named the "bye bye" bridge since it is to be blasted away and the remainder will be underwater.

We were taken up the Darling river in a small boat in order to view some of the small gorges. There was a group of Chinese people on another one of the small boats, and they were there to entertain us with songs. It is difficult to find words that can express the wonderful views.

Our cruise continued on through the other two gorges on our way to the dam. We went through the locks at the dam, which is a time-consuming ordeal. We were taken on a tour of the dam site.

Suzhou is a small town outside Shanghai. We had a nice boat ride through the canals there. There were some people living on boats in the canal. The architecture of the bridges across the canal and the homes on either side was intriguing. We spotted one fisherman under a bridge who used cormorants at night with a light for catching the fish.

The number of bikes here brings back memories of my first trip to China. Now in the big cities, however, there are fewer bikes and more automobiles. We were told that there were now more Buicks and Chevrolets being manufactured in China than in the United States.

The Suzhou Museum was designed by I. M. Pei, who was born in this city. His parents supposedly lived nearby the museum.

Our final stop of the tour was in Shanghai. A visit to Shanghai is not complete without a stroll on The Bund. I can remember on my previous visit that if I were to look across to the other side, there wasn't very much to see. It was all slums and contained no high-rise buildings. Now, when one looks across, there are several large skyscrapers with neon lights everywhere.

We visited the Huxingting Teahouse, which was built in 1784 by cotton merchants. The zigzag bridge here is to protect the structure as evil spirits are not supposed to be able to turn corners. We also visited the Shanghai Museum and a carpet factory.

The traffic here was horrendous, but on the major thoroughfares they had very modern up-to-date lighted signs across the highway indicating the traffic conditions ahead. If someone were on their way home, these signs would enable them in making a decision as to which road to take. If the sign for your exit was in red, it meant that the traffic was at a standstill; if it were yellow, moving slowly; and if it were green, it was moving all right.

We took the new maglev train from Shanghai to the airport. It travels at about 260 miles per hour. The trip to the airport took about seven minutes. Then, of course, it was time for our overseas flight that would take about ten or eleven hours.

I arrived in San Francisco early the next morning. The two friends who picked me up at the airport were friends I had met on the *Queen Elizabeth 2* trip. Believe it or not, even after an overnight flight from Shanghai, I actually went with my friends for a matinee performance of Jersey Boys that same afternoon. For the first few minutes I didn't know if I was going to be able to keep my eyes open. However, the familiar songs in the production kept me awake.

As soon as the show had finished, we were going to have dinner. My friends asked me what kind of food I would like. My response was obvious—anything but Chinese! I had had Chinese food every meal for three weeks! Yes, the giant cheeseburger was delicious and, the French fries were scrumptious!

2008

Queen Victoria cruise, Dubai, Albania, and Trans-Siberian Railway

In January 2008, I flew to California to join the new *Queen Victoria* for a segment of its first world cruise. The segment I chose was from Los Angeles to Singapore, and it was for seven weeks. This was to be another around-the-world adventure. Upon leaving the ship in Singapore I had already planned to fly to Dubai for a few days. At this point my travel agent asked me if there was any place that I had not visited between Dubai and Washington. I said that the only place between Dubai and Washington that I had not visited was Albania. He immediately turned to his computer and said, "Well, we'll just send you to Albania for a few days!"

The new *Queen Victoria* was absolutely beautiful with its three-story lobby, the Clock Tower steps, and especially the Royal Court Theater. The inside of my deluxe room was huge, and I really appreciated having all the extra space.

The first stop on the tour was Hololulu, where we docked at the Aloha Tower. I spent the day there with my longtime friends. We left Hawaii and headed south to Pago Pago, American Samoa. We were greeted with musical and dancing entertainment.

I enjoyed our tour of the island in the "big green bus." I remember seeing this large rock protruding up out of the water. They called it the Flower Pot Rock.

I think this was the first place I had seen graves in people's yards. We were told that they do this to signify that the deceased person is still part of the family. I did, however, wonder what happened when the house was sold to another family?

The residents of the village we visited gave us demonstrations on weaving, cooking, and other daily activities.

Lautoka, Fiji, was our next stop. Five of us from the ship made a deal with a driver, who took us sightseeing. We visited the Viseisei Village, where the first Fijians arrived almost 3,500 years ago. The President lives in the village.

Not too far from here was the Garden of the Sleeping Giant. This garden was founded by Raymond Burr in 1977 to house his own orchids. The garden now displays Fiji's largest orchid collection.

Auckland, New Zealand, was the next stop. Since this was my fourth time here, I tried to find new things to do. I was really looking forward to the next stop in Napier. I had never been in this town before. We were lucky that we just happened to be there on their big weekend of the year—the annual Art Deco Weekend! The city has many buildings with wonderful examples of true art-deco architecture.

In addition to that, there were almost eight hundred antique cars there for the weekend. Several of them drove out adjacent to our ship to welcome us. Many of the residents dress up in period costumes of the 20s and 30s and show-off their classic cars. There are three hundred members of the club in Napier alone. Many cars came here from other parts of New Zealand and Australia.

There was a big park in town with a shell where they usually have concerts. For this weekend, in addition to entertainment, there was a fashion show with the wonderful old fashions.

Wellington, New Zealand, was our next port of call. It was great to be back in this city and to see how it had changed since my 1989 visit. I took the cable car up to the Botanical Gardens, visited the cable car museum, and enjoyed the lovely gardens and the old cemetery on the way back down to the city.

A group of Maori dancers and musicians came aboard the *Queen Victoria* and gave us a folklore show before our departure for Australia.

Upon arriving in Melbourne, Australia, I met and spent the day with two guys that I had met on the *Queen Mary 2* cruise three years earlier. They had also been on the Prinsendam cruise that I was on in Africa.

We visited Miss Marple's Tea Room in Sassafras outside Melbourne. There were pictures on all the walls of Margaret Rutherford who portrayed the Agatha Christie character. We enjoyed our tea and scones.

Our drive through the Sherbrooke Forest and the Dandenong Mountains was a real treat with their fern trees and very tall hardwood trees.

Back into the city I was able to visit the nice home of my two friends. We also saw the tallest apartment building in the world and the Botanical Gardens.

The sail away in Melbourne was out of this world. The pier was filled with people, and as the ship was ready to sail there was a wonderful fireworks display.

We arrived in Sydney and docked across from the Opera House and next to the huge Harbor Bridge. Here I was again in Sydney and was trying to figure out what there was to see that I had not seen previously.

I walked through the Botanical Gardens and took some pictures of the Sydney skyline from a different viewpoint. There I saw the Music Pavilion, and the Cactus Garden. It was a first to tour the Government House.

Our departure from Sydney turned out to be an historic spectacle! The *Queen Victoria* had just had its first visit to Sydney and the *Queen Elizabeth 2* was visiting for the last time. Both ships left their berths at the same time. The space that the *Queen Victoria* had been occupying was to be occupied by the *Queen Elizabeth 2.* Consequently, we passed each other in the harbor.

There were hundreds of thousands on the piers that day to witness this. Everywhere you looked there were throngs of people waving and yelling. Helicopters from the television stations were circling above during all this. As we exited the city there was a flotilla of about three hundred boats escorting us. It was truly an occasion that I will never forget.

Moving up the east coast of Australia, the *Queen Victoria* made a stop at the Gold Coast where many of the passengers planned to spend the day at the Barrier Reef. Since I had been to the Barrier Reef twice previously, I decided that it would be nice to take a tour into Brisbane and also visit the Australia Zoo.

The city tour included seeing the Town Hall, the Customs House, and the Art Museum. We had lunch at the Ettamogah Pub, which evidently was the most popular spot in all of Queensland at that time.

After lunch, we went to The Australia Zoo where several aboriginal dancers gave a performance and demonstrated their way of starting a fire. Of interest in the zoo were the ostriches, kangaroos, and koalas. And yes, I do have a picture of me holding one of those little cute animals!

The *Ultimate Wildlife Adventure* show at the Australia Zoo was the section that was established by Steve Irwin. There we saw snakes, alligators, and many colorful birds that were trained to perform various acts.

Our next stop was in Port Douglas, which is outside the city of Cairns. That day also they offered tours to the barrier reef and several other sites that I had previously enjoyed. And knowing that 95 percent of the passengers would be off the ship for the day made it a perfect day for me to do laundry. When you are on a ship with over two thousand people there is never a good time to do laundry.

Kota Kinabalu is the capital of the Sabah State in Northern Borneo in Malaysia. Mount Kinabalu was visible from the upper deck of the ship. On the tour, we visited the downtown area with its Clock Tower. Outside the city we visited the State Mosque of Sabah, the Sabah Museum, and the Sabah Art Museum. In the Heritage Village near the Sabah Art Museum typical stilted homes were displayed. We saw several modern office buildings, one of which was called the "floating" building because of its architectural structure.

Hong Kong (again) was the next stop. This was the first time that I had been in Hong Kong and witnessed the terrible smog. The welcome entertainment was a huge dragon carried by several boys with musical accompaniment. There was an enormous exhibition hall set up to promote the upcoming Olympics in Beijing.

I found a park here that I had not visited on my previous trips. The flowers and the waterfalls were a photographer's dream! It was soothing to just sit in this environment and observe various groups participating in their daily exercises, some of which actually included swords.

Some of the birds could talk. While I was sitting to take a rest I was able to observe families walking by and they would hear a "hello." Sometimes it took a few minutes for them to realize that it was actually a bird saying it and not a person. The bird would say "hello" and, of course, a kid would try to look and see where it came from. When the family would begin to walk away the bird would say "good-bye."

The *Queen Victoria* docked in Da Nang in Vietnam. I chose an excursion here whereby you left the ship for a few days and then rejoined the ship outside Ho Chi Minh City.

First was our sightseeing in Da Nang and Hue. The Imperial Citadel in Hue was built in 1804-35. There we saw the Royal Library, the Noon Gate, the Palace of Supreme Harmony, and The Heavenly Lady Pagoda, which is the most revered and visited Buddist shrine.

There was a short ride on a dragon boat on the Perfume river. We saw the Truong Tien Bridge that was built by the French as a gift to the Emperor. We disembarked from the dragon boat and had lunch at a local restaurant overlooking the river.

We flew from Hue to Hanoi, where we stayed at the Daewoo Hotel. From my hotel window the next morning I have never seen so many bikes and scooters in my life! And the way they maneuvered in making turns was breathtaking to watch.

We were treated to a tour of a certain section of the city while riding a pedicab, which was another adventure! I still can't understand why we weren't hit by the wreckless drivers on scooters and motorcycles! In one of the areas that we were driven through, there must have been a gazillion shoe shops. We visited a silk factory and the gift shop where various silk items were for sale.

The Ho Chi Minh Mausoleum is huge and draws many, many tourists. The guards expect you to respect this as a holy place—no talking! I saw several young school kids being asked to stop talking.

The Presidential Palace area not only includes the Presidential Palace, but also a history museum, the house where Ho Chi Minh lived and worked from 1954 to 1958, and another house where he lived from 1958 to 1969.

We visited the Temple of Literature that is adjacent to the University. It was built in the late eleventh century and is dedicated to Confucius. There were many courtyards with open pavilions used for various schools of learning. There were steles in one section on giant stone tortoises to recognize those doctoral candidates.

The prison in Hanoi where John McCain was imprisoned was sometime referred to as the Hanoi Hilton. In a large courtyard there were bronze plaques depicting the life at the prison. Inside one could see a guillotine used by the French, a typical cell, and typical bed, etc. John McCain's flight suit was in an exhibit and there were pictures of him receiving medical assistance. There were also pictures of John McCain visiting the prison, as well as Bill Clinton, and George W. Bush.

While touring through a certain section of the city we asked our guide about the very narrow homes we saw. We were told that they pay taxes on the width of the lot. Therefore, they would build a narrow house, but it might be five floors high. This reminded me of the regulation in Turkey, whereby the residents don't pay taxes until the house is finished.

We flew from Hanoi to Ho Chi Minh City (Saigon). There we stayed at the Renaissance Riverside Hotel. Just up the street was where I had stayed on my previous visit in 1991. My hotel from that trip had been torn down and a new hotel was there in its place. The building in the middle of the street before was just a theater and was very black from the pollution. Now it was the opera house and had been cleaned. The hotel where I had had my nice French dinner in 1991 was still there!

The Museum of Vietnamese History in Ho Chi Minh City covered the history from the Stone Age on through the colonial period. There was one special exhibit made of flowers. In the middle of the arrangement was an 8 and a 3. We asked why those numbers and were told that on August 3rd Women's Day is observed—8/3. The highlight of the visit to this museum has to be the performance by the Water Puppets. The puppets are attached to long sticks and are maneuvered by the human performers behind the screen.

We visited a lacquer factory and saw the different steps needed to produce an item. After having seen this process, it makes me appreciate the piece that I bought there. After the lacquer factory, we visited the Sea Goddess Temple. It is said that this temple is the home of the Sea Goddess who travels on the clouds rescuing seafarers from storms and shipwrecks.

In 1991, I wasn't even allowed to take a picture of the Reunification Hall, the former Presidential Palace that is now a museum. Now, it is possible to even tour the facility and its huge meeting rooms.

Our group was then taken by bus to Vung Tau, the beach city where I stayed in 1991, in order rejoin the *Queen Victoria*. On our way there I noticed that the dirt highway from 1991 had been replaced by a four-lane highway. As soon as we boarded the ship, we were off to Thailand.

The remainder of the *Queen Victoria* cruise was to Pattaya and Ko Samui in Thailand and ended in Singapore.

I flew to Dubai where I stayed at the Taj Palace Hotel. It is always interesting to return to this city to see all the new buildings that have "sprouted" up since the last visit. The tallest building in the world was almost complete at this time.

It was a longtime wish to be able to go to the Mall of the Emirates, which is purported to be the largest mall in the world, to see the indoor skiing. I had planned to ski; however, the wait time was such that it wasn't that important. I settled to watch and take pictures.

The Al Mahara Restaurant in the Burj Al Arab Hotel was the highlight of this visit. The elevator takes you from the lobby level to a lower lever. The entrance is designed to give you the feeling that you are entering a submarine. In the center of the restaurant there is an aquarium from floor to ceiling. As your meal proceeds you can sit and watch a numerous variety of fish. The tables are spaced so that you have a feeling of privacy. I found it interesting that there was a large blue crystal fish adorning the table that I discovered later was actually for sale if you so desired. It was a wonderful meal. Unfortunately, on the night of visit it happened to be a holiday in the United Arab Emirates and no alcoholic beverages were served.

The tourism desk at my hotel arranged for an English-speaking guide/driver to pick me up at the hotel for an all day excursion in order to visit the Emirates that I had not previously visited. I had been to Abu Dhabi and Dubai. On this day I visited Sharjah, Ajman, Umm Al Qaiwain, Ras Al Khaimah, and Fujairah.

In Sharjah, I saw the new "intown" palace for the emirate and the huge mosque. Many people who live here work and commute to Dubai each day and have to face terrific traffic jams in doing so.

The Al Bidiya Mosque in the Emirate of Fujairah is the oldest functioning place of worship in the United Arab Emirates. The mosque is unique in design with its four small domes. It was constructed as early as AD 1446.

We visited the Fujairah Fort that was under reconstruction. From the fort one has a good view of the city. We also visited the Fujairah Museum, where some of the exhibits included typical living quarters, pottery, and drugs that were used in the early years.

On our drive back to Dubai, we saw large mountains on our left side that were in Oman. There were several oil refineries along the drive back. A new tunnel had been opened, which aided in cutting the number of miles needed to drive and the amount of time needed in order to arrive back in Dubai.

Now it was time to leave Dubai and proceed to my next stop in working my way back to Washington. I flew from Dubai to Munich where I would connect with my flight to Tirana, Albania.

There was to be a long layover at the airport. Even that departure was delayed for a few more hours. There was a gentleman sitting near me at the airport who was on his way to Tirana. He asked me if I was going there on business and I said no and that I was a tourist. Since we were to be arriving very late in Tirana, he offered to give me a ride to the hotel with his relative who was picking him up at the airport. They also offered to come back to the hotel two days later to take me sightseeing.

My first day in Tirana was spent walking through Skanderbeg Square, seeing the Albanian National Culture Museum, the Mosque of Etehem Bez, the Opera House, and the Tirana Art Museum. One particular street was literally filled with people because of the many different kinds of interesting shops. I found the architecture of some of the elder buildings particularly interesting since they were obviously a carryover from the socialist regime.

The new friends picked me up the next day and we drove to hillside city of Kruja. There we visited the old city and the Skanderbeg Museum that was actually in the middle of the castle.

There had been a bomb explosion the week before my visit in a small town outside Tirana and several people were killed. This bombing made headline news around the world. The Red Cross had set up tents to aid those affected by the explosion. In fact, a relative of my "newfound friends" had been killed and that was the reason I couldn't see them the day before. They had to attend a funeral. The gentleman I had met at the airport in Munich had come from Florida to attend the funeral.

From Kruja we drove to the seaside city of Durres. In Durres, we saw the Amphitheater that dates back to 2,500 BC. I was able to get pictures of the old city wall, the monument to one of the city heroes, and a beautiful sunset at the beach along the Adriatic Sea.

Without the aid of those friends, my stop in Albania would have never been the same. They even offered and had planned to take me to the airport on Monday morning. However, a few hours after arriving back at the hotel, I received a call informing me that my flight had been changed and that I would be leaving almost four hours earlier than planned. The only sad note in this is that I didn't have any telephone number in which to call them to let them know.

In June and July, I was busy doing my homework in preparation for my next adventure. I knew that I would be flying into Sheremetyevo airport in Moscow, which is used mainly for international flights and is on the northwest side of the city. However, in leaving the city for Vladivostok I would be flying out of Domodedovo airport, which is used mainly for domestic flights and is on the southeastern side of the city.

Since the cost of transport from the airport into the central part of the city where my hotel was located was exorbitantly expensive I decided that I would try to complete that ordeal by using the metro. Even though all the signs were written in Cyrillic, I kept looking at maps and making notes as to what line and what stations I needed to use. It worked!

I remember asking the lady at the front desk of the hotel how much it would cost to go to the airport and she said that it would be at least $100. I made it on the subway and it cost about $4. It was well worth it, not only monetarily, but also for the adventure of proving to myself that I could do it.

This was my third visit to Moscow and it was still exciting to walk around and see places that I had seen thirty-seven years before.

But now it was time to leave for my overnight flight to Vladivostok where I would join approximately ninety other tourists to begin our Trans-Siberian Railway trip. Upon arriving in Vladivostok, we were taken to the hotel and given instructions as to what time to meet in the lobby for a city tour.

We stayed at the Hyundai Hotel in Vladivostok. There was a wedding at the hotel the evening we were there. It was interesting to sit in the lobby and watch the people who were coming to attend the wedding. All the ladies were dressed to the nines in their elaborate dresses, extremely high-heeled shoes, and tons of makeup. The gentlemen, however, were very casual in ordinary pants and shirts—no big deal for them.

On our city tour we visited a submarine that had been used in World War II. There was a monument for World War II nearby. We were taken on a cruise in the harbor where we were able to realize just how busy this harbor really is with its many ships coming and going.

We had lunch at the Versailles Restaurant in a Vladivostok hotel, and it was regally decorated. At the Vladivostok Fortress, we had a nice overview of the city. There we visited the Arsenyev Museum where there were many pictures of the war and the equipment used. We were able to see the house that Yul Brynner lived in when he was a boy.

At the end of our city tour, it was time to go to the train station where we would board the Golden Eagle Express for our private journey of almost seven thousand miles through Siberia with a side excursion into Mongolia. Everything about this train was top notch—the guides, the cabins, the bar, everything. One of the dining cars was a replica of a room in Pushkin Palace.

Our first stop was in Khabarovsk. Strategically located in a main square was a large statue of Khaborov, who was the city's founder, and a memorial to World War II. We walked down an embankment to the Amur river, which was quite scenic. We went into a Russian Orthodox Church here while they were having their Sunday service. The music was pleasant to listen to and it was interesting to note that nearly all of those in attendance were women. And unlike our churches, these have no pews, which mean that you stand during the entire service. The church itself was similar to others—extremely ornate with lots of gold and icons.

As the train progressed from one stop to the next it was exciting to stand at the windows and watch the countryside pass. Many of the homes were painted in vibrant colors with the lace-like shutters on the windows. There would be elder apartment buildings covered on the outside with satellite dishes. The countryside in Siberia was far greener than I had anticipated. However, we were told that in about a month the frost and the snow would probably begin. One interesting sight that I observed that showed the old and the new was when I observed a lady coming out of the outhouse using her cell phone.

George Kennan in his 1891 journal wrote that you can take the whole of the United States . . . and set it down in the middle of Siberia without touching anywhere the boundaries of the latter's territory, you can then take Alaska and all the countries of Europe, with the exception of Russia, and fit them into the remaining margin like the pieces of a dissected map. After having thus accommodated all this you will still have more than three hundred thousand square miles of Siberian territory to spare . . . an area half as large again as the Empire of Germany.

The train headed south for the border of Mongolia. Going through customs was time consuming and was in the middle of the night.

Upon our arrival in the city of Ulan Bator, we visited the Gandantegchenling Monastery. The main building here contained 108 volumes printed in the fourteenth century in gold ink on black paper. There were several stupas inside. One section had a long row of large brass prayer wheels. While walking through the monastery, I saw monks in their daily costumes and had the feeling that this is the same way things looked several hundreds of years before. And just as this feeling is sinking in,

I looked down and realized that one of the monks was looking at his cell phone to see if he had received any e-mails or text messages!

Outside the city we went to Terelj National Park. As we entered the park it reminded me of what the old Wild West would be like. There were large herds of cows, sheep, and various animals with several men on horseback keeping them together and or moving them from one location to another. A little later we were able to see several yak.

This park is very popular for Mongolians who like to come here for their vacations. The area for the accommodations includes a series of yurts for rent and a large dining area. This dining area is where we had lunch that day. We were able to go inside some of the yurts in order to see how they were decorated.

Before our return to the city, we were able to see a gentleman with a large eagle. One could have a picture made with the eagle. Protective covering for the hand and arm were provided.

Before returning to the train, we had time in the city to see some of the major government buildings, the opera house, a theater, and the Museum of Mongolian National History.

We saw a building that had been burned. We were told that this building was burned after a series of rioting. Each month, I receive the International Travel News magazine and one of the sections in each issue relates to turmoil in various countries and indicates those countries who have received warnings from the state department regarding upcoming visits. Just after my return, I noticed an article about this same building. It seems that there were allegations that the majority party had interfered in the recent election. Several people died from the rioting and the next day the campaign offices of the Mongolian People's Revolutionary Party were ransacked and set afire.

Several large modern buildings were under construction. And no major park in Mongolia would be complete without the ever present statue of Genghis Khan.

The train retraced our route that took us back north where we visited Ulan Ude.

There we saw what is referred to as the largest statue of Lenin's head.

Outside the city of Ulan Ude we made a visit to The Old Believers Village. The Old Believers are a religious sect who fled to Siberia from the persecution of Russia's seventeenth century tsars. Optimism and religion helped these people persevere under the tsars, under communism and in an area dominated by Buddhism and Shamanism. Having preserved their traditions and religious rituals, in 1991, they were recognized by UNESCO as one of the nineteen cultures of the world.

The ladies were in their traditional costumes and performed several musical numbers for our group.

The train proceeded up the west coast of Lake Baikal. This segment of the rail tracks had been constructed in the early years of the twentieth century. This entailed a lot of concrete supports and many tunnels in order to complete.

Lake Baikal contains one-fifth of the world's fresh water, enough to supply all the world's fresh water requirements for forty years, with ninety miles across at its widest point and 395 miles long. The depth in some places is over a mile deep. During the extremely cold winter months, there can be ice three of more feet deep.

Listvyanka is a small village on the banks of Lake Baikal. Here we were able to visit the Museum of Wooden Architecture. There were several very interesting buildings completely made of wood. One was a typical schoolroom. There were even examples of old wooden snow sleds.

We were taken to visit a typical home. I, myself felt that this home was a little above the average. There was a beautiful garden in front with many beautiful flowers of which we were told would only last another month or so because of the approach of cold weather. They even had a large greenhouse. I found it interesting that there was a refrigerator magnate from Colorado!

Irkutsk is one of Siberia's oldest cities, once known as the Paris of Siberia. The discovery of gold caused the city to become a boom town and proclaimed itself as the capital of Siberia. The area covered an area twenty times the size of France. There was a fire in 1879, which destroyed almost the entire city. However, because of its importance in the financial world, it rebounded. Its population was made up of fur traders, gold prospectors, tea merchants, exiles, and convicts. Those who became rich on gambling had huge homes, were able to have French tutors for their children, and wore clothes made in France.

The Irkutsk Museum of Regional Studies contained many old items such as typewriters, cash registers, musical instruments, snow sleds, and clothing apparel.

The museum was located in an area known as the Gagarin Embankment, which was alongside the Angara river, the only river flowing into Lake Baikal. The embankment was named after the Russian cosmonaut who was the first in space.

Near the approach to the river were the World War II Memorial and the eternal flame for World War II. Many couples come here as part of their marriage ceremony.

We visited the Maria Volkonsky House in Irkutsk. This house was occupied by the Decembrists who took part in the uprising in Senate Square, Saint Petersburg in December of 1825. Five revolutionaries were hanged and over hundred sentenced to penal servitude followed by exile to Siberia. The mansions seem rather palatial and exile for them perhaps wasn't all that difficult to endure. We were given a candlelight opera concert followed by champagne.

Some of the homes in this area were elaborately decorated with lavish woodwork, especially along the roofline and around the windows.

We visited the Mineralogical Museum outside Novosibirsk. Our guide at the museum explained a large map and the kinds of minerals that came from certain districts. The guide was very knowledgeable and by the end of the tour we discovered that all his children now live in the United States.

We visited the Railway Museum in Novosibirsk. Here we saw numerous old trains and were able to walk through them. The one I found most interesting was the one car that was used as a hospital and displayed some of the instruments that would have been used in operations. Also of interest was the car that included the large pots for soup in the kitchen.

Yekaterinburg is synonymous with the murder of the Romanov family by the Bolsheviks in 1918. The tsar and his family were imprisoned in the house of a merchant. In July, the Bolshevik government ordered the tsar's murder. At midnight on July 16, they were taken to a cellar and shot. They thought they were going to be photographed. The bodies were then taken to a mine some twenty-five miles outside the city and were disposed of. The remains were doused with gasoline and burned. These remains were discovered and through DNA samples they were matched with blood samples taken from Prince Philip who is a blood relative.

In the city of Yekaterinburg we were able to see the Opera House, the concert hall, a monument to various states of the area, a ever-present huge statue of Lenin, the monument for Prosperity and Agriculture, and several large apartment buildings under construction. There was a shopping area that had surrounding it a large sports complex and a theater. It was interesting to note that one of the upcoming shows was to be *Mamma Mia.*

One thing I noticed here while driving around was the number of automobiles that were extremely dirty as though they had been driving on dirt roads. A friend of mine was looking at my photo album of the trip. When he turned the page with the pictures of the dirty automobiles, he said, "It looks like North Dakota." That was his home state. He explained that the reason was—"Why wash the car, tomorrow it will just be dirty again."

On our drive out to Ganina Yarna, the spot where the bodies of the royal family were found, there were lots of tall birch trees along the way. In the area where the bodies were found are now located several monasteries.

The Cathedral of the Blood was built on the spot where the bodies of the royal family were shot. The interior of the church was probably one of the most elaborate I had ever seen with lots and lots of gold and many, many icons. Outside the church in the courtyard were large pictures of the royal family.

We were still on the bus from our sightseeing when we arrived at the spot where one leaves Asia and enters Europe. A stern-looking Soviet policeman comes on the bus and our guide tells us that we all need to show our passports. Of course, we didn't have them with us as they were still on the train. This conversation goes back and forth saying that he will accept a bribe. He then indicates that he doesn't take any bribes and that in order to pay our fine, we must exit the bus and have a glass of champagne to celebrate! It was all a joke they love to play on tourists! It was a great photo op where we all had to have our photo taken with one foot in Europe and the other foot in Asia.

Our next major stop was in the city of Kazan, the capital of Tatarstan. Here we saw the Tatarstan Presidential Headquarters. Nearby was a huge mosque, the Kul Sharif Mosque. Along the Kremlin wall in Kazan was the Spasskaya Tower and a large monument to the prisoners.

The Soyembika Tower or leaning tower in Kazan was where legend has it that the Kazan queen threw herself off from the highest level. Of course, it is just a legend.

We also visited the Cathedral of Peter and Paul here.

We had lunch in Kazan in a large room of a hotel with musical accompaniment. After lunch, we had time to walk around the city. Just outside the hotel where we had lunch was a walking street with a huge bell tower that was built in 1897.

Feodor Ivanovich Shaliapin was a noted bass opera singer. He was born in 1873 and died in 1938. There was a hotel named after him in Kazan along with a large statue of him out front. In the afternoon, we were given a concert of Shaliapin's repertory. We were able to take a short cruise at the point where the Volga river heads toward Moscow.

Our train arrived in Moscow, where were taken to the Marriott Hotel, and we had our farewell dinner. Early the next morning, I departed Moscow for my return home.

Kruja, Albania 2008

Trans Siberian Railway 2008

Europe-Asia Border 2008

Brisbane, Australia 2008

Ha Noi, Vietnam 2008

The Harbor Bridge, Sydney Australia 2008

Samarkand, Uzbekistan 2009

Esfahan, Iran 2010

Tehran, Iran 2010

The Dead Sea, Jordan 2010

Kyrenia, Turkish Cyprus 2010

Lemur Madagascar 2010

Lake Titicaca, Peru 2011

Moai Statues, Easter Island 2011

2009

Caribbean Cruise, Central America, the Five 'Stans, and the Caucasus

To begin the year 2009, I was invited to go on a short cruise as a guest of two friends that I had met on a trip to South Africa. They live in Florida in the winter and upstate New York in the summer. They were celebrating fifty years of "sailing through life" together and had asked several of their friends to accompany them on a four-day Caribbean cruise. I was fortunate to be one of the invitees. We left Fort Lauderdale and our first stop was Key West. Then, we continued on to Cozumel and back to Florida.

In March, I took a Globus tour to Central America. The tour started with a city tour in Managua, Nicaragua of Republic Square. This square is made up of the Presidential Palace, the Old Cathedral of Managua, and the National Museum. The National Museum had extensive exhibits including art, dinosaur bones, pottery, and prehistoric remains.

We also visited the Monument for Independence and the War Memorial. Near the Freedom Statue, there was an obelisk commemorating a visit by Pope John Paul II in 1983.

The Ancient Footprints of Acahualinca was a small museum where they had preserved fossilized footprints of humans and animals in the dust and mud from a previous volcanic eruption. This seemed to be a popular location for school children to come on field trips.

Nicaragua is known for its volcanic activity. On our drive from Managua to Grenada we stopped at the Masaya Volcano National Park. It is about a five-mile drive off the main highway. On the way to the top there were lava fields on both sides. We were able to look into the crater. We also visited the Santiago Crater.

Our hotel in Grenada, Nicaragua, was located right on the main city square. Horse-drawn carriages just outside the hotel were there to offer you a nice ride around the city. Across the square was the main cathedral. We visited the old convent there, and at the rear section of the convent there was a museum with prehistoric statues.

The La Merced Church was built in 1534. It isn't far from the main square and is well worth the visit. The highlight of the visit to this church is to walk up to the top of the tower and savor the magnificent view it offers of the city.

On walking through the shopping area of the city and the market place, we discovered a small preschool. Being a former teacher I was curious. The teacher recognized that the three of us were tourists and asked where we came from. We were invited in and the young students were excited to meet us and have their pictures taken.

Many residents of Grenada own their own island in Lake Nicaragua. This is the second largest freshwater lake in the world and there are many small islands not far from the city. We took a boat ride through the many small islands and were fascinated by the architecture of some of the homes. The foliage was conducive to this tropical setting with an abundance of beautiful flowers.

Another person in our group and myself decided that we would check out the real estate office near our hotel. The lady there was very pleasant and showed us houses that were for sale. We found out that we could own an island for about $35,000.

After years of travel and especially after having participated in several group tours, it is apparent that at some point you will be in a group and realize that you have been in a group with a person on a previous trip. That happened here in Nicaragua.

We were talking about previous experiences in travel. I was telling a story about what happened on a cruise. A lady in the group realized that the same thing had happened to her. It turns out we were both on the same cruise from Lisbon to Cape Town, when our ship hit a sandbank upon our departure from Douala in Cameroon, which caused the ship to begin listing to one side. It was a rather frightful moment, but the Captain came on the public address system and explained what happened.

We flew from Managua to San Salvador. We visited the Cathedral and the crypt in the lower lever.

It just so happened that our visit coincided with the day of the election for their new President. We drove by several voting booths and were impressed with the number of people that were out to vote.

We were supposed to visit the Mayan ruins outside the city on our way to Honduras, but they were closed because of the election.

We continued on to Honduras and visited the ruins in Copan. I remember the colorful birds that welcomed us at the entrance. It seems that every time you turn in a place like this your camera is telling you to take another series of pictures of the various temples, pyramids, courtyards, etc.

On our way out of the city, we stopped along the road and gave various items, like toothpaste, soap, etc., to some of the local poor people. We then drove through a large banana plantation.

Our first ruins in Guatemala were at Quirigua. Some of the monoliths here weighed sixty-five tons and the steles are some of the tallest.

In Antigua, we stayed at the Hotel Casa Santa Domingo, which was a converted monastery. In walking through the hallways of the main building in the evening there are thousands of candles lighting the way. Each room had its own fireplace. The courtyards were filled with lots of shrubbery and flowers. From one lookout, it is possible to see a volcano in the distance with some plume escaping. It did have a small eruption while we were there. Several politicians and movie stars from the United States had stayed at this hotel. I found it interesting that on the wall of the bar was a large painting of *The Last Supper*.

The Chapel of Our Lady of the Rosary was part of the hotel complex. Church services as well as weddings still take place here. Adjacent to the chapel is a museum containing a large display of religious figures.

After our city tour here in Antigua, we also visited Chichicastenango, which has the largest outdoor market in all of Guatemala. We also visited Lake Atitlan. We then drove back into Guatemala City, where were toured the main square, had lunch, and headed to our next ruins of Tikal.

When visiting the ruins at Tikal, be prepared to get your exercise and be prepared for an unexpected downpour of rain. At one point there is a very long series of steps to climb. However, at the top, the view makes it worth the climb. We did get caught in one of the downpours and everyone was soaked through and through. We were able to get to a shelter to wait it out.

Our tour continued on to Belize and our last ruins for our trip was at Caracol. I haven't gone into the details of the ruins—that would be another book!

In August and September 2009, I combined two tours into one. MIR Corporation had a tour to the Five 'Stans (Kazakhstan, Kyrgyzstan, Uzbekistan, Tajikistan, and Turkmenistan) and another to The Caucasus (Azerbaijan, Georgia, and Armenia).

A neighbor friend of mine and I flew from Washington to Almaty in Kazakhstan to begin the tour. My friend and I are both members of the Circumnavigators Club for travelers who have circumnavigated the globe in a single trip and the Travelers Century Club for travelers who have traveled in over hundred countries. When one participates in travel to locations that are considered "out-of-the-way" or "not normal" by many non-travelers, it turns out that the majority of the members of that group will have traveled for many years and will have seen most of the major places there is to see in the world.

The city tour of Almaty started with a visit to Panfilov Park. Panfilov was the General of twenty-eight Kazakh soldiers who died outside Moscow during World War II. A monument in the park honors the soldiers and an eternal flame memorializes those who died during the war.

The Zenkov Cathedral is an orthodox church built out of wood without a single nail being used in its construction. Nearby were the State Central Museum and the Museum of Musical Instruments.

The Medeo Sports Complex is in the mountains north of the city. The drive there is quite picturesque in that you reach an elevation of about five thousand feet.

Many world records have been set at the Olympic-size skating rink there. The tall ski jump was impressive against the mountainous background.

We were treated to a Kazahk welcome lunch with musical entertainment in a yurt near the stadium.

The following day we drove through Charyn Canyon or "valley of castles" on our way into Kyrgyzstan. The river from the mountains has carved this deep and beautiful canyon that is about fifty miles long.

The Karven Issyk Kul Hotel was located on the shores of Lake Issykul. The only lake that is higher than this one is Lake Titicaca on the Peruvian and Bolivian border in South America. On the opposite side of the lake were the Tien Shan Mountains with snow-covered peaks.

Following the old Silk Road, we stopped at the Buryan Tower, one of the only existing watch tower remaining. We had lunch at the home of a former school teacher. The food was plentiful and delicious. Following our meal, we were treated to a series of horse games. One of the games seemed similar to polo except the two teams were trying to see whose team could place a sheep in the goal.

Our next stop was the capital of Kyrgyzstan, Bishkek. The city has wide boulevards and lots of trees. Snow-covered mountains were also visible from here.

We flew from Bishkek to Osh, which is the second largest city of Kyrgyzstan. There we were invited to a luncheon at the home of one of the local residents. During lunch, we talked to a gentleman from the United States who was working as a volunteer there.

In the afternoon, we visited a large outdoor market and then continued our drive in Uzbekistan. We spent the night in the Fergana Valley.

The only part of the tour that I didn't participate in was the tour for the next day. I seemed to have come down with a one-day stomach virus. I didn't feel that I missed a lot because the tour that day was to include a visit to a pottery factory and see a demonstration on ceramics making. Included in the sightseeing was also to be a visit to a silk workshop to observe the process of silk making. Since I had had the pleasure of seeing both of these in other countries, it was okay to miss one. It also made me feel good when a few of the people came back and said that I should feel grateful that I had been sick. It not only had been an extremely long day of sightseeing, but the bus was not air-conditioned and the temperature was high with a lot of humidity.

The people at the Club 777 Hotel could not have been nicer to me that day. They brought me hot soup. They brought me hot rice and tea. About every hour or two one of the people from the hotel would come and make sure that I was all right.

The next morning, we had a wonderful scenic drive through the mountains on our way to Tashkent, the capital of Uzbekistan. This city was taken by the Arabs in 751 and by Genghis Khan in the thirteenth century. Tamerlane was here in the fourteenth century. The Russian Empire took over in 1865 and the city was not an independent country again until 1991.

On the first morning here, I just happened to look out the window from the hotel and saw all the children on their way to the first day of school. This is a big day for these people. The parents go to school with the child for the first day to meet the teacher and all of the children were carrying huge bouquets of flowers.

Later that afternoon we were on our way to a show. While waiting for a traffic light I noticed a lady standing on the corner, who had to have been a teacher! She had two other people with her in order to be able to carry all the flowers home from that first day of school.

Even though there was an earthquake here in 1966, most of the city has been rebuilt since then. However, there are still several large twentieth century Soviet buildings remaining. We visited the Square of Independence, the Navoi Theater, where we had our lunch, the Palace of the Peoples Friendship, the Kukeldash Madrassah, and the Kaffal Shashi Mausoleum.

I was really looking forward to our next stop. Samarkand, which has been designated a UNESCO World Heritage Site, has been a prominent name that we remember from our early history lessons. The Registran is still considered on of the noblest public squares in the world. We also visited the Gur Emir Mausoleum, where Tamerlane and his three sons are buried.

Ulugh Beg's Observatory displayed how he was able to pinpoint the position of the moon, the planets, and many stars with infinite precision. His work has been compared to that of Copernicus. There was a museum adjoining the observatory that had a ceiling that looked almost like being in a planetarium.

Upon our leaving there was a group of young school children on a field trip. I found it interesting that one of the backpacks was of Mickey Mouse, one of Hanna Montana, and another of Betty Boop.

The next day took our group to the Tajikistan border. Our guide, being Uzbek, wasn't able to accompany us. We were met on the other side of the border by a local guide.

We visited the archaeological site at Old Penjikent that was founded in the fifth century. We toured the Shakristan, two Zoroastrian temples, the citadel, and the Rudaki Museum of History and Regional Studies.

On our drive to Bukhara the next day we had a stop at Shakhrisabz, the birthplace of Tamerlane. We saw the ruins of Ak-Saray or White Palace that was built in the fourteenth century and was one of Tamerlane's most expansive undertakings. The palace complex included a massive portal with blue, white, and gold ceramic tiles and is over 130-feet high.

A local artist was sitting nearby painting. I was fascinated by his artwork and have one of them in my home now.

The city of Bukhara is also a UNESCO World Heritage Site and is considered to be like an oasis for those travelers on the Silk Road years ago because of being able to offer a cool place to stop and rest. The center of the city has a large pool and a plaza where people can meet to eat and shop. There were several mulberry trees adjacent to the pool, which are hundreds of years old. Several madrassas, or schools, are located around the square. We had dinner here one night at the plaza and were treated to a fashion show.

Our hotel for three nights in Bukhara was the Sasha and Sons Bed and Breakfast and was located near the plaza. The property had been the home of a Jewish merchant in the sixteenth century. The rooms of the hotel were unbelievable. They were decorated in the traditional Bukhara style that showed-off the intricate plaster work and painting skills of the craftsmen! Our room had actually been the dining room before an extension to the hotel was completed. Just outside our room was a large open courtyard.

On our walking tour of the city, we visited the Kukeldash Madrassah, which is the largest Koran school that dates from the turn of the fifteenth century. In some of the classrooms, we were serenaded with song.

We strolled through the old market place where they were making the ever-popular caps that some of the people still wear. We visited the Kalon Mosque and Minaret that can be seen from almost anywhere in the city. In the afternoon, we visited the Zindan Prison. The prisoners were treated badly and had to contend with all kinds of "creepy-crawlies" that led it to be called "the bug pit."

We visited the Summer Palace of the last emir and also the Palace of Moon and Stars. This palace for the emir was located outside the city in order to give the emir some privacy. It was elaborately decorated.

We left Bukhara and begin our drive to Khiva. On the way we cross the Red Sands Desert and have a chance to see the Amu Darya river that runs along the border of Turkmenistan.

The city of Khiva dates back to the fifth century BC and was a strategic stop on the old Silk Road. We walked around the city and saw the Old Town, the Tash-Hauli Palace, the Djuma Mosque, and the Kunya Ark. The Djuma Mosque is also called the Friday Mosque and contains many, many wooden columns.

We leave Khiva and cross the border into Turkmenistan. Upon completing the customs proceedings, we had some time to spend in Tashauz. In the afternoon we flew to Ashgabat.

Because of the 1948 earthquake that killed almost two-thirds of the population, many of the buildings in Ashgabat are fairly new. There are many buildings made of marble. We asked our guide about this and his answer was that it seems that they need marble and Italy needs oil.

We saw hundreds of satellite dishes on the sides of apartment buildings. We also asked about the cost of those. We were told that they pay a small price for them. Once they have them they don't have to pay a monthly fee. It seems that their electricity costs are extremely low.

Saparmurat Niyazov was born in 1940 and died in 2006. He named himself "President for Life" and lived a lavish lifestyle. There is a huge monument for him called The Arch of Neutrality. It is possible to take an escalator and elevator to the top. It is over two hundred-feet tall and has a thirty-six-foot gold statue of him at the top that rotates so that it is always facing the sun. His Presidential Palace was nearby and can be seen from the monument along with its many acres of manicured grounds and many fountains.

There is a memorial statue for the victims of the 1948 earthquake, and also another statue that has ten horses to celebrate the tenth anniversary of independence. It seems that no matter where you have a monument there will be a gold statue of the President for Life.

Just outside the city of Ashgabat and in the city where Niyazov's mother was born, he built one of the largest mosques in all of Asia. Next to the mosque is a mausoleum that was built for his mother. His tomb is there as well.

The Museum of Carpets and Textiles displays an enormous number of handmade carpets, kilims, cushions, and costumes. One of the carpets on display here is supposedly the largest hand-knotted carpet in the world.

After our lunch, we were taken to an art gallery that actually was part of someone's living quarters. In one of the large rooms, we were given an opera concert by two singers who were very professional.

We flew to Mary and then drove some twenty miles to Merv. Merv dates back some four thousand years. The earliest of five ancient cities at Merv is attributed to Cyrus the Great in the sixth century. Merv was the center of civilization and was a thriving section of the Silk Road until the Mongols burned it down.

We visited another UNESCO site at Nisa. This was once a major center of the ancient Parthian Kingdom. More than two thousand years ago the Parthian Empire spread out from Nisa and took its place among such kingdoms as the Achaemenid under Cyrus the Great and the Macedonian under Alexander the Great. This place also thrived until it was devastated by the Mongols.

The Tolkuchka Oriental Bazaar is probably one of the most interesting open air markets I have ever seen in all my travels. Where else would you find a market that is auctioning off camels. Yes, hundreds of them! There was also sheep, goats, chickens, birds, ducks—you name it, they had it! There were also sections for housewares, tools, clothes, carpets, and items for children. Because of this market, my automobile now has floor mats in it from Turkmenistan.

The 'Stans journey has come to a close and it is time to say farewell to those fellow travelmates who will be returning home. My friend and I will be flying out to Azerbaijan to continue the second part of our journey to the Caucasus.

Since my friend and I were arriving in Azerbaijan a couple days prior to joining our next tour group, we were able to spend a day sightseeing in Tbilisi and arrange a day trip on our own to Nakhchivan.

Our day in Baku began with a nice long walk from the Hyatt Regency Hotel to the waterfront. Fizuli Square, named after the sixteenth century Azerbaijani poet, Muhammed Fizuli. A large statue of him overlooks the square. There is another statue here of Nizami Ganjavi, another poet and philosopher. At the far end of the square is the Museum of Literature.

We sat alongside the Caspian Sea to take a small break near the large Exhibition Hall. We strolled through the Old Town section where we chose a pleasant restaurant where we could sit outside.

The next day we had an early flight from Baku to Nakhchivan. Nakhchivan is an autonomous region of Azerbaijan. However, it is separated by a strip of Armenia, which makes it almost impossible to visit. We flew from Baku and returned the same day. We were met at the airport by our guide and taken on a tour of the city.

The Momina Khatum Mausoleum is probably the most famous one here. Ajami, an architect, built it for his wife in the late twelfth century; however, he died before it was completed. The tomb consists of parts above and under the ground. From the outside, it is ten-sided in shape and round on the interior and has a dome.

The Yusif Ibn Kuseir tomb was built by the same architect. It is octagonal in shape and also has an underground burial place. The top of this tomb is slanted to a peak in the middle.

The Cave of the Seven Sleepers is about four miles outside the city and is accepted as a sacred place for pilgrimage based upon a story described in a chapter of the Koran. From the entrance to the top where you can go into the cave there are almost five hundred steps! Coming down is easy. At the top there are two small mosques—one for men and another for women.

Another mausoleum was visited outside the city of Nakhchivan in Garabaghlar. This small village was a bustling caravan town and had numerous mosques and minarets and was a major stoping point on caravan routes. On our way back into the city we were able to tour an old salt mine. It had been used as a hospital for asthma sufferers.

The Nakhchivan Memorial Museum contained an enormous amount of pictures in an exhibit about the residents of Nakhchivan who fought against the Armenian genocide against Azerbaijan. I found it interesting that we never heard one word regarding the genocide of the Armenians by the Turks. And in Armenia you never hear a word regarding the genocide of the Azerbaijanis by the Armenians.

On our first day in Baku, the capital of Azerbaijan, we drove passed acres and acres of active oil wells. We were on our way to see the flaming natural gas vents on the Absheron Peninsula. These flames may have been the reasoning behind the inclusion of fire in the Zoroastrian religion.

We also visited the Old Town including Shirvanshah Palace, Fountain Square, and the State Museum of Azerbaijani Carpets and Applied Folk Art. The Old Town was at one time the entire city and was encircled by a city wall. There are still mosques, schools, private residences, embassies, shops, and restaurants located within the walls.

On our way out of the city of Baku we stopped at The Bibi-Heybatr Mosque that was built on the shores of the Caspian Sea. It was a rather ethereal feeling to see this in the early morning just as the sun was rising.

Further out of the city we stopped at Gobustan, another UNESCO site, where one can view ancient petroglyphs. These rocks were discovered in the early twentieth century. There was a small museum nearby.

The scenic drive from here to Sheki was filled with many views of beautiful snow-capped mountains. Sheki is one of the oldest towns in Azerbaijan—some say as early as more than 2,500 years ago. A mudslide destroyed it in 1772 and it was moved. It was an independent Khanate until the eighteenth century when the Russians moved it.

Kish Village is all that remains of the original Sheki. We had lunch in an old winery that had been making wine for about three hundred years. Our luncheon included some of the wine and musical accompaniment. Craftsmen in this area create many different kinds of wooden chests. Some of them are used by a new bride to store her trousseau.

We visited the Palace of the Sheki Khans. The walls and ceilings are decorated with intricately detailed tile work and meticulously painted war scenes. Most of the windows were stained glass.

The next day we drove into the country of Georgia. There were many vineyards along the way as well as many herds of animals, some of which mandated a wait.

Our tour began with a visit to the Metekhi Church of the Virgin that was built in the late thirteenth century. From this point, the view of the Narikala Fortress, along the Kura river, was excellent. It was built in the fourth century. From almost any point in Tbilisi one can spot the large statue of Mother Georgia. She holds a sword for her enemies and a bowl of wine for her guests.

Another prominent building is the huge Parliament Building. We visited the area where there are several old bath houses. My friend and I decided to try one later on that afternoon. It was quite an experience and very different from others I had visited in other countries.

We had some free time to walk around in the old section. We were just in time to witness a wedding at one of the large cathedrals. One bar located in this old section was named KGB with a subtitle of "still watching you."

We left Tbilisi for our long drive to Gudari, which is a famous skiing area. On the way there we toured the Jvari Monastery, which is a Georgian Orthodox Monastery built in the sixth century. Nearby in the small city of Mtskheta we visited the Svetitskhoveli Cathedral. We made another stop in Ananuri where there is a castle complex and inside are two churches. And yet two more stops in Signagi and Gurjaani.

After spending one night in Gudari, we began our return to Tbilisi. We had a stop in Gori, the birthplace of Stalin. There is now a Stalin Museum and it has the birth home of Stalin, his private railway car, a replica of his old office, and other memorabilia.

Just outside the city of Gori are the caves at Uplistsikhe. The caves are carved from sandstone and were actually occupied until the early part of the twentieth century. It is fun to explore them and to see the church at the top.

Also in this area are several large sections of homes that were built to accommodate those people who were displaced with the Russian intervention with nearby South Ossetia.

The David Gareja Monastery was named after one of the thirteen Syrian Fathers who in the sixth century lived in a natural cave. By the twelfth century, over two thousand monks lived here. However, it seems that it meant trouble—it was ransacked by the Mongols in the thirteenth century; by Tamerlane in the fourteenth century; and later by the Soviet army because they wanted to use the area for training since the area resembled that of Afghanistan.

On the way out to the monastery from Tbilisi we had to stop several times in order to allow the large, large herds of sheep cross the highway. The country scenery; however, was well worth the drive.

Before our departure from Tbilisi we had a treat in store. We were guests at the museum that had been opened in the home of Elene Akhvlediani. She was a printer, a graphic artist, and had great interest in theater and music. A lot of her artwork is on display in the house. We were able to sit and enjoy a musical concert. I distinctly remember this one child who played the violin and he could not have been more than about nine years old.

Our first stop in Armenia was at Haghpat. This complex was built between the eleventh and the fourteenth centuries. Included in the complex are not only a monastery, but a church, a seminary, and a mausoleum.

The drive from here into Yerevan, the capital of Armenia, offered excellent views of the snow-capped Aragat Mountains.

Our first full day in Armenia took us to Echmiadzin, which was once the capital of Armenia. The Cathedral here was built in 301. In the treasury there are relics including a piece of wood from Mt. Ararat thought to be from Noah's Ark. In another display there is an elaborate cross made of gold and jewels and supposedly includes a piece of wood from the cross.

The Zvartnots Cathedral is actually a ruin from the seventh century. At the time of its existence it was the largest round church in the world. It was ruined by Arab invaders because they didn't want any building higher than their mosque. From this location there is a wonderful view of Mount Ararat.

The afternoon was spent touring the Genocide Museum, which was built in memory of those killed in the genocide. Over one million people perished between 1914 and 1918.

The Monastery of Khor Virap is about forty miles south of Yerevan. Along the way there you can see several towers indicating the Turkish border. It also offers spectacular views of Mount Ararat. Saint Gregory was imprisoned here for many years along with other Christian ministers. It is one of the most visited sights in all of Armenia.

The Temple of Garni looks vaguely similar to the Parthenon on a smaller scale. It was once the summer palace of King Trdat I in the first century. It was destroyed by an earthquake in the late seventeenth century and has been restored by Armenian architects and craftsmen.

Geghard Monastery is almost in a category by itself in that it is carved on the side of a mountain. The monastery was started in the fourth century; however, it wasn't until the early thirteenth century that some of the other churches in the complex were built. By the fact that they are carved from stone, the acoustics are excellent. We were treated to a mini-concert by a quartet of Armenian ladies.

We visited the Ashtarak region, which is on the southern slope of Mount Aragats. The Saghmosavank Monastery is in this location on the edge of the gorge made by the Kasagh river. There happened to be a wedding taking place here when we visited. We were surprised to see several Hummer automobiles in the parking area for wedding guests. We had time before our departure to speak to several local residents.

Our next day took us to Lake Sevan. On our drive out we saw an Olympic village where athletes train for the games. We had a stop in the city of Dilijan where a lot of craftsmen have shops.

Our seafood lunch was served in a restaurant just below the Sevan Monastery. The monastery is situated, as most are, at the top of a hill. It took quite an amount of stamina in order to climb to the top because of the high altitude (puff, puff!).

On the way back to Yerevan, it was snowing most of the way! Yes, and this was the twenty-eighth of September, the day before my birthday! That evening we had a nice farewell dinner at the restaurant just across from our hotel in Yerevan and they did have a cake for my birthday. I stayed in Yerevan for another week with a longtime friend who now goes there every year for a couple months.

2010

Iran, Jordan, Syria, Lebanon, Cyprus, Copenhagen to Warsaw, and the Indian Ocean

When one begins thinking of planning a trip to Iran, interesting stories seem to evolve. First of all, it is almost impossible to go alone. Even the tour company that I was planning to have my travel agent use would only set up a trip with a minimum of two people. Being only a single person, I called a friend in New York that I had met on the Central American trip the year before. Fortunately, he was interested in going.

It seemed like forever and many, many communications to finalize the plans. Once the plans are made, it was necessary for us to wait for the travel company to receive a letter with the entire itinerary from the tourism department in Iran.

I took all the information including passports, applications, pictures, and letters from the company with our assigned number, and checks for the visas to the Iranian section of the Pakistan Embassy in Washington. When I was called back to the window, I was told that they couldn't issue the visas until they received an actual letter from the tourism department in Iran. Matters were further complicated, since it was only a couple weeks before we were to depart and a full week of that was a holiday in Iran and the offices would be closed. We finally received our visas just in time for me to return my friend's passport to him in New York.

My friend flew from New York and I flew from Washington and we met in Germany. From there we flew to Tehran. We were standing in line for passport control when a gentleman standing behind us asked if we were Americans. We said that we were. It just so happened that he was a businessman and told us that he had been coming through this area for customs control at least once a month for ten years and this was the first time that he had seen any Americans.

My friend went through customs first. While I was waiting for the customs control employee to scrutinize my passport, I noticed that the passport of my friend had been kept and wondered why. A few minutes later we were asked to go to another section. From there we were asked to follow another gentleman down a long corridor where we were asked to wait. We didn't know how long we had to wait or why we were waiting. Finally, he came back and took us into a small room where we had to have each of our fingers fingerprinted. Once the entire procedure was completed we continued through to meet our guide. The first question he asked of course was why did it take so long!

The Enghelab Hotel in Tehran was our home during our stay in Tehran. We had a local guide there for the two days of sightseeing. While he was showing us the city our other driver/guide was in the process of driving from Tehran to Kerman, where he would meet us in order to be our guide from that point back to Tehran.

The first thing one need while visiting another country is some of the local currency. Our guide stopped along the street and we were able to exchange money with a gentleman while we sat in the car.

There were several places in the city where large banners would be displayed. They were quite decorative and upon closer observation we discovered that they actually contained sayings from the Koran. The cost for some of them had been paid for by local companies.

We saw the huge banner hanging on the side of a building near an expressway that we had both seen in the Rick Steve's video of Iran. The saying on the banner says, "Down with America."

It was interesting to have seen this sign, since everyone we met while we were there seemed to like Americans. The interaction between us and the locals would usually go through the same routine each time in that we were asked if we were British. Upon discovering that we weren't British, the next guess was whether or not we were Australians. When we would finally let them know that we were Americans, the first thing we would hear is that they loved us and were glad that we had come to see their country and see what it was really like instead of what we were told by the media.

We visited the National Museum in Tehran. Many of the exhibits in this museum had come from the ruins in Persepolis, Shiraz, and Esfahan.

The local market was very crowded and contained a wide variety of items, including herbs, olives, nuts, clothing, rugs, and restaurants. We were told that unfortunately most of the items in the market nowadays come from China. Through my years of travel I have been teased by fellow travelers about being able to find an ice cream cone anywhere, and it was in this market that I was able to have my first ice cream cone in Iran!

We drove to the Azadi Freedom Monument in order to take pictures. The streets and the subway were overcrowded. In the streets there were hundreds of scooters along with automobiles. With traffic circles instead of cross streets, the need for traffic lights was practically unnecessary. And in all of this, pedestrians would be crossing the street and zig zagging between all of it!

The Sa'd Abad Palace Complex contains eighteen different palaces, including the White Palace, the Green Palace, and the Queen Mother's Palace. The shah used this as a summer home. The complex is now a museum and can be toured in order to see how the shah and his family lived at one time. Many of the rooms have mirrored walls and ceilings. In one room, we noticed that there were pictures of foreign visitors, including the Pope and Presidents Eisenhower, Nixon, and Johnson.

We drove through the northern suburbs of Tehran where it seems that the more wealthy people live. Some of the apartment buildings here are very nice. It was also interesting to note that there were more women drivers in this area than in some of the other areas.

We continued toward the Alborz Mountains and the ski areas. We had hoped to take the ride up on the chair lift. However, it closed at 2:00 p.m. and we arrived at 2:15 p.m. C'est la vie. It was nice to have a view of the city of Tehran from this vista.

While having lunch at the ski slopes, we saw people eating something that we had never seen. We asked out guide what it was. Instead of responding, he proceeded to a nearby kiosk and returned a few minutes later with three of them. It was a long skewer with a potato that had been spiral cut and placed on the skewer. It was like eating potato chips, but from a one-foot long wooden skewer.

The next day, we had an early flight to Kerman, which is in the southern part of the country. Upon our arrival, we were met by our local guide for Kerman. We checked into the Pars Hotel and were told that in about an hour we should meet in the lobby for our city tour.

Our first stop on the tour was the city library. Near the library was our first sighting of an Ice House. The ice houses in Iran are large domelike structures with one entrance. The basic plan is of a large chamber set deep into the ground. Beneath are inner beds along the outside. In the winter months, water is let in to fill these beds and freeze. The ice is then broken up into blocks for storage and insulated with straw to be used in the summer.

The Moshtaghie Mosque, sometimes called the Three Dome Mosque, was built in the nineteenth century. The walls are typical for the mosques in that they are made of glazed tiles and many are blue and turquoise. The Masjid-e-jame Mosque is also called the Friday Mosque.

The Ganjali Khan Bath House had been converted into an anthropological museum. The waxed figures are displayed in various rooms depicting daily rituals in that time period.

Upon our return to the hotel we were able to meet the person who had driven from Tehran while we touring there. He was to be our driver and guide for the remainder of our visit to Iran.

The next morning we drove to the city of Bam. Bam had one of the largest mud structures in the world at one time. Unfortunately, in 2003, there was a terrible earthquake there that destroyed a lot of it. The most devastating thing about this earthquake was that twenty-six thousand people perished because of it. There is a large cemetery here for those victims. An eerie feeling comes over you when you realize that all of the dates of death are the same for all of them.

We stopped on our way back to Kerman at the Qajar Gardens and Pavilion outside Mahan. It was built by the governor as a retreat around the end of the nineteenth century. There are terraced fountains descending from the pavilion. It seems rather strange that here in the middle of desert country is a beautiful oasis.

The other stop was at the shrine of Shah Ni'mattulah Vali Kirmani. There are several buildings in the complex including the sanctuary. The large and dome and several minarets were added later.

Just outside Yazd we visited a Zoroastrian Temple and Burial Place sometimes referred to as "Towers of Silence." When someone died their body would be taken to the top of a mountain-like hill or tower. There the body would be eaten by vultures. Afterwards the remains would be burned. This practice was stopped because of environmental reasons. Now the bodies are buried in a grave that is lined with yellow bricks and has a headstone or marker.

Iran is known for its pistachio nuts. We drove passed several orchards of pistachios and could see how they looked before they actually matured into what we usually associate with their appearance.

In Yazd, we stayed at the Dad Hotel. This was a very nice hotel that was built with a large inner courtyard, which contained many flowers. Here we visited the mosque, a Zoroastrian Temple, and the water museum. Several buildings have large wind towers on top to channel the breezes down into the building to cool the air. I remember seeing similar wind towers when I was on a tour in Bahrain. However, they are becoming a rarity with the invention of the air-conditioner.

We visited the Saheb A Zaman Club, where several of the local gentlemen were undergoing rigorous exercises. Some of the instruments they used in these exercises resembled giant bowling pins. Every exercise they completed was accompanied with very loud music played by a DJ. It was almost like a religious ritual.

Pasargadae was at one time the capital city. Its construction was begun by Cyrus the Great in 546 BC. He died before it was completed; however, his tomb is located in the ruins of Pasargadae. The capital was moved to Susa at one time. Darius eventually moved it to Persepolis.

The construction of Persepolis was started by Darius the Great in 515 BC and finished in 330 BC. Near the entrance is a long stairway that leads to a large reception area. It is believed that these stairs would have been used for horses to bring carriages up to the upper level.

After the death of Darius the Great, his son Xerses the Great was instrumental in the construction of additional buildings.

There were military quarters, a treasury, private rooms, and large reception halls. The building that housed the harem is now a museum. On an adjacent hill to the ruins are the royal tombs.

Throughout the ruins there are several statues of a griffin. Some statues have a double griffin. The griffin has the body of a lion and the head of an eagle and is meant to exemplify that it is the most powerful creature. It is interesting that their national airline uses the griffin in its logo.

Our visit to Shiraz began with a visit to the Koran Gate. At one time the gate was damaged and restored. In the restoration there is a room at the top that holds a copy of the Holy Book. Therefore, as one enters the city through the gate they receive a blessing.

Out next visit in Shiraz was to the Eram Gardens. This large area is like taking another biology class. There are trees, bushes, and flowers of all kinds here and they are clearly labeled. There is a large pavilion on the grounds also. Here we were approached by more than one group of Iranians curious as to our origins and, as always, were pleased that Americans had come to visit. This would then lead to our taking their pictures and them taking our pictures.

While in Shiraz we visited the Vakil Mosque with its large prayer hall with many elaborate columns and a stairway made of one giant piece of marble. The Atigh Jame Mosque from the ninth century of one of the oldest mosques. The Friday Mosque, also known as Masjid-i Atiq, was first built in 875. It was damaged and restored many times after that because of earthquakes. The Khoday Khaneh, also known as "God's House," was built in the fourteenth century and is located in the large square next to the Friday Monque. We were welcomed to tour the Theological School of Shiraz.

The Arg-e-Karim Khan, or the Citadel, resembles a medieval fortress and covers an entire city block. It was built as a residence for the king. Most of the paintings and frescoes were plastered over when it was used as a prison. Now, they have been restored and are part of the museum under the auspices of Iran's Cultural Heritage Organization.

My friend and I were on our way to another sightseeing venue when we noticed this man sitting along the sidewalk with a small table. He had a bird and a small box filled with pieces of paper. After you gave him a dollar the bird would use its beak and pull out one of the pieces of paper with your fortune on it. Once we knew our fate, we continued on to the tomb of Aramgah-e Hafez, a highly respected Shiraz poet.

Just outside Shiraz are the Achaemenid Tombs of Persian Kings. Here carved into the walls are the tombs of Darius the Great (486 BC), Darius II the Great (405 BC), and Artaxerxes (424 BC).

Esfahan has to have been my favorite place in all of Iran. It is a beautiful city with many historic bridges and one of the grandest squares anywhere in the world!

The Zayandeh river was just down the street from our hotel. The local residents were there so peacefully strolling along the riverbank. This park-like garden setting contained many flowers along the walkway and a giant fountain in the middle of the river.

Esfahan is known for its bridges. The Si-O-Se Pol, or Allah-Verdi Khan Bridge, was built in 1629 and has thirty-three arches spanning the river. It is good to see in the daytime, but even better to see it while it is illuminated in the evening. The

Khaju Bridge was built in 1660 and has two levels. The other two major bridges of historical note would include the Shahrestan Bridge and the Joobi Bridge.

Vank Cathedral is located in a section of the city where many Armenians moved to after the Ottoman War at the turn of the seventeenth century. In addition to the beautiful cathedral, the grounds include a museum and a monument to the genocide. A statue of Saint Mesrop Mashtots is located just outside the entrance to the museum. He is the founder of the Armenian alphabet. Many religious artifacts and paintings are displayed in the museum.

The Pigeon Tower is similar to a large silo. It is round and is usually constructed out of brick. It seems that at one time these towers were built in order to attract the pigeons. This led to a large accumulation of pigeon droppings, which were a good source of fertilizer for the crops. Of course, any amount that wasn't used could be a money maker by being sold to others. My friend of mine and I visited one of these and were able to walk to the top which offered excellent views of the city and the nearby mountains.

The Chehel Sotoon Museum is sometimes called the Pavilion of Forty Columns. It should be pointed out that there aren't actually forty columns. It seems that forty is sort of a lucky number to these people that commanded respect and admiration. When the twenty columns are reflected in the waterway as one approaches the pavilion there are forty. The pavilion was used for entertainment and receptions for the king. Inside is a throne room. Many frescoes and paintings are displayed.

As in any city, the best has to be kept until the end, i.e., save the best till last. The Naqsh-e Jahan Square built by Abbas I at the turn of the seventeenth century and is one of the most magnificent squares in the world. The square is approximately five hundred-feet wide and 1,500 feet long. Shops are located in areas surrounding the square.

The Sheikh Lotf Allah Mosque was one of the first built on the square and is now known as the mosque for the harem or women's mosque. Directly across for this mosque is Ali Qapu, the palace built in the early seventeenth century by Shah Abbas the Great. The palace was used for entertainment. There is a large music room on the top floor with an interestingly designed acoustical ceiling that contained several large holes. These holes were supposed to diffuse the sound in order to make it more soothing to the listeners. From the balcony on the front of the palace overlooking the large square, the shah and his guests were able to view sporting events or large parades.

My purchases in the bazaar here allow me to keep this remembrance vivid every day as I look at my beautiful silk and wool carpet and the meticulously painted clock with Farsi numerals.

Outside the city of Kashan, we visited a complex consisting of several houses. One of them had been built by a wealthy merchant, Boroujerdi, for his wife. It seems that the family of the wife, the Tabatabaeis, was wealthy also. The same architect was employed for the construction of both houses. Later, the family built another house for their daughter.

In all of the houses the plaster work was ornate and the grounds were beautiful with pools, flowers and trees.

A group of young ladies spotted us at this location also. When they discovered that we were Americans they began asking many questions. After many questions and several photos my friend and I finally had to tell them that we had no more time. It was almost like a politician telling the news reporter that we only have time for one more question.

Our final stop before arriving back in Tehran was at the Mausoleum of Ayatollah Khomeini. There are three major buildings at present. The center building resembles a mosque in that it has a large gold dome and four minarets. The sarcophagus is located directly under the gold dome.

We had to go through security and were told that no pictures were allowed in this area. However, our guide evidently was able to say the right words because I was the only person at that time taking pictures and no one said anything.

In order to continue our trip to Jordan, we had to fly from Tehran through Bahrain and connect there with our flight to Amman. Otherwise we would have had to fly over Iraq. We obtained a visa for a day in Bahrain and hired a driver to take us to the places to visit in the capital of Manama. The weather for that particular day was quite typical for Bahrain. It must have been at least a hundred degrees and the humidity was just about the same. It had been the same on my previous visit.

Our flight arrived in Amman and we were met at the airport by our driver. The drive into the city will be one that neither my friend nor I will ever forget. It just so happens that our arrival coincided with the end of a major soccer match. It took us over an hour to get to the hotel. Traffic was at a standstill. People were hanging out the windows of cars while yelling, waving flags, and blowing horns.

We arrived at the Landmark Hotel a day earlier than our tour was to begin. We spent that first day walking into the downtown area. On our way there we passed the Turkish Embassy. In the downtown, there were many shops including several that sold nothing but water pipes, shoe and clothing shops, and several antique shops.

The next day we joined our fellow travelers and were taken to the Citadel that overlooks the city of Amman. Within the Citadel is an old Byzantine Church dating back to the sixth century, the Temple of Hercules, and the Umayyad Mosque. The National Archeological Museum comprises ancient skulls almost six thousand years old, coffins, artwork, and some examples of the Dead Sea Scrolls.

Looking from the Citadel over the city of Amman, one can see the Presidential Complex at the top of yet another hill. It seems that every city we visited had an amphitheater and Amman was no different. We made a tour of this theater and the nearby Folklore Museum.

Our group was taken to a restaurant for dinner. The restaurant was previously an old caravanserai. The food was plentiful and pleasing to the palate.

Our drive north the next day offered views into nearby Syria, the Sea of Galilee, and the Jordan Valley. Israel could be seen from the outdoor veranda where we had our lunch. After lunch, we had a stop at the spot on the Jordan river where John the Baptist supposedly baptized Jesus Christ.

Today, I was finally able to fulfill a longtime dream, which was to be able to float in the Dead Sea. We were like kids with a new toy, taking pictures of each other and laughing hysterically at how difficult it was to maneuver in the salt water and how crude we appeared with mud all over our bodies.

Ajloun Castle was built in the late twelfth century as protection from the crusader attacks. Through the years it was taken over by Mongols, used as storage, and suffered from several earthquakes. The antiquities department of the Jordanian government is now completing the restoration work.

The extensive ruins at Jerash cover a large expanse. Excavations have been found that date back to the Bronze Age. It is one of the most complete examples of a Roman city. Just after we had walked through the main gate known as Hadrian's Gate to a large open area where there was a large contingency of musicians in period costumes performing. We got our exercise at this place because it entails a lot of walking. We saw the main gates to the other sides of the complex, the Hippodrome, the Oval Forum, and the Cathedral.

Madaba, the city of mosaics, is located south of Amman. We visited the Greek Orthodox Church there and the mosaics museum where a sixth century Byzantine map was on display, completely made of mosaics.

Our trip continued to Mount Nebo where Moses was first to have seen the Promised Land. The remains of a church or monastery along with several pieces of tiles are preserved here. A cross with a snake is sometimes referred to as the Brazen Serpent Monument and was created to symbolize the serpent created by Moses and the cross of Jesus.

We drove to the scenic Wadi Mujib and Kerak on our way to Petra. The large difference in elevation creates a pleasant picturesque scene as one is driving through this area. The large crusader castle in Kerak was built in 1142.

Our hotel in Petra was just outside the entrance gates. Our day there began very early and didn't end until almost 7:00 p.m. On my previous visit, time was of the essence since we had to retrace our steps and arrive back in Aqaba to board the ship for our departure to Egypt.

We visited the Treasury, the Royal Tombs, the Amphitheater, and the Urn Tomb.

Also on this visit, I was able to visit the Monastery. To do this requires some determination and stamina as there are nine hundred steps to climb in order to reach that destination. Everyone is our group made it and agreed that it was worth the climb. One gentleman in our group decided that he would do it by donkey. However, not far from the starting point, he decided otherwise. It seems that he felt the ride was so uneven he was afraid he was going to fall off.

Wadi Rum is a large valley comprised of sandstone and granite. Many different people have lived in this area; however, the area now is occupied by Bedouins. We were fortunate enough to be asked to have tea with them under a large tent while they were assembled in their native costumes. This area was used in the making of the film, *Lawrence of Arabia.*

We were driven to the border the next day where we said good-bye to our Jordanian driver and proceeded through customs. On the other side of customs, we were greeted by our Syrian driver. Near the border we stopped at the town of Bosra. Here we toured the old amphitheater, the mosque, and the walled ruins.

Upon our arrival in Damascus, we were driven up Mount Qassioun where we were able to take nice pictures overlooking the city. I was really impressed at how large the city is and how many new buildings had been completed.

Our hotel in Damascus was in the old section of the city, where several of the homes that were once owned by wealthy merchants and had now been converted to boutique hotels. The Beit Al Wali Hotel was one of them. There was a large atrium just outside our room with marble floors and period furnishings. The area for having breakfast was outside, on an upper level. The hotel provided Internet service for the guests, which made it convenient in keeping up with friends and relatives back home.

Our driver recommended a restaurant near our hotel. We heeded his recommendation and had dinner in what was a large inner garden. The food was typical Syrian and was delightful. Many diners in Syria have a hookah, or water pipe, next to their table and partake during their meal. Two ladies were sitting at a table on the other side of the restaurant from us and they both had their individual hookahs.

Some of the highlights of our city tour included the National Museum, the Old Railway Station, a giant covered bazaar, an old bath house, and the walls of the old city.

The Umayyad Mosque is called the Great Mosque and is one of the largest mosques in the world. There is a shrine inside the mosque and supposedly contains the head of John the Baptist. This particular mosque is one of the holiest sights in all of Islam.

The tomb of Saladin who died in 1193 is located in the outside courtyard. He was a famous leader of Muslim and Arab opposition to the crusaders. The area of his sultanate included Syria and Mesopotamia and even as far as Egypt and Yemen.

Azem Palace was built in 1750 as a residence for the governor. It was built in such a way that one wing was used for living, and the other wing was used for entertaining. The palace now is a museum of arts and folk traditions.

Just outside Damascus on our way to Palmyra we stopped in Maaloula at the St. Thecla Monastery. She was a student of Saint Paul and was one of the first female martyrs. It seems that she was to be married and had heard of St. Paul's discourse on virginity. She was to be burned at the stake. However, a wild storm came and put out the fire and she escaped. Lightning struck a wall of rock and split it open allowing a passage. She lived the rest of her life in a cave. This monastery is built within a large rock and serves as a sanctuary for nuns and orphans.

In Palmyra, we toured the ruins including the Bel Temple, the Valley of Tombs, the funerary towers, the castle, the amphitheater, the Monumental Arch, and the Great Colonnade. The castle is high upon a hill where vistas of the surrounding areas are spectacular. It seems that everyone gets the word and is supposed to be at the castle for sunset. There were several tour buses there at the time. At the amphitheater they were in the process of making a musical video for a local singing artist, which was interesting to watch.

On our drive to Aleppo, we stopped in the town of Hama where we were able to see several water wheels. It seems this city is known for its water wheels. At one time there were many. They were used to raise water into the aqueducts. Their use was terminated in the mid-twentieth century. However, the Syrian government still provides money for their maintenance in order to keep their historical value alive.

Visiting the Citadel in Aleppo was the highlight of the visit there. It is considered to be one of the largest and oldest in the world dating back to the third century. Many different groups have maintained control throughout the years, but today it is merely the tourist attraction for Aleppo.

Several of the buildings near our hotel still maintain the old wooden balconies. We visited an old caravanserai that had been converted to a hotel. And we walked through the shops in the bazaar.

Our next stop was at Apamea. These ruins date back to 300 BC. It has been said that Cleopatra actually visited here. The architecture is Roman and Byzantine, and some of the columns are unique in that they have twisted fluting from top to bottom. The main colonnade was over one mile long! Much of it was destroyed in the twelfth century by a series of earthquakes.

The epitome of castles has to be Krak des Chevaliers. It has thirteen majestic towers and two outside walls with a moat between the two. This crusader castle was originally built in 1031.

After our visit here my friend and I were taken to a nearby place to have our dinner. We didn't order anything. However, several plates of food arrived at our table. We were astonished at the amount of food and were taking pictures. And as though that weren't enough, several other plates of food arrived. Now, we were not astonished, we were flabbergasted! It was a memorable feast.

On our drive into Lebanon, we saw several fields of tents and were told that these were occupied by the gypsies. The line of cars at the immigration station was not to be believed. We thought it was bad coming from Syria until we saw the other side and it was twice as long with an enormous number of vehicles, mainly trucks, coming from Lebanon to Syria.

The first day in Lebanon was spent driving to the southern part of the country just north of Israel. We saw several manned military checkpoints on our way.

The ruins in the ancient city of Tyre included a cemetery with several sarcophagi above ground made out of large slabs of stone. There was a large plaza, which would have been where the shops in the agora would have been located. There was a sports arena that had probably been used for spectator sports such as chariot racing.

Just north of Tyre is the city of Sidon. Both Sidon and Tyre are located alongside the Mediterranean Sea and offers exquisite scenery. The most famous structure in the city of Sidon was the Sea Castle. A causeway from the main street connects the castle, which is located on an island. It was built in 1228 by the Crusaders.

Beitteddine Palace is about thirty miles southeast of Beirut and was built in 1788 by Emir Bashir to be used as his residence until 1840. Since 1943, it has been used as a summer residence of the president of the republic. One wing of the palace is a museum.

On the way back to Beirut we stopped in the small town of Deir el Qamar. This small town served as the residence of former governors. Emir Fakhreddine Maan was the first prince of the State of Lebanon. The mosque and the palace here in Deir el Qamar bear his name. A Deir el Qamar Synagogue dates back to the seventeenth century.

It doesn't take long to recognize the amount of destruction that has been caused by the recent conflicts in Lebanon. As you walk through a section of the downtown area, it is possible to witness a statue for martyrs that contain several bullet holes. Then you see a building with the windows missing and also bullet holes all over the side.

The National Museum in Beirut suffered from the war because of its strategic location. However, most of the archeological items were saved and are on display in a renovated building. A temporary memorial has been set up to honor Rafiq Hariri and those who were killed along with him.

Aanjar is a small town in Lebanon where many Armenians settled from the Musa Dagh section of Turkey. Many Armenians make a pilgrimage to this place every year. The ruins here are well worth a visit.

Baalbek is located about fifty miles from Beirut. This is definitely the one place in Lebanon that no one should miss. It has to be considered one of the wonders of the world. It is difficult for words to express the enormity of the palaces and temples. The large columns are some of the tallest I have ever seen. There are temples for Venus, Bacchus, and Jupiter. An international festival is held here each year with one of the structures as a backdrop of the stage. They were in the process of constructing the stage for this when we visited.

The Ksara Winery produces many wines that are sold all over the world. We took a tour of the winery including a section of the two miles of underground caves that are used for storage and aging of the wines.

Our driver took us to the top at Harissa. This area offers spectacular views of the bay area below. There is a large white statue here called The Virgin of Lebanon. It can be seen as one drives on the highway below. There are two large churches located at the top—the modern St. Mary Church and the Basilica of St. Paul. We were able to take the cable car on the way down where we rejoined our driver.

This comprehensive visit to the country of Lebanon also included a visit to Byblos, Tripoli, the Khalil Gibran Museum in Bcharre, and the Cedars of Lebanon.

We flew from Beirut to Cyprus. We stayed in Larnaca and visited the sights of that city including the Archeological Museum, the Pierides Museum, and the Church of Saint Lazarus.

We drove to Paphos on the far end of the island where I was able to join a friend from the *Queen Elizabeth 2* world cruise for lunch. While in Paphos we toured the harbor area, the castle, the catacombs, and the Tomb of the Kings. On our journey back to Larnaca we saw the Rock of Aphrodite.

We drove into Nicosia the next day. We visited several shopping areas and the Cathedral of St. John. We were able to obtain a visa to go into the Turkish section of Cyprus. We had been told to expect a long wait and that we would probably have to pay for the visa. However, we were lucky in arriving to this point rather early in the day. There was no wait at all and there was no charge.

We hired a taxi that took us to the city of Kyrenia. We toured the castle there and wandered around the harbor. This is an extremely beautiful place.

We returned to the city and were quite surprised when we observed the long lines waiting to go through customs. We were glad that we went early.

The last day was spent driving to Limassol where we toured the castle, the harbor front, and an old Greek Orthodox Church. From Limassol we stopped at an old monastery on our drive to the top of the Troodos Mountains. We were high enough that we could see clouds below us.

From Cyprus, we flew to Munich, Germany, to connect with our flights back to the United States. During most of our visit my friend and I were quite concerned about our return. A volcano had erupted in Iceland and the ash had descended upon most of Europe and several of the airports had been closed.

Upon entering the terminal we noticed that one entire wing had been filled with cots for people to use who couldn't get home. While waiting for my flight, I discovered that several of the people in line with me had been at the airport for several days waiting to get a flight. I was fortunate that I was only delayed for about four hours. The one thing I couldn't figure out though was that our flight then took us directly over Iceland on the way home.

The only country in Europe that I had not visited at this time was Belarus. In searching the computer for tours I discovered that Globus had exactly what I was looking for.

My departure at the airport from Washington was quite a routine. When it came time to board the plane I began my usual trek toward the middle or rear section of the plane. It was then that I realized I had already passed my seat assignment. I was pleasantly surprised on discovering that I had been upgraded to a business class seat. By not having the lady at the check in counter say anything about it even contributed in making it more of a surprise. What a nice way to begin the trip.

The tour began in Copenhagen. There was an orientation meeting the first day, which allowed all of the members of the tour group to meet each other and to hear a brief overview of what we were to expect in the next few days. After the meeting, we had dinner together in the dining room of the hotel, which allowed us the opportunity of getting to know each other a little better.

Our tour in Copenhagen took us to the usual places—Christiansborg Palace, Amelienborg Palace, the Little Mermaid, and a visit to Tivoli Gardens. We saw the changing of the guard at the palace and view several of the reception rooms.

I felt a little sorry for those in our group who had not been here before. The Little Mermaid had been taken to Shanghai for the World Expo. In the place where you would normally see her, there was a large video screen that was showing an live picture of the statue being transmitted from China.

On my own I took a canal tour where we were able to see the Royal Yacht, the Performing Arts Center, the Opera House, and several of the spires for which the city is known.

The next morning we drove north to take the ferry to Sweden. On the way, our guide was giving us an overview of the remainder of our trip. He asked if anyone had been to Russia previously. I sheepishly raised my hand. He then asked what year I had visited. I said, "1971, 1976, 1992, and 2008," Needless to say, the other travelers were quite impressed and wondered what had enticed me to return so many times.

There were a couple of places we visited in Stockholm that I had not visited on my earlier trips. We went to the City Hall and toured the banquet hall where the Nobel Prizes are awarded. In other parts of the City Hall building, we saw the room where the Stockholm City Legislature meets and several large reception areas some of which were adorned with large murals done in mosaics using a lot of gold.

The other new place for me was Skansen Park, which is an open air museum and zoo. There we were able to see dwellings from the past, an old school, and a wooden church. In the area of the zoo, we saw rabbits, bison, leopard, bear, and elk.

From Stockholm, we took an overnight boat to Helsinki. I had read and had also been told by a friend who had taken one of these overnight boats a couple times that it was extremely noisy. I thought he had just been unlucky. It seems that a lot of the young people go on this boat ride as a right of passage from being a teenager to adulthood. My friends were right—it was noisy!

In Helsinki, we toured the typical tourist sights including the Rock Church, the Lutheran Church, the harbor, and the memorial to Sibelius all of which I had seen before.

This tour offered us the option of taking a day trip to Estonia. Since I had been there before, I decided to remain in Helsinki and spend most of the day going to the National Museum. The exhibits there included elaborate antique altars, home furnishings, musical instruments, clocks, and several miniature dollhouses complete with furnishing and people. One of the documents displayed that I found quite interesting was the peace treaty between Russian and Finland.

The Angleterre Hotel in Saint Petersburg could not have been more centrally located. It was directly across the street from the St. Isaac's Church. While in Saint Petersburg, we visited the Hermitage, which can be an all-day affair and still not see everything. We drove to Pushkin and toured Catherine Palace. The first time I was here in 1971, they had just begun the restoration. By having seen it in that condition helps to make one appreciate what has been accomplished since.

Our journey continued from Saint Petersburg with an overnight stop in Novgorod. Our hotel, the Beresta, was supposedly the best in town. There was a long list of all the television stations that were available in the room and in what language the station was telecast. Strangely enough all of them indicated that they were broadcast in Russian.

Our sightseeing tour included the old city wall by their Kremlin, the Yuri Monastery, St. Sophia, the monument of the Millennium of Russia, and the Museum of Wooden Architecture.

In Moscow, we toured the Armory and the Kremlin. The items in the armory never cease to amaze me. Even after having visited it twice before I was still in awe. The different churches in the Kremlin with their gold onion domes are always a "Kodak moment." It was interesting to see the area that the president uses as his offices. The Kremlin Palace Theater brought back memories of having seen the *Carmen* ballet there in 1976—thirty-four years earlier! Yikes, I'm getting old!

We visited the Cathedral of Christ the Savior. Tsar Alexander I signed a manifesto in 1812 to build a church in honor of Christ the Savior. Plans were drawn and work began in 1839 and was finished in 1883. However, during the Stalin years when religion was not looked upon very favorably, it was demolished with dynamite. Then this area was just a big hole. During the Khrushchev years, it was used as a swimming pool. Then, in 1992, after the fall of communism, a group began raising money to rebuild it. It was completely rebuilt and opened in 2000 and is probably the largest orthodox cathedral in the world.

I had hoped to see the Novodevichy Convent and the adjacent cemetery when I was in Moscow in 2008, but was out of time. I knew there would be another time. This was it! The iconoclast in the cathedral is one of the most ornate I have seen.

The famous names in the cemetery include Khrushchev, Chekhov, Shostakovich, Stalin's wife, Chaliapin, Gorbachev, and Yeltsin.

While driving back into the downtown area of Moscow from the area where the university is located there is a "new city" comprised of many new skyscrapers. Some are for business and some are condominiums.

On our drive from Moscow to Smolensk, we stopped to see the area where The Battle of Borodino was fought. This battle was the largest and bloodiest day of the French invasion of Russia. There were 250,000 troops and seventy thousand casualties. This was called the Patriotic War of 1812. Peter llyich Tchaikovsky wrote his 1812 overture in 1880. It was to be presented at the Church of Christ Our Savior in Moscow to commemorate Russia's defense of Moscow against Napoleon's advancing Grand Armee at the Battle of Borodino in 1812.

Katyn Wood is an area in western Russian near the border of Belarus where mass graves were found of 4,500 Polish soldiers massacred by the Russians. Locals knew that the Russians had a dacha at that location, but it was closed off to outsiders. They also knew that it was being used to get rid of people who were opposed to Stalin. Polish soldiers were brought in by the carloads and killed. They were buried in mass graves. It wasn't until later when outsiders discovered the location that the Russian government finally acknowledged what had happened.

Our brief overnight stop in Smolensk didn't allow much time to tour. We were able to see the Cathedral of the Assumption that was built between 1676 and 1740. The interior was very ornate and workers were in the process of doing some restoration.

After our dinner, we did walk around the town and took some pictures of the monuments.

There had just recently been a plane crash here where the President of Poland was killed. Upon our departure from the city we were driven to the spot where the crash occurred and saw several tokens of appreciation that had been made for those who perished in the crash.

We drove out of our way in order to see a World War II memorial. On March 22, 1943, there were twenty-six houses burned by the Nazis killing 149 people. During the siege, 2.2 million people were killed, 209 cities, and 9,200 villages were destroyed. The memorial opened in 1969. Josef Kaminski was out-of-town when the houses were burned. Consequently, he was the only survivor. There is a statue of him carrying his dead son.

I was pleasantly surprised at the city of Minsk. I had thought it would be an old city with blackened buildings. It was completely the opposite. The large central square was just outside my window of the Minsk Hotel. Around the square was a large Catholic Church, a large statue of Lenin, and other buildings. There was a large dome in the center of the square and there is a shopping area located underneath.

We saw theaters, opera house, the parliament, the old KGB building that is still in use, the Victory Column, and the World War II monument. The guidehad pointed out to us the apartment building where Lee Harvey Oswald had an apartment at one time.

The monument that was most memorable to me was the one called Island of Tears. It is located on a small island in the Dnieper river. The monument is for the soldiers who were killed in the war with Afghanistan from 1979 until 1988. Guarding the memorial that contains four small chapels inside are statues of the widows, mothers, and sisters who had someone killed.

Our last stop in the tour was Warsaw. Not much had changed since my last visit in 1998.

The one place that was new for me was the Umschlagplatz Monument. This is the spot where Polish Jews were to assemble to be placed on trains to be transported to death camps.

Since my last visit, Poland had a Catholic Pope. Yes, John Paul II was Polish and a statue of him was on the outside of a church near the old section of town.

—2010 is not over yet! There is still time to take a nice tour of the Indian Ocean. First, I had to fly to Paris—spend one night—and fly the next day to Mauritius where I landed at the Sir Seewoosagur Ramgoolam International airport. I was met at the airport and transported to my nearby hotel, the Blue Lagoon. I had the remainder of the day free, and I really needed it after the long, long flight from Paris. The views from the hotel were breathtaking!

My English-speaking driver/guide arrived at the hotel the next morning to take me on a tour of the island. It just so happened that this was a national holiday in Mauritius. Indian Arrival Day is a holiday commemorating the arrival of the people of the Indian subcontinent. It is celebrated in several countries, but in Mauritius it is celebrated on November 2, when the indentured slaves came from India.

One of the things they do during this day is to take flowers to the cemeteries for their friends and relatives who have died. We saw a large Hindu temple where the people were making offerings, and celebrating with lots of food and dressed in their finery.

My lunch was at a restaurant in the mountains with a spectacular view. The buffet lunch was superb. From this location we traveled to see the Seven Colored Earth. This site shows how different colored stones having been made into sand and resembles a rainbow.

We saw a large coffee plantation, and I was able to take some pictures of the blossoms of the coffee plants. At the Grand Bassin, there were several beautiful white beaches.

My second day was spent flying to Rodriguez Island. This island is governed by Mauritius; however, being almost three hundred miles away, it operates rather independently. My guide for the day drove me around the island. We stopped at the Catholic Church. The gravesites in the cemetery next to the church contained an overabundance of fresh flowers that had been left there the day before.

It is interesting how much one can surmise by just riding around the island with a few stops. It was obvious that the average annual income for the residents was quite low. I was told also that there is only one service station on the entire island.

There is a small town that includes a market, several shops, churches, a post office, and the college. There were other small colleges on the island, which would be considered to others as a technical school where various trades would be learned.

Being a small island also lends itself to the fact that everyone knows everyone else. It would be difficult to do something wrong and not have others know about it.

I had a nice lunch at one of the only hotels on the island. The lunch was served adjacent to a swimming pool with a nice view of the ocean. Then, it was time to return to the airport and fly back to Mauritius.

The next day I was driven into Port Louis, which is the capital of Mauritius. Tourists from other hotels around the island were arriving at a central location. Once everyone had arrived, we were separated into groups according to language. In my English group we only had three people—myself and a couple from Cape Town, South Africa.

We visited the Pamplemousses Royal Botanical Gardens. Most areas in the park were quite typical with various flowers and trees. We did, however, spot a tree that had many bats hanging from it.

One large pond was filled with giant lily pads some of which had blooms. One section displayed various plants and herbs that could be used for medicinal purposes. For example, some would be good for headaches, some for diarrhea, dysentery, or constipation.

The tour continued to a large sugar factory. There we were asked to participate in sugar tasting. There were many different kinds of sugar with different consistencies ranging from extremely course to the fineness of powdered sugar.

Our lunch was served in a restaurant at the sugar factory with an outdoor setting. We found it interesting at the number of birds there were flying around the eating area waiting for crumbs. Some of them, however, were very colorful.

Our driver had told us that we would now be continuing our tour by visiting the Citadel overlooking Port Louis. However, the road that we needed to use had been closed because of an overabundance of smoke from a fire. We had to turn around and proceed with plan B.

The citadel, an abandoned fort, does offer excellent views overlooking the capital city. There were large cannons still there. The waterfront area that could be seen from this vantage point was to be our next stop.

The waterfront area in Port Louis reminded me a lot of the waterfront in Cape Town. My fellow tourists for the day agreed with me and they were from Cape Town.

My next flight would take me to Antananarivo, the capital city of Madagascar. The drive from the airport passed several large rice fields. A canal was alongside the road and many of the local residents were in this area to wash clothes and lay them on the grassy hillside to dry. For as far as you could see, there were clothes.

The exchange rate in Madagascar was about 2,000 Ariary to a dollar. In exchanging $40 I received about 77,000! I kept a copy of my dinner bill at the hotel, which was 53,900!

I stayed at the Carlton Hotel in Antananarivo. It was a very nice high-rise hotel. Across the street were a couple office buildings. Adjacent to the hotel and also across the street were several small housing structures that served as homes for poor people—quite a diversity!

From the window of my hotel room was a panoramic view of the lower part of the city with a large lake in the center. The lake was encircled with Jacaranda trees and their beautiful blue blossoms were at their peak! A tall statue with an angel on top in the center of the lake served as a memorial for World War I.

This city is separated into the low city and the high city. I was given a tour of the high city in the afternoon. In that section we stopped at an Anglican Church, a Catholic Church, and the Queen's Palace, which is now a museum.

Upon our return to the low city, I couldn't believe all the selling happening on both sides of the overcrowded streets. It seems that no matter what one would want to buy, they could find it here—clothes, food, cooking utensils, auto parts—everything!

I found it interesting that in the midst of all this, there was a large monument with a giant red ribbon on it remembering those who had died from AIDS, and to also serve as a reminder that safe sex can help to solve this problem.

At the end of this street was the old railway station. It is used only for freight these days, no passenger cars.

We left the next morning to drive down the eastern side of the island where I would spend time visiting several nature parks. On the way out-of-town, I was amazed at the number of old French Citroen cars that were being used as taxis. Alongside the street, I noticed butcher shops with raw meat hanging in the open air.

Continuing our drive outside the city, we passed many rice fields where workers would be tending to the fields. There were several places for brick making. It seems that the mud can be formed, dried, and baked, making it perfect to use in the construction of homes. Many homes are still made of mud and suffer greatly during the rainy season.

It was very interesting to drive through a small village and see a sign on a dilapidated building indicating that it was a hotel. Of course, these aren't the ones that one finds in the Trip Advisor suggestions on the computer! They would only be used by locals in moving from one city to another. It seems that their most common method of transporting people or merchandise was with a hand-pulled cart.

We stopped at the Marozevo Private Zoo, where many indigenous animals were on display. There were chameleons, alligators, petit-colored frogs, a boa snake, and several brightly colored lizards.

My stay at the Eulophiella Lodge was pleasant. The location was quite remote.

My driver had to drive for about three miles from the main road to reach this venue. There was a large reception building that had a nice lobby with a fireplace, a restaurant, and a large porch for resting.

Each guest has their own completely separate dwelling. It was like having your own home. Mine had a porch that encircled three sides. There was a large bed with a net, a sitting area, and a bathroom that was separated into three rooms. Yes, there was one room with the shower, another with the lavatory, and the other with the commode.

In the afternoon, we drove to the Vacona Private Reserve. There I was able to see my first lemurs. Not only see them, but I had them crawling all over me while a person from the reserve was hysterically taking several pictures of me with the lemurs.

The next day, I spent the morning walking through the Mantadia National Park. This rain forest contains different species of lemur. The most common types would include the brown lemur, white-fronted lemur, and the ring-tailed lemur.

After lunch we walked through the other section of the park called the Analamazoatra Reserve where we were able to see several indri, the largest of the lemurs. The loud sounds that the indri make is almost deafening! They are quite territorial and protective of their own family if another family tries to move in.

I flew from Madagascar to Moroni, the capital of Comoros. Comoros was under the control of France for many years. They received their independence in 1975.

Most of the people raise many kinds of vegetables, which they can sell at the market and use that money to buy other items. The island grows a lot of bananas and coconuts. Vanilla, cloves, and perfume essences are also quite popular. The local market was very active. It isn't uncommon to see many of the ladies with sandalwood on their faces. It is supposedly good for the skin and helps in protection from the sun.

While touring the island we saw the French Embassy, the home of the president, the Friday Temple, and the port section where large boats can dock. Many houses are made of corrugated metal. Some of the elder homes were constructed from carved volcanic stones.

Many sections of the road would have clothes hanging alongside. I asked if they had just been washed and were drying and was told that those items were for sale.

Planes land at the airport in Dzaoudzi when flying into Mayotte. One must then take a taxi to the ferry station where you ride a ferry across to the city of Mamoudzou. My hotel, the Trevani, was located a few miles north of the city. Each guest has their own little home that consists of a large bedroom, a dressing room, a bath, and shower and they are all painted in different colors. Mine was lavender. These living quarters also have a porch in the front that overlooks the beach and the ocean. Who couldn't just stay here for a while and do nothing but walk around on the beach.

My guide in Mayotte was Attoumani Harouna. His picture was included in the travel promotion brochure for the island and he was proud of that.

Our tour of the island included a visit to the botanical garden. There we saw a cinnamon tree, bamboo, and palm trees with thorns, breadfruit, and the frangipani flowers.

The Ylang Ylang flower is used in making perfume. We visited a place where I could see the process of extracting the oil. Some of this is exported to France.

When a boy reaches the age of fifteen in Mayotte, he has to leave home. In doing so, he is expected to build what is called a banga. This banga is to be built in such a way as to impress the girls and prove to them that they would be able to build a home for them and take care of them. The banga is used for their first "rendezvous." During the time that the boy is living in the banga, he still has his meals with the family.

The Vanilla and Ylang Ylang museum offers it visitors an opportunity to "test their nose" in determining what it is you are smelling. Evidently my nose needs repair. I would be able to determine a certain smell, but couldn't seem to be able to pinpoint exactly what it was.

We visited the largest baobab tree on the island and possibly the largest of any in the Indian Ocean. It was gigantic. My photo makes me look like a midget.

On our way back to the hotel there was a section of housing just outside Mamoudzou that depicted where very poor people may live. I asked the guide about it. His response was that that particular section was where a lot of illegal immigrants live. It didn't seem to make a lot of sense because at the top of that hill was the government offices.

My next stop on my tour of the islands of the Indian Ocean was to the island of Reunion. St. Denis is the capital, and there I stayed at the Best Western Hotel. Just up the street from the hotel was the central part of the city. There was the Catholic Church, The Victory Monument, the Town Hall, and many shops. The residence for the head of the government was also located here.

A nice surprise awaited me as I was picked up for my first day of touring in Reunion. I found out that I would not be traveling alone for the day. Instead, I would be joining with about twenty other travelers. After having been several days as a "group of one," it was comforting to share the experiences of the day with others.

Soon our bus was leaving the coastal area and the scenery began to change from the coastal vegetation to forests, then to desert-like areas in the high mountains.

Our first stop was to have been a view of an active volcano. However, as we neared the entrance to the road leading to the volcano, we noticed a number of fire trucks! We were informed that there had been a fire in an area on the way to the volcano and the road was closed. All was not lost in that we retraced our steps a little and visited the Maison du Volcan, a volcano museum.

We stopped at one location, which offered views of the valley that cuts through the mountains. The view was breathtaking! And at the bottom of the valley, you could see that there was a small village there.

We were taken to a nice place where we had lunch. It was an experience in that the group consisted of people from the United States, from Australia, from Italy, and from Africa. It was like a "mini-united nations" of languages.

After lunch, we were taken to a volcanic area where there had just been an explosion not long before we were there. Lava everywhere!

The area adjacent to the front of my hotel in St. Denis lent itself for a nice stroll. To the left were tall cliffs that descended almost straight down to the ocean. A major highway followed these cliffs as one drove to the south of the island.

Walking north, there were two large cemeteries alongside the ocean. One was a military cemetery.

I flew from St. Denis on the island of Reunion to Mahe in the Seychelles for my last major stop on this Indian Island adventure. Victoria, the capital of the Seychelles, is a quaint little town on the island of Mahe.

In the center square in town is a small replica of Big Ben. They just refer to theirs as "Little Ben." A large white statue consisting of three pieces is to commemorate freedom where three continents are joined—Africa, Europe, and Asia.

At the Justice Department the judges still wear the wigs from the colonial days.

Victoria has three major churches downtown. There is the St. Paul's Anglican Church, the Cathedral of Immaculate Conception, and a Hindu temple.

The local market had several choices of fresh fish. Many fruits, spices, and vegetables were available. And don't forget the peppers. From what we were told, some of the peppers are extremely powerful.

The major touring company here on the island has a central office in the downtown section. One of the buses for the company will follow a route each morning to the various hotels in collecting those tourists who have signed up for a tour with them. Once at the central location, the tourists are separated according to the particular tour they are taking for the day.

My tour the first day included a visit to a large manufacturing plant that processed tea and packaged it for distribution. It was nice to be able to drive around the island and see the other hotels. I remember the guide pointing out a section of cottages on a hillside. It seems that this is an exclusive place for the wealthy to stay where each cottage comes with its own private swimming pool and rents are about three thousand Euros per night.

We had a nice buffet lunch by the beach. One of the fascinating things about these tours was that the participants were from all over the world. One gentleman on the tour was from New Zealand, but he was now working in Dubai and was just here for a little break. Another gentleman was from England and we had just met the day before at the local market. Others were from Africa, Europe, and Australia.

The next day, I had finished breakfast and was ready for my tour for the day. I ask the gentleman who was standing near the tourist desk if he was waiting for a tour. When he replied, I could detect that he had an accent. It just so happened that he was from Siberia. He couldn't believe it when I told him that I had been to Siberia. We enjoyed spending the day together and we still keep in touch through e-mails.

The tour for today began by taking a boat to Praslin Island. We visited the Vallée de Mai Nature Reserve. The natural palm forest provides a pleasant place to walk. The one palm that is endemic to the area is the Coco de Mer. The nuts from the palm are supposed to be the largest nuts in the world. Some of them weigh as much as twenty pounds. And interestingly enough there is a male and a female nut. If you ever see one you will know which is which.

A traditional schooner took us from Praslin Island to La Digue Island where we had our buffet lunch. My newfound Siberian friend and I were enjoying our buffet lunch, when he noticed that the couple sitting across the table from us had a Russian accent. He asked where they were from. The gentleman was from Canada and the lady was from Russia, but they are now living in the United Arab Emirates. The Russian lady was surprised also that I had visited Russia several times.

We drove passed a large pit of giant tortoises. Then, we drove through an area where the huge rock formations were unbelievable. The afternoon was spent at the Anse Source D'Argent beach and then we returned to Mahe.

The last day in the Seychelles was spent going to Moyenne Island. We went there on a glass bottom boat where we could observe the ocean life below. At one point we stopped and were given bread to throw overboard. Needless to say the hundreds and hundreds of fish were glad to see us.

The island was purchased in 1964 by an Englishman named Brendon Grimshaw. He purchased the island for some 10,000 pounds. A book was written about this adventure called *A Grain of Sand: The Story of One Man and an Island.*

It seems that the island was quite barren when he purchased it. During the years he has planted many trees, palms, and other plants. There are now a number of giant tortoises living there with him on his island.

There is a small chapel on the island along with a couple tombs. It is believed that the tombs are of pirates but no one knows for sure.

While we were there for our buffet lunch, Brendon came out and talked to us. He is now ninety years old and still enjoys his interactions with the people who visit the island.

Today was yet another day of international couples. There was a gentleman from the United States and his wife was from South America and now they are living in Saudi Arabia. By observing this, one gets a new meaning of a melting pot society.

2011

South America, New Guinea, and Bhutan

In February, I flew to Quito, Ecuador where I spent a couple days sightseeing before flying to the Galapagos Islands. I stayed at the Quito Hotel. The room on the top floor of the hotel that is used for the breakfast buffet offered spectacular views of the city. In the lobby of the hotel, there was a flower arrangement that must have had ten dozen roses in it! During our morning tour, we were told how inexpensive roses are in Ecuador and that many of them are exported to other countries.

There were several other tourists that were going on the city tour that day. It was good to be with other people for a change.

La Basilica del Voto Nacional is a large cathedral in Quito. Some of the gargoyles on the cathedral are animals conducive to the ones that would be found in the Galapagos Islands. Near the cathedral was the University. Independence Plaza is the central square in Quito and around the square are the Cathedral, the Presidential Palace, and the Mayor's Place. Overlooking the city is the giant Winged Virgin Statue. Also, on the city tour we went to the San Francisco Monastery.

Our group then flew via Guayaquil to the Galapagos Islands. The next four days would be spent cruising around on the *Galapagos Legend*, a nice tourist ship that accommodates one hundred people.

Most of the visitors to the islands seem to come for one reason more than any other and that is to finally see The Blue-Footed Boobie! We were able to see several. Some of the animals that we saw would include iguanas, lizards, sea gulls, frigate birds, sea lions, crabs, blue herons, porpoises, and giant tortoises. From the deck of the ship at night, we were able to see flying fish and sharks.

From here I flew to Lima, Peru, where I stayed at the Sol de Oro Hotel located in the Miraflores section of the city.

My city tour here included the Parque del Amor thatwas located near my hotel overlooking the ocean. There is a statue in the park called The Kissing Couple. From the park to the sea is a very high cliff. One can walk down to that area if you are in good shape. I did it in the afternoon in order to get some photos. It seems that the highway that goes through that area is always crowded!

The Huaca Huallamarca is a pyramid that was only discovered a few years ago. It apparently dates back to 200 BC and has been used by various groups during those years. Some of it, of course, has been restored.

In the central part of the city, I was able to see the Basilica de San Pedro, the Presidential Palace, the Palace of Justice, the Museum of Italian Art, and the San Francisco Church and convent.

My next stop was the city of Cusco where I stayed at the Novotel Hotel. One section of the hotel was at one time a monastery. Some of the old stone walls remain. Just outside the hotel on the narrow street were two llamas for photo ops.

The Church of Santo Domingo contains the Temple of Coricancha, which has been made into a museum. In the courtyard of the museum are several flowers. One of them, Cantuta, is the national flower of Peru. The grass in a section of the courtyard had been manicured to reveal "the three levels of life"—the condor, the puma, and the snake.

The main square of Cusco consists of the Church of the Holy Family, the Cathedral of Cusco, the Church of La Compania, and a large shopping arcade. Outside the city, I was able to tour the ruins of Sacsayhuaman Fortress, the Tampumachay ruins, the Kenko ruins, and the Puca Pucara ruins.

On our drive to the Sacred Valley, we stopped at what I would call a family-operated outdoor zoo and museum. The zoo area included several animals that you can feed. There were llamas, alpacas, groundhogs, and chinchillas. There was also a shop, a demonstration of how wool is dyed for weaving, and a weaving demonstration.

We had a stop in Pisaq, where we strolled through the market. At one location in the market there was a large group of local residents serenading with music while dressed in their native costumes.

We spent several hours climbing the ruins in the Sacred Valley of the Incas and receiving a history lesson of the area.

In driving through the countryside of Peru, it isn't uncommon to see snow-covered mountains in the background. Some of the houses would have a large section painted as an advertisement of for promoting a political candidate. On the top of several houses there would be a small statue consisting of two bulls. This adornment is supposed to bring good luck.

My visit to Cusco ended with a nice folklore show. The next morning, I took the train to Machu Picchu. Upon arrival, we were taken by bus up to the ruins. I had been here once before; however, that was forty-two years back. Much more had been excavated since my last visit. On my first visit the sun was shining. On this visit it was pouring rain! I was worth seeing—either way!

The next day I spent most of the day walking around the small city of Aguas Calientes. There was a small square with a statue in the center and a church on the side. For several blocks around that area were a lot of restaurants and places to buy souvenirs. I noticed that there were many places in which to get a therapeutic massage using the hot waters of the area. In the afternoon, we took the train back to Cusco where I spent another night at the Novotel Hotel.

Early the next morning I left of the Andean Express train to Puno. The train was delightfully decorated, and the food was extremely palatable. It was a ten-hour train ride. The last car of the train is an observation car with lots of glass and brass with an open space that facilitates the taking of pictures. There was a demonstration in the bar as to how to make a pisco sour. We also had a music concert and a fashion show on our way.

La Raya Pass that the train passes through in the early afternoon is an elevation over fourteen thousandfeet. The scenery through this area was unforgettable. We arrived in Puno, the city adjacent to Lake Titicaca at 6:00 p.m. Of course, the lake is the highest lake in the world and is situated between the borders of Peru and Bolivia.

In Puno, I stayed at the Sonesta Posado del Inca Hotel that was situated on Lake Titicaca. Behind the hotel, it was possible to walk out to see the Yavari, a British ship was had been disassembled and brought here in 1862.

A certain tribe of people live on floating islands in the lake. The islands are made from the roots of the reeds. We toured one of the islands and saw inside one of their dwellings.

We had a visit to Taquile Island. The people who live on this island are quite self-sufficient. They grow their own vegetables, raise cattle, and do a lot of fishing.

The men on the island begin knitting at an early age. It is possible to see them sitting in the square talking to their friends, but they will be knitting at the same time. While they were walking through the square they would be knitting! The women do the weaving. Located on this particular square was a large gift shop where the items could be purchased.

The island is divided into six sectors. Each sector has their own representative. This representative would be in charge of taking care of any problem that arises. The motto of the island is "do not steal, do not lie, and do not be lazy." I was told that there is almost no crime on the island. And if someone does something that is deemed wrong—they have to appear before the representatives and plead their case. If they are found guilty, they can be deported from the island.

On my last day here, I was able to go to see the chullpas, or funerary towers, at Sillustani on my way to the airport. The towers were built by the Colla tribe even before the Incas and are located alongside the Umayo Lagoon.

I flew from Juliaca through Arequipa to Lima. My local guide met me at the airport and took me to a park in Lima where they have a light show with lasers. We had talked about this before I left for Cusco and he wanted to know if I would be interested in seeing it. I said that I would love to see it. So we did. I had never seen anything quite like it before. There would be a huge screen made of water and behind it laser images would be transmitted to allow you to see it on the other side.

The park is very popular, consequently, it was crowded. The park contains many fountains. One of the spumes is supposed to be the highest one in the world and is in Guinness' Book of Records. There was even a tunnel of water that you could walk through without getting wet. I remember also a large topiary teapot where you could see the water coming from the teapot into a cup, and it was all made out of a plant and was illuminated with changing colors of light.

The next day I flew to Santiago, Chile. The downtown tour included the Plaza de Armas, the Presidential Palace, the Justice Department, and the local market. The architecture of this market resembled that of the Eiffel Tower in Paris.

There were two large buildings near my hotel that were architecturally appealing. One was a bank and the other was a telecommunications building. A couple of other buildings in the neighborhood were ecologically correct in that they were completely covered on the outside with greenery. Another building was under construction, and when finished will be the tallest building in South America.

I was driven outside the city to have a tour of the Concha y Toro Winery. We saw the mansion where the first owner had lived. We walked through some of the vineyards and were informed about the different kinds of grapes. We then toured the cellars. In the evening there was a folk show.

The next day I flew to Easter Island. The passengers of the plane were greeted with floral leis similar to what you would receive if you went to Hawaii. I stayed at the Iorana Hotel and the view from the restaurant was perfect for watching the sunset in the evening while having dinner.

Our first stop was Vinapu located near the runway of the airport. There were two moai statues here; however, it was just the head. One of the members of our English-speaking group asked our guide about the horses we could see walking nearby. We were told that there are more horses on the island than there are people!

Our next stop included the Rano Kau crater and the Ana Kai Tangata cave. This cave was located near my hotel. Inside there were still petroglyphs depicting the Birdman cult.

Ahu Akivi has seven moai statues facing the ocean. Because of the location of Easter Island, these moai statues are facing the sunrise during part of the year and facing the sunset at other times.

The Ana Te Pahu caves were once levels of molten lava. Once drained, they created empty lava tunnels and provided living quarters for the Rapa Nui natives. They also provided a place to hide from enemies.

Akahanga is a large area where the moai statues are thought to have been carved. There is some still lying that is partially carved.

The Ahu Tongariki moai statues were flattened at one time by a tsunami and have been restored to their former locations. These are probably the most photographed of any of the statues here. Out last stop was at Anakena Beach. Just up from the beach are the Nau Nau moai statues.

Another trip comes to a close and its now time to fly back to Santiago, where I will connect with my flight back to Washington, D. C.

Papua New Guinea

My trip to Papua New Guinea began with a flight from Washington, DC to Dallas/ Fort Worth, Texas. That was followed by a 16-hour flight to Brisbane, Australia and continued on to Port Moresby, New Guinea. Fortunately the Airways Hotel was nearby. After checking into the room the first thing that I wanted to do was to take a nice shower and try to feel like a human being again. The main part of the hotel was separated from the restaurant and the swimming pool which were located up on a hill behind the hotel. To get there one has to take an elevator from the main part of the hotel to the seventh floor and use the walkway across to reach the pool and the restaurant. To the right in the open space between the main part of the hotel and the hill was an old airplane which gave you the impression that it was coming in for a landing at the nearby airport.

The first night we had an orientation meeting where we met our guide for the tour and the other members who would be traveling together for the next two weeks.

Since the single supplement for this trip was nearly $1,000 I decided that I would opt for a roommate. My travel agent called the tour company to find out if there was another male single traveler who would be willing to share hotel accommodations with me. The company called the next day and told my travel agent that there was indeed another single male traveler who would be willing to share. The main drawback or concern to me in choosing to do this was whether or not the person was a snorer!! Fortunately he didn't. The first morning he made the comment that I was a very silent sleeper. I replied that he was also. I think we were both relieved. Evidently he had had the same concern.

After having breakfast the next day we flew to Mt. Hagan where we would enjoy seeing the annual Mt. Hagan Cultural Show. Fifty different groups dressed in distinctive traditional attire come together to perform their respective dances. Needless to say the camera got a real work out here!

All the various forms of makeup – the use of feathers, shells, mud, and grass offers a plethora of photographic opportunities. One group even had a large snake and another group had a collection of exotic birds. Since this is an annual affair it draws thousands of onlookers.

For our stay in Mt. Hagan we stayed at the Rondon Ridge Lodge situated high in the mountains with fantastic views of the surrounding area. However, early the next morning one could only see a thick layer of fog in the valley below.

We arrived back to the sight of the festival early the next morning in order to witness the makeup process. It was really interesting to see the various groups preparing for the show. We were told how various seeds, plants, and flowers are used in order to maintain several bright colors. One group of the male participants had their entire bodies covered in tan mud while another group was completely covered in a black tar-like substance.

One incident happened which could have been a spoiler for our visit here. One member was focusing to take a photo when an individual came running by, snatched his camera from his hands, and was running away with the camera! Almost instantaneously members of the security began using their walky-talky means of communication to alert those at the various entrances. It seemed that several people who witnessed this event knew the person who did it. Within an hour the camera was retrieved and returned to its rightful owner.

The next morning we flew to Karawari on a small plane that would only accommodate about five people including the pilot. I was lucky in being chosen by the pilot to sit in the front seat alongside him. The view was spectacular. We landed on a grassy runway. The air terminal consisted of a thatched roof supported by four poles. A sign at the terminal, which we found quite amusing, indicated that Gate 1 to the left was for arriving passengers and Gate 2 to the right was for departing passengers.

Several local residents were hanging out there, I think, just to see the foreigners arriving and also to see the plane land. Most of the young kids were wearing no clothes.

The Karawari Lodge supported a large display of artwork similar to our previous hotel. Even the bar stools were held up by carved statues of men displaying their manhood.

We visited the Tangambit Village where we were able to meet some of the local people, see their church, and go into the spirit house. The spirit houses are for men only. At a certain point in their life they go through a ritual into manhood.

We flew to Timbunke where the small plane again landed on a grassy runway, however, with lots of rain the runway was extremely soggy! As we landed we were going into deep ruts caused by the landings of the previous flights. I had to take some photos of this as the plane even had mud all over the wings, etc.

From here we boarded the air-conditioned Sepik Spirit boat which would be our home for the next four days as we visited several other villages along the Sepik River. This river is the third largest river in the world volume-wise.

For our sunset visit to the Kiminibit Village we were entertained by dances performed by the locals in their native costumes again using lots of feathers, shells, and makeup. Several of the men had giant penises attached as part of their costumes.

The Palembe Village differed from the previous ones in that we were able to see the cutting designs on the male bodies of those who had been through the rid of their former life and preparing them for manhood. During this period of time there is to be no contact with a female. Even when the mother prepares food she has to leave it outside to be picked up by one of the elders.

In order to enter the Village of Yenchen we had to walk across a segment of water using small canoes that had been strategically placed one after the other. Keeping ones balance was essential in completing this task!

The highlight of the visit to this village was a crocodile dance performed by men from the village in crocodile costumes. The children sang their national anthem for us.

The Kanganaman Village also performed a dance for us by two gentlemen in extremely tall costumes made possible through the use of stilts. Upon completion of their performance we were allowed to enter their spirit house. Sometimes there will be a carved statue of a woman over the entryway depicting her as she would be during childbirth. This was to show the importance of the woman.

At the Yessimbit Village we saw several young men who were in the Spirit

House awaiting their initiation ceremony the next day. These men performed a dance for us.

The Sangriman Village was another one where we had to enter through a waterway. We were able to see inside the school for the children where they learn English, math, etc. We gave them several items that could be used in the school including pencils, books, maps, flags, etc.

Our last village to visit while on the Sepik River was the Memeri Village, which happened to be the village of our local guide. At this village the school children again sang their national anthem. They were really surprised upon the completion of the song when the members of our group sang it back to them! We had been practicing for a few days in preparation for this.

Now it was time to return to our small plane for yet another adventurous flight. This time we had a runway that ran up the side of a mountain. This was extremely helpful for slowing down the plane upon landing.

The Ambua Lodge was to be our accommodations here for the next couple of days. The rooms were individual cottages with thatched roofs and windows that went almost two-thirds of the way around. This offered a nice view of the surrounding mountains and all the beautiful wild flowers. Since we were at an elevation of nearly 7,000 feet the evenings became quite brisk. To compensate for this each cottage was provide with an electric heating pad for each bed. It seemed somewhat of a frivolity initially. However, the second day we looked at it in an entirely different perspective and were grateful for having it.

During the nature walk here it was raining. It was nice to see the two waterfalls, but by the time we returned to the lodge we were soaked to the core! And, our shoes were completely covered with mud! The lodge is accustomed to this. We were to leave our shoes outside the entrance to the main lodge. They were then cleaned and placed adjacent to the fireplace where they would dry.

Early the next morning several of us opted for a tour to try to see if we could spot one of their 'birds of paradise.' We saw two – the King of Saxony and Stephanie's Astrapia. It was well worth getting up early just to see the King of Saxony fly across the road with its long feathers waving behind.

Our group then visited the Huli Clan, sometimes known as the 'wig men.' Their hair is allowed to grow long and when it is cut it is used to make wigs that they sell.

We were given a talk by one of the ladies from the lodge that explained the life of a woman in this society and what their daily chores consisted of doing. One lady showed us the process of preparing a meal for the family and cleaning the utensils afterward. They also are responsible for maintaining the garden where they grow their own food. Even when a lady is contemplating marriage, one of the things that enter into the process is how many pigs she possesses.

We visited the Spirit Doctor and were shown some of the items he uses in healing the sick. There was a gentleman here for his service during our visit. Later a group of men here also performed a dance for us.

Now it is time to fly back to Port Moresby where we would do a whirlwind tour of the city including the Parliament Building, the United States embassy, the downtown area, and the section of homes built on stilts.

My return flight was designed to give me a couple days in Sydney, Australia before returning. I took advantage of this time to have dinner with a lady that I had met on my trip to Scandinavia and Russia in 2010. The next evening I had dinner with a couple that I had met on a trip to Central America in 2009.

Bangladesh/Bhutan/Sikkim/India

In the fall of 2011 I flew through Mumbai, India where I spent one night and the hotel had a feature that I had never encountered previously. There was a glass wall between the bedroom and the bathroom! I was always under the impression that a bathroom should provide a degree of privacy! Evidently not here!

I flew Jet Airways from Mumbai to Dhaka, Bangladesh. The monsoon season had passed and there wasn't a great deal of rain. However, from the airport to the Pan Pacific Sonargaon Hotel we did have a little downpour. My first inclination was whether or not this was an omen of things to come. Fortunately, it wasn't. We hardly had any rain after that.

The traffic there can be horrendous with many automobiles, several extremely old buses, small taxis, and lot of carts being propelled by people and animals. At one point we were sitting in traffic and I noticed the gentleman in the automobile adjacent to our vehicle was reading the newspaper. I saw many buses that were traveling at a slow rate of speed allowing people to jump onto the bus, climb the ladder at the back, and sit on top. That way it was probably a free ride. Sometimes there would be a bus with not only people on top, but people with animals.

While touring the city it became obvious that their electrical wiring was not performed by skillful electrical engineers. I took several photos of poles where the wires were dangling down while not being attached to anything. Hopefully the children won't get hold of a live one while playing.

My tour in Bangladesh was set up through Bestway Tours and since there were no other people signed up for this particular tour I was doing it as 'a group of one.' I had a local English speaking guide and a driver.

As part of the city tour I visited the Shahid Manar monument. This monument was built to commemorate the uprising there in 1952 to protest the fact that the government wanted them to change their language. Of course they wanted to maintain their native language. Many people lost their lives in this uprising.

My next visit was the Tomb of Bibi Pari. In this large garden-like setting there was also an old bath house and another building that is now being used as a museum. The square reminded me a little of the huge square in Isfahan, Iran.

The National Memorial for Martyrs of the Liberation was quite an impressive monument and I was happy that I was able to see it.

United Airways flew me from Dhaka to Jessore where I met another guide and driver. They would be with me for the duration of the trip. Our first stop was to visit the Bagerhat Museum where items were displayed to assist you in understanding their way of life through the years.

Nearby this museum was the 60-dome mosque which was built in the 15th century by Khan Jahan Ali. His tomb was in a nearby area along with an old school and a graveyard with several prominent people entombed there.

The weather was very hot and extremely humid. Therefore, it was easy to become dehydrated. To compensate for this, we would treat ourselves to a drink whereby a gentleman would use a machete to cut off the top of a coconut allowing us to drink the fresh juice.

Once outside the big city of Dhaka many of the roads we used to travel from one sightseeing spot to another were not paved. They were dirt roads. Because of this there was a tremendous amount of dust and many of the plants alongside the road would have so much dust on them they all looked the same shade of gray.

The Sundarban Mangrove is one of the largest in the world. It covers almost 300,000 acres and drains into the Bay of Bengal. We drove to a departure point where we boarded a small boat which took us to a larger boat on the other side of the river. Food for lunch was taken since we did not return until later in the afternoon.

We had an escort to take us through part of the mangrove. He was well equipped with a rifle just in case we encountered a problem. Fortunately we didn't have to use it.

There was a navy ship anchored in an area near where we were touring. Several sailors from the ship were seen fishing at one point during our visit. We asked later where they were from and several of them had actually been to the United States.

Just before we were getting ready to leave the area in our boat we discovered that the sailors were having a problem with their small boat. We gave them a ride back to their large ship so that others could assist them in solving their current dilemma.

There was a small zoo adjoining this area and the compound had a display of several crocodiles, deer, monkeys, etc.

Now it was time to hit the road again in order to arrive at our hotel in Khulna before dark. Driving along these roads one sees how the locals live. I remember seeing a large sawmill where wood was being processed into lumber which could be used for home construction, furniture, etc.

There were many towers alongside the road and I was told that these are used in the process of making bricks.

My next hotel was the Castle Salam Hotel in Khulna. My guide and driver would stay at another location which would probably be more economical for the tour company. The first night I was to be ready to be picked up at 7 p.m. in order to go to dinner. I entered the van and we began on our way to the restaurant. I didn't know exactly how far away it was going to be. Was I surprised when we merely drove across the street to another hotel where I was to have dinner. I still have never been able to determine why it was necessary to drive! I was told that the restaurant in this hotel was much better than the one in my hotel. My guide made sure that I conquered the ordering process and then went over and sat in another section of the restaurant where he visited with the owners.

One of the things I remember about my stay at this particular hotel was that the electricity would go off randomly for a few minutes and then come back on again. Strangely enough, the second night I had dinner at my hotel and actually I liked it better than the one we had gone to across the street the night before.

During our drive on one of the dirt roads the next day we encountered a large truck where the driver had tried to turn around and had become stuck in a ditch. We had to wait for several minutes while people pushed it out of the ditch. Many of the men in Bangladesh wear a large piece of cloth wrapped around their waist called a lungi. It is also common for some of the men to use henna in their hair and/or beard which causes it to be a bright reddish orange color.

One of the highlights of this area was our visit to the grass-covered religious site called Gokul Medh. It contained many cells that were used by monks. However, the site that overshadows this place was the Buddist Vihara at Paharpor. This was at one time the largest monastery in the Himalayas. The ornamental bricks and terra cotta plaques used in its construction were beautifully and intricately carved.

During our visit here my guide met a person with whom he had attended college and had not seen in a long time. He was now the governor of his village. Another gentleman with him was one of the youngest magistrates that the country had ever elected. My guide and I were invited to the governor's house for a meal in the afternoon. Even though they ate with their fingers they were cordial in asking if I would be more comfortable eating with a fork. I condescended and ate with a fork. The food was delicious and consisted of chicken and rice with fruit to follow.

Our last visit in this area before driving to Bogra was to the Kusumba Mosque which was built in the 16th century alongside the Atrai River. This mosque contained similar intricately-carved bricks in its construction as we had seen in some of the other places.

The Hotel Naz Garden in Bogra was a delight! Not only were the rooms extremely well-decorated, the exterior of the hotel was beautifully landscaped. Even the entryway of the hotel was impressive. Thus, many photos were taken of the surrounding gardens.

One of the most interesting places visited in this area was the Tangail Village. This is a weaver's village and there were many workshops to visit in order to witness the weaving of saris, lungis, and linens. Gentlemen of the village learn this trade at an early age and utilize that knowledge in supporting their life and family.

My guide took me to a school in this village where I was able to meet the principal. He showed me some of the classrooms. Since my profession was that of a teacher, it is always nice to be able to visit schools and classrooms in foreign countries and not only make comparisons but distinguish differences.

This visit coincided with their lunch break. The students look forward to this as they do in any school. Many of the students go home for lunch and then return for the afternoon session.

The principal gave me some lunch while we talked about the school. Several of the teachers were over in a corner having their lunch.

The Atia Mosque built in 1609 was my last visit before returning to Dhaka where I spent one more night at the same hotel as when I arrived. The next morning I was taken to the airport for my departure to Bhutan where I would meet a friend for our visit there.

Bhutan

The window seat of my flight from Dhaka to Paro, Bhutan afforded me the opportunity to witness the beautiful mountain ranges as we flew over. The airport in Paro was typical Bhutanese architecture with carved wooden shutters, etc. The architecture of the fairly new Hotel Tenzinling Resort was the same and offered nice views of the mountains in the background. The somewhat small city of Paro is located in a valley.

Just about two weeks prior to my departure there was a sizable earthquake that was centered in Sikkim, a place that was interestingly enough on the itinerary. The friend that I was to be traveling with and I were concerned about whether or not the trip would be canceled. My travel agent called the representative of the company and we were assured that all the roads where we would be traveling were open.

Bhutan is known for its monasteries and the Kyichu Lhakhang was the first one that I visited. It is one of the oldest. There was a section of this monastery that was damaged by the earthquake.

One of the most recognizable venues in Paro is the giant Fortress which is now used as a school for the monks. My tour of the Fortress allowed me to view the magnificent artwork inside.

There was a museum just up the hill from the Fortress. However, it was closed because of damage suffered from the recent earthquake.

Just outside the city of Paro I visited the Drukgyel Dzong Fortress which was built in the 16th century. Surrounding the area of this Fortress were hundreds of varying colors of prayer flags. It is possible at one point on the drive here to see the highest mountain in Bhutan, the Gangkhar. It is the fortieth highest mountain in the world.

Archery is probably the most prominent sport in Bhutan. I was fortunate in being able to go to an area of a sport complex to witness a couple matches. I was surprised to see the kind of bows that were being used – not like the old bow and arrows I was accustomed to seeing. They were metal. The other thing I found fascinating was that when one of the competitors would hit 'the bull's eye,' his teammate would immediately perform a little song and dance routine.

My guide took me to the airport where I would welcome my friend who would be accompanying me for the remainder of the trip—not a 'group of one' any more.

The one tourist site in Bhutan that one cannot think of visiting here without seeing is the Takstang Monastery, also called the Birds Nest. Yes, it is one that is depicted in all the travel brochures for Bhutan and looks as if it were literally hanging on the side of a mountain. However, most tourists don't realize what a strenuous climb it is to even hike to the halfway point. It is possible to do the climb using their donkeys, but that didn't look like it would be very pleasant either. Even though it does require a degree of effort to see it, most people would agree that it is worth it.

The large stadium in Paro was being used by several groups of high school students to rehearse for their participation in the celebration of the marriage of their King, which was to take place a couple of days later. The ceremony was to take place at a palace in the countryside. Afterwards the couple would return to Paro for the celebrations there. It was exciting to be visiting there during this festive time and to see all the large posters around the town with pictures of the bride and groom. The Presidential mansion was decorated for the affair.

Our drive from Paro to Thimpu was another memorable journey. To say the roads were extremely rough would be an understatement. We were told that most of it was a result of the earthquake!

High on a mountaintop overlooking Thimpu was a giant statue of Buddha. The area around the statue was under construction and when finished will have areas for various outdoor activities.

The library contains hundreds and hundreds of old documents. In order to preserve these valuable documents, they are wrapped in cloth and are stored on shelves located behind glass doors. Inside the library was supposedly, according to the Guinness Book of World Records, the world's largest book.

We were taken to a factory where they made stationery and other various paper products. It is really interesting to see the process from the beginning until it becomes a finished product. An adjoining small gift shop allowed one to see all the products and also an opportunity to purchase them.

The visit to the School of Traditional Arts allowed us to view the students as they were busy at work with carving masks, sculpting, weaving, painting, and embroidering. A large store here also exhibited the finished works of the students and those objects were available for purchase.

The takin is considered the national animal of Bhutan. As legend has it – Drukpa Kunley, a Tibetan saint, was asked to perform a miracle. He asked for a goat and a cow. After the goat and the cow were eaten, he asked for the bones and the head of each. He joined the head of the goat and the bones of the cow. Miraculously they came to life, they rose, and began to graze—thus, the takin!

The National Folk Heritage Museum covers a large area and displays what a farm would have looked like many years ago. Outside were storage places for grain, an old water mill, and the gardens where vegetables were grown. The large house was built on three levels. Sometimes the first level would be used to house the animals, especially in the cold months of winter. On the upper levels would be where the family lived and cooked. It was possible to see examples of their clothing, their cooking utensils, and various pieces of furniture.

From Thimpu to Phuentshoing we drove on yet another extremely bumpy road partly caused by the earthquake and rock slides. Here we would spend the night before driving into the Western Bengal part of India the next day.

The first memorable sight on this segment of the journey to Kalimpong was the elaborately colored Coronation Bridge. The bridge was named in honor of the coronation of King George VI. Construction began around 1937 and was completed in 1941. It is painted a bright pink and one end of the bridge has two large lion statues.

We stayed at the Silver Oaks Hotel in Kalimpong. It was a beautiful old hotel with lots of charm throughout the hallways, the restaurant, and the manicured gardens.

Nearby we visited a nursery owned by a prominent family and their main product is the orchid. Not only could one see many orchids, they also exported bulbs to other parts of the world. After our visit here, we visited a cactus nursery where many varieties were shown in large greenhouses.

A large monastery here had several cracks in the walls from the earthquake. Through one of the cracks it was possible to see all the way through to the outside. The monks here had a ceremony and we were able to listen to the beautiful music and chanting, even though it was a bit strange to our ears.

The small roadway entrance to the Norkill Hotel in Gangtok had been damaged by the earthquake. Our van could barely squeeze through on the part that hadn't collapsed. In fact as we were leaving, my friend and I were asked to walk across instead of riding since our bodies would only add more weight to the vehicle. We took photos of the van as it came across. Just to the side was a deep crevice created by the washing away of part of the hillside.

The lobby of this hotel looked as though it could have been a museum. It was filled with period pieces of furniture and exquisitely woven carpets, etc. Even the dining room had a feel of English influence in its architecture.

Here we visited the Enchey Monastery and the Dodrul Chorten Stupa on our city tour. The stupa visit gave us an opportunity to test our skills in turning the many prayer wheels.

The Mayfair Hotel in Darjeeling was like a dream come true. It contained several buildings, meticulously manicured gardens with beautiful flowers, and museum quality statues everywhere! One cupola on the premises was always occupied by an extremely large dog! The dog was usually asleep. We just assumed that it must be owned by one of the owners.

When you are told to be ready to go sightseeing at 3 a.m. you can't help to wonder—why? That was the case the first morning here. We drove and drove to a mountaintop location along with a multitude of other tourists so that we would be there at sunrise and be able to witness seeing the most famous mountain range in the area. From this vantage point it was possible to see the Khang-Chen-Dzod-Nga Mountain range. There are several peaks one of which is the third highest mountain in the world.

From this same viewpoint we were able to see a distant view of Mt. Everest. Even on our itinerary we were forewarned that this adventure might not be possible. If the area were fogged in, it would not be possible to see anything, thus the excursion would be canceled. Lucky for us we had a perfect day. We were told that the group the day before had to cancel.

On our visit to the zoo we were able to see a black bear, a Himalayan goral, a tahr, a yak, a Bengal tiger, several birds, a red panda, and an aquarium full of colorful fish.

There was a large group of school children at the zoo at the same time that we were there. Some of the school children, I think, were as fascinated by the fact that they were actually seeing Americans as they were to see the animals! Therefore, they kept asking us if they could take a picture of us and have a picture of them with us.

We had a ride on the Darjeeling Himalayan Railway, sometimes referred to as the "toy train." The ride proceeded through the area to a turnabout point where you are given a few minutes to get off and take pictures. The train is a narrow gauge train and was built near the end of the 19th century.

From here we drove through the countryside and saw many large tea plantations on our way to Bagdogra where we would get our Jet Airways flight to Kolkata.

We stayed at the Vedic Village Resort in Kolkata. To reach the resort one has to drive what seemed like several miles down a dirt road that was full of large holes caused by the monsoons. It was a lovely resort, but we couldn't figure out why we were staying here as opposed to staying in a place closer to or in the city. Our suite at the hotel included a living room, a bedroom, large bath with two entrances, and a kitchen.

Our first stop in sightseeing was the Jain Temple which was built in 1867. The walls of the temple were elaborately decorated with mirrors, colored stones, and glass mosaics.

We had a stop in a section of town where clay statues and masks are made to be used in parades. We had tea in a large upstairs room near the university. We saw the headquarters of the Tata Corporation, the Victoria Memorial, and the St. Paul's Church.

There had not been any rain during the visit until the afternoon that I was to return to the airport for my flight home. The dirt road mentioned earlier was a big mud hole! We even saw one vehicle that had overturned! Because of this my driver and I had to make a detour. Since we were being directed to a different route and the fact that there were no street signs anywhere, my driver would have to stop at each turn and ask which way to the airport. It was dark at night and pouring down rain and I just knew that I was going to miss my flight! I didn't! I flew from Kolkata to Mumbai (3 hours), from Mumbai to Frankfurt (9 hours), and then to Washington, DC (9 hours).

Festival in Papua New Guinea, 2011

Lake Bled, Slovenia, 2012

Nan Madol, Micronesia, 2012

Stone Money, Palau, 2012

Lake Geneva, Switzerland, 2013

Tenerife, Canary Islands, 2013

The Matterhorn, Switzerland, 2013

The Matterhorn, Switzerland, 2013

Oslo, Norway, 2014

The Faroe Islands, 2014

Tulip Fields, The Netherlands, 2014

Parliament House, Berlin, 2015

Rila Monastery, Bulgaria, 2015

Savica Waterfall, Slovenia, 2015

Stanley, The Falkland Islands, 2015

2012

Ethiopia, Rwanda, Uganda Caribbean Cruise, Micronesia, and the Balkans

My friend from New York and I started this excursion by flying to London and spending a few days before flying to Ethiopia. While there we did a lot of walking to see the tourist sights. In addition to the usual sights we found time to participate in a "Jack the Ripper" night tour from the Tower of London.

We took the train to the north side of London where we were able to have lunch with a lady that I had met on the Queen Elizabeth 2 cruise around the world in 2005. It is good that several people from that cruise and I still keep in touch.

The time came to make our way to the airport for our departure to Addis Ababa where we would join others for our tour of Ethiopia. On the way to the airport I was standing and looking at the newspaper that a gentleman sitting next to me was reading. On one page was an article which really became important for some reason. The title of the article was – "Two Tourists Killed in Ethiopia!" When the gentleman finished reading the newspaper and was going to dispose of it, I asked if I could have it. Once he gave it to me I proceeded to open it to the article which I quickly showed to my friend. Our first thought was why are we going?

We had a small group who had not only come to Ethiopia to see the country,

but also to be there for the Timket festival, which is one of the largest celebrations during the year.

The Ethiopian Orthodox Church celebrates the Epiphany of Christ baptism in the Jordan River. The festival is celebrated all over the country, however, the largest is in the capital, Addis Ababa.

The festival gets underway with a large celebration at a church. At the end of the ceremony here the Ark of the Covenant is carried from the church through the streets to a large exhibition area.

Participants walk on a red carpet for the parade. Since the carpet isn't long enough to cover the entire route, volunteers run to the back and roll up the carpet at the end and carry it hurriedly to the front. One has to constantly be alert to the fact that at any minute another group might be approaching from the rear while carrying another roll of carpet to the front of the parade route.

The parade consists of many different groups in brightly-colored costumes. Some of the groups are playing stringed instruments while others play drums. This celebration continues until late in the night.

The festival the next day begins very early. Clergy from other countries visit to be a part of the celebration. Behind the main stage for the speeches is a large pool of water which has been blessed. Adjacent to the pool is a large statue depicting the baptism of Christ in the Jordan River by John the Baptist.

A fence separates large crowds of people from the pool. Volunteers take jugs of the holy water from the pool and offer it to those on the other side of the fence who would like to be sprinkled with it.

These festivities are carried live on the local television stations. My friend and I were chosen to be interviewed. We were asked where we were from and what our impressions of the festival were. Who knew that we would actually be on Ethiopian television during our visit?

Our group tour in Addis Ababa took us to the National Museum of Ethiopia. The highlight of the museum is to see the remains of "Lucy" which is an exhibit of bones that are more than three million years old. The Haile Salassie memorabilia displayed in the museum included thrones, robes, crowns, etc.

It seems to be a common practice in several restaurants where our group would be having lunch or dinner that a lady would be in view making the tea. She had to keep the coals underneath the pot going at all times.

We departed Addis Ababa and flew to Bahir Dar. The airport terminal there was under construction. Therefore, we had to pick up our luggage outside the terminal.

Our accommodations in Bahir Dar were at a lodge where each person had their own quaint little house with a front porch. In this large compound there were many species of birds. There were also monkeys. It seems that one of the members of our group had kept a sandwich from breakfast. It was lying on a table inside her front door. While she was sitting on her porch with the door open, a monkey darted in, took the sandwich and ran.

We were to leave the next morning after breakfast for a tour. The time came for us to leave and our guide had not arrived. We kept waiting to find out that since there was such a large crowd celebrating in the area that our small bus wasn't able to pass through. So, we had to walk quite a distance from the hotel to get to the area where our bus had to stop. The rural area that we were walking through was interesting to observe how the local people lived. Their houses were very basic with thatched roofs. However, they seemed to be self-sufficient in that there were cows, chickens, pigs, etc. living in the proximity of their dwellings. Many kinds of vegetables were being grown in their gardens.

We took a boat ride on Lake Tana in order to reach the island monasteries. We visited the Vra Kidane Meret and the Betra Mariam monasteries. Both had extensive paintings of vibrant colors depicting various religious events. We were able to see the area where the monks lived. I found it interesting that the weather vanes on the top of the domes of the monasteries consisted of a ring-like exhibit of several ostrich eggs.

At the end of our return boat ride we spent some time meandering in a nice area adjacent to the lake where local residents come to relax, spend their day off, and play games. That particular day there was a ball game being played. There was a large fence surrounding the stadium. Those who could not afford to pay the admission were standing on the outside peering through holes without paying.

Many of the residents here, especially those in the cities, depend on small tuk-tuk like taxis for getting around. There are many stalls along the streets and the roads where people sell their wares especially fruits and vegetables.

As we began our sightseeing the next day we were fortunate in that it was the time of the morning when the ladies would be preparing bread for the day. Our guide stopped and asked a lady if we could watch. She agreed. It was fascinating to see a large circular pan placed over the coals to be used for the process. She would pour a quantity of liquid, stir it into a large circle, and wait for that side to finish. It would then be turned and when it became done it would be removed and another would be started. The children of the family were anxiously awaiting the finished product.

The children were also fascinated by the members of our group and enjoyed having their pictures taken.

In order to visit the Blue Nile Falls, we had to get off the bus and take a small boat ride to an area next to the falls. We were told that there were two reasons that the magnitude and force of the falls were not as great as it was previously because a dam had been built upstream and because of the lack of rain. However, it is still exciting to view because of the context of it actually the actual beginning of the longest river in the world.

Before returning to the hotel we drove to the Old Palace grounds. It was not possible to go in, however it was nice to see. The view from the palace grounds was spectacular with the river below. One could see large hippos in the river.

The next day we left early for our drive to Lalibella. On the drive there it was obvious that not many people own their own car. We would see many people walking along the road on their way to the markets. There would be small towns with huge outdoor markets. Some of the sections of the road would not be paved and the dust was almost unbearable.

The rock-hewn churches in Lalibella are known all over the world. Most of them are quite large and it is hard to believe that they were able to complete this magnificent feat. They were built in the 12th century and it is thought that Lalibella had tried to create a 'new Jerusalem' since Jerusalem had been taken over by the Muslims. Bete Medame Alem is the largest, Bete Maryam is the oldest and Bete Golgatha contains artwork and the tomb of Lalibella. Bete George is the most famous and is built in the shape of a cross. At one time it was considered the 8th wonder of the world.

On the drive the next day to visit the Cave Church we had a flat tire. While our driver and guide changed the tire, we had a moment to see the topography of the area. Once the tire was fixed, we were on our way again.

We visited the Cave Church and were able to observe a service there. Outside the cave at the conclusion of the service inside, several people were there in brightly-colored attire carrying large elaborately decorated umbrellas and singing.

Our guide stopped at a local school on our return. Being a retired school teacher, I was interested in seeing the inside. On one wall was the flag of their country and on another was a large chalk board. The desks were very basic. The mission of the school was – "enrich all the children in the Kebele with knowledge, skill and attitude." The vision of the school was – "creating to see that students are able to solve social, political, and economic problems of the Kebele society." Outside the entry door was a large sign with one word for each letter of the word TEACHER – T for Technical, E for Eager, A for Accountable, C for Counselor, H for Honest, E for Ethical, and R for Responsible.

We flew from Lalibella to Axum. We stayed at the Yeha Hotel. One of the first sights we saw here was a small lake that was the bath of the Queen of Sheba. Later we saw the ruins of her palace.

Axum is considered the holiest city in Ethiopia. The Ark of the Covenant is housed there. There is an old Mt. Mary of Zion Church and a new one. Inside the new church one can see 17th century manuscripts showing their vibrant drawings. Outside is a large bell tower.

The giant obelisks in Axum are of noted importance. These obelisks were carved and erected around the 4th century and are located in an area not far from the above mentioned church complex. One obelisk fell and is broken in several pieces. It is believed to be approximately 33 meters in height and weighed nearly 5 tons. It has never been established exactly as to why they were built and how they were erected. However, some believe that they were markers for underground burial chambers. In fact, legend has it that the large broken one was the tomb of the Queen of Sheba.

Our next stop on this Ethiopian tour was the city of Gondar. The highlight of this stop was the Palace of Fasilades, the Yohannes Library, and Iyasu's Castle.

We visited several other places of importance in this city. The Bath House of Fasilades was quite elaborate and was erected so that it stands in a surrounding pool of water. The Debre Berhan Selassie Church was built in the 17th century and has a beautiful painted ceiling of angels. There are separate entrances for men and women. We also saw the ruins of Queen Mantowab's Palace.

An early stop the next day allowed us to visit the Jewish village. There we were able to see their way of life, the kind of houses they inhabited, and the way they shopped and prepared their meals. The children were busy trying to sell some of their many craft-type objects and having their picture taken.

Our long drive that day passed many local markets. The roads were very basic and mostly dirt. Since there had been no rain for some time, it was necessary to close the windows of the small bus as we approached oncoming vehicles. We got our exercise for the day by opening and closing the windows.

At the conclusion of our long drive we arrived at the hotel in the Simien Mountains. While we were having our lunch we observed baboons running around outside. This initial observance motivates one toward the camera for a photo moment. However, if we had known that later in the afternoon we would see hundreds and hundreds of them, we would have waited.

The Simien Lodge is the highest lodge in Africa at 10,700 feet in elevation.

Just after dinner the electricity went out. We managed to make our way to bed and tried to pack our bags in the dark. Even breakfast the next morning was in the dark also.

We departed from the hotel that morning after breakfast and had only driven a few minutes when I wanted to take a photo. I reached for my camera in the location where I always kept it and it wasn't there. I told the guide that I must have left my camera in the room. We returned to the hotel and I had to make the difficult trek of climbing the hill again at a high altitude. I looked in the room and the camera was not there. Upon returning to the bus and letting my guide know that it wasn't there the next step was to pull down my luggage from the top of the bus and check it. Voila! There it was in that bag. It must have fallen into that bag during the night while we were trying to repack the bags in the dark. Anyhow, it was good to know that it was there.

We flew back to Addis Ababa where most of our group left that evening for their return home. My friend and I were not leaving until the next evening. We spent the next day driving north of the city to a monastery.

We then flew to Kigali, Rwanda. We were met at the airport by our guide and taken to the hotel. Our first inclination as we drove was how modern the city was and how good the roads were! We weren't in Ethiopia anymore!

On our drive to The Chez Lando Hotel we realized that it was located in a very nice section of the city. Several foreign embassies were located nearby. The hotel was very nice and had several large beautifully landscaped gardens.

We told our guide that we needed to exchange some money into the local currency. He took us to a local shopping center. There we had to go through security before entering. Inside was not only a bank but a large department store that also carried groceries. A lot of the items in the store were very common to us—the same kinds of things we would see back home.

Later that afternoon we were taken to an area where many people had been killed during the genocide. There were bullet holes on the outside walls of the building. There was a monument dedicated to those who died. Inside the building were several posters that told how many people lost their lives and compared that to other genocides through history.

The next morning we were taken to the Kigali Genocide Museum. Pictures and narrations of the genocide of 1994 were shown in several rooms as one walked through. It was a very moving experience. Some 250,000 are buried in mass tombs located outside in the garden setting.

Our next stop was the Gorilla Mountain View Lodge in Puhengeri, Rwanda. Upon checking into the lodge my friend and I were given separate 'houses.' We were not given any reason for this. Even our guide was surprised the next morning when we told him that we had separate rooms. The lodge had made a mistake. Each accommodation was a large stone house. Inside was a large room with a sitting area, a bedroom area, and a fireplace.

Not long after we arrived we were invited to a singing and dancing presentation by a local troupe attired in their native costumes. Later that evening we had our dinner outside with a welcomed large fire blazing since the weather was a little chilly. The food was served buffet style and was quite tasty. While we were at dinner the housekeeper came into the house and built a roaring fire in the fireplace.

The next day we had what was one of the most tiresome, exhausting days that I have ever spent in my years of travel. We hiked up a steep mountain for approximately three hours through high bush. Our guide was ahead with two other gentlemen who would use their machetes to cut down enough of the bush so that we could walk through. One gentleman also carried a rifle just in case we needed it.

The moment that one realizes that they are standing in close proximity to an entire family of large gorillas makes the whole trek worth it. I could not believe how close we were to them. The father of the family, the silverback, weighs about 400 pounds. At one point as we were leaving, one of them even brushed against my leg.

One slight drawback! Just about the time we were approaching the gorillas, my camera went on the blink! Somehow the entire lens was turned and the camera would not function or turn off. Fortunately my friend had just bought a new camcorder which also functioned as a camera. So I took the chip out of my camera and placed it in his extra camera and continued using it to take pictures for the remainder of the trip.

After our excitement of seeing the large family of gorillas it was time to hike three more hours to return to the bottom of the mountain. I must admit that I was thinking about how sore my legs were going to be the next morning. However, I must have been in better shape than I gave myself credit for because I wasn't sore at all.

The next day we drove from Rwanda into Uganda. The scenery along the way was quite enjoyable. There were large tea and banana plantations. I won't ever forget seeing those young boys pushing a bicycle along the road and have three or four large stalks of bananas on the bike.

Going through customs was uneventful as we were in an extremely rural setting and there wasn't any others going through at the same time.

We arrived at the Katara Lodge where we would spend the two nights. Again we had our own separate home, but this time it was a log cabin instead of being constructed of stone. We had a wonderful view overlooking the animal park. One of the beds had wheels on it and could be rolled onto the patio where one could literally sleep under the stars.

The next two days we spent exploring Queen Elizabeth Park. Our game vehicle looked like something you would see in an old movie. It was painted a bright color of green and had a large opening in the roof to make it easy for photography. In this park we saw warthogs, many species of birds, water buffalo, river bucks, elephants, lions, and hundreds of hippos.

While we were having our picnic lunch we were joined by several mongoose who were more than willing to share our food.

The highlight of this visit for me was the boat ride on Lake George in the Kazinga Channel. In that seemingly short period of time we saw hundreds of water buffalo, hippopotamus, grey herons, elephants, monkeys, eagles, egrets, pelicans, and alligators. It was a paradise setting for a photographer!

Early the next morning we departed in hopes of seeing a lion. After having driven a few miles we had a flat tire! Fortunately another vehicle came along about the same time and offered to give my friend and me a lift while our guide equipped our vehicle with another tire. Not long after that we saw two lions. This was definitely another photographic opportunity to say the least!

We later visited a large salt lake where we had a local guide who explained the process of salt mining.

On our drive from the park to our next stop we had yet another flat tire! In a situation such as this there isn't much one can do except to sit and wait. Once it was finished, we made it to the Boma Guest House in Entebbe.

I have visited many countries, however, I had never seen television antennas like the ones we saw here. They were on very long poles and resembled the ones we installed on our homes in the 1950s.

We visited the National Museum in Kampala which is only about 30 kilometers from Entebbe. The museum was quite extensive and included clothing, recreational exhibits, pottery, and musical instruments.

There were many modern buildings in this capital city. The sign on the front of the Parliament Building indicated that Uganda became independent on October 9, 1962.

Religion seems to consume a large segment of their daily lives. There was an old-time tent revival meeting happening as we drove into Kampala. There were Anglican, Catholic, Protestant, and several other denominations represented in this area. Even the religion part is carried over into the naming of business establishments. For example, God Cares Salon, Divine Grace Wholesalers, and the Blessed Furniture Center.

It seems that investors from other countries have a tendency to want to come in and buy property. Hence, there were many large signs in the front of homes stating, "Land Not For Sale."

On the last morning of the trip in Entebbe we walked from our hotel to a nearby park. There we were given a nice tour by a local guide. He explained all the various trees, flowers, and animals that we saw. The tour ended in the edge of Lake Victoria where we were able to capture some photos documenting the occasion. On our way back to the hotel we saw a large military parade.

Another trip comes to an end and now it was time to fly back to Addis Ababa, on to London, and back to the United States.

Caribbean Cruise. Not long after my return from that trip to the three countries in Africa I departed on yet another Caribbean cruise that consisted of four places that I had not previously visited.

The first stop was in Samana, Dominican Republic. There I participated in a ship-sponsored excursion. We drove through the downtown part of Samana and then visited the Whale Museum. The island had received a large amount of rain the evening prior to our visit and our small tour bus had to contend with driving through large pools of water.

Many beautiful and colorful flowers dominated the scenery as we drove to the outdoor museum which depicted the history of the life of the people of this island. The exhibits were well presented and the individual documentary that went along was well written and spoken.

Our next stop was Tortola, which is part of the British Virgin Islands. There really wasn't a lot to see on this island. Most of the people usually come to get away from everything and spend a week lying on the beach. They did, however, have a new airport that we toured.

Our next stop allowed us the opportunity of exploring both St. Martin (French) and St. Maarten (Dutch). We were given time for shopping, which seems to be a part of any ship excursion. In addition to this we saw shipwrecks and an old fort.

On the island of Antigua we toured the entire island and saw large pineapple plantations, old sugar mills, and Nelsons Dockyard.

Dominica was probably one of the lushest of any of the islands that I have visited. There was a large rain forest, waterfalls, banana plantations, and a wide variety of flowers. Near the botanical garden where we saw bamboo and the cannonball tree, there was an old school bus with a tree lying on it! The tree had fallen during a hurricane in 1979 and fortunately, there were no children on the bus at the time.

Since I had visited Barbados on previous trips, I chose to spend the day with a couple people from Canada that I had met on the ship. We had a pleasant visit and I took pictures of things that I probably already have from previous visits including the Parliament Building, the riverside, Independence Square, and several old churches.

On St. Kitts, our last stop, we visited the home of John Gardiner. He was the Attorney General at one time. After several disputes with the government regarding elections and religion, he decided to leave the island. However, he put his property in a trust. We also toured the large fortress on the hill.

Micronesia. In June I spent a few days with my friends in Hawaii on my way to Majuro in the Marshall Islands. The hotel there had individual houses with porches that overlooked the ocean. The first afternoon I was taken on a tour of the island. The island is only about 16 miles long and is shaped somewhat like a boomerang. The international airport is located near the bend. Joe, my guide, pointed out that the highest point on the island in only about 30 feet high. As we were driving along what is the only road there, it was quite obvious that at certain locations one could see the ocean on both sides of the road. Near the end of the island there was a memorial to the Japanese.

Many families bury their relatives in the front yard of the house. This seemingly is to show that the deceased person is not forgotten.

From Majuro I flew to my first stop in Micronesia. What a difference from Marshall Islands. In Majuro everything was so flat and here there are actually big mountains!

My individual home at the Village Resort offered spectacular views from the many windows. There weren't any glass windows—only screen. The bed had a nice net over it.

The highlight of my visit here was the tour to Nan Madal. Ward, my guide, maneuvered the small boat for about an hour in reaching this site. In the entire time that I was there I only saw two other tourists. They were from Russia.

It is somewhat of a puzzle as to how Nan Madal was constructed. Large sticks of basalt-like rock logs were used. There are theories as to where they came from, but it is not certain. The other mystery is somewhat similar to the mystery surrounding the moah statues on Easter Island in that they are not sure how the large logs were manipulated in building the structures.

A city tour prior to leaving Pohnpei included the sports stadium, the university, and some World War II remains. In the distance was what is referred to as Manure Mountain as it is composed of chicken droppings.

My next stop in Micronesia was Chuuk. The road from the airport to the hotel brought back reminisces of my drive to the airport in Kolkata, India. There had been terrific rainstorms and there were large puddles to attempt to drive around. Even during the first night at the Blue Lagoon Hotel, I thought that the roof was definitely going to blow off. Not only was it pouring rain but accompanied with extremely high winds. It seems that this is the norm in Chuuk. Most of the visitors to Chuuk come here for diving. In fact there was a ship located near the hotel and is actually a diver's hotel.

I arrived early in the restaurant for dinner and was seated in a nice table in the corner with a nice view. Not long after another couple came in and were seated at a nearby table. They started a conversation by saying, "Where are you from?" I responded by saying that I live in Washington, DC. It was then that I discovered that they live in a suburb in Virginia just outside Washington. Sometimes it is a small world!

My full day in Chuuk was spent going on a boat ride to a nearby island. There I saw many sunken ships from World War II, a catholic school, and several items left over from World War II including a hospital, a communications center, bunkers, and an old power station.

From Chuuk I flew to Saipan in the Northern Marianas. The extensive gardens of the hotel here were exquisite. There were small lakes, fountains, birds, flowers, and even a chapel. I saw one couple there in their bridal outfits taking photos. They were also getting photos on the nearby beach. My photos of the sunset the first night there were unbelievable.

My tour in Saipan the next day included Red Beach Night where during World War II approximately 1,000 Japanese infantrymen died, 40 tanks were burned, and a total of 3,500 casualties.

The golf course here was well manicured as most golf courses are. However, this one was completely encircled by flame trees that were in full bloom.

My guide and I had lunch in a tall office building with a revolving restaurant on top. It seems that many local politicians patronize this restaurant. In fact, several of them knew my guide.

In the afternoon we drove past a large garden that was dedicated to Haruji Matsue, who was known as the Sugar King. He contributed a lot in using his knowledge from his education in America to instruct natives as to how to improve their production of sugar cane.

We also saw the ruins of an old Japanese jail where supposedly Amelia Earhart was imprisoned. We drove to the top of Mt. Tapochau where it was possible to view almost the entire island. Forbidden island can be seen from here. Legend has it that it was once the bearer of evil spirits. Today it is mostly used as a bird sanctuary.

Included in our afternoon tour was a visit to the Blue Grotto and the Bon Zai Cliffs. One should not visit here without witnessing the suicide cliffs. These cliffs were used by the Japanese to jump to their death rather than be captured and tortured.

I flew from Saipan to Koror in Palau. The Cliffside Hotel commanded a nice view of the waterfront and the bridge that connects this part of the city to the other side. My room was cavernous and included a nice Jacuzzi. In order to use the swimming pool one had to cross the street and walk up a steep hill. However, the view from here was well worth the climb.

It seems that Koror is a stopover for several airlines. For my tour of the island the next day I was joined by two lady stewardesses who were enjoying a two-day layover here. I have never considered it a negative to be traveling alone yet it was nice to have the company for the day of sightseeing.

We first visited a clam farm. Then we visited the local aquarium. This was an excellent exhibit for the various fish of the island.

We drove to the capital in Melekeok. Strangely enough, the capitol building and its environs are built in the middle of nowhere country. We toured the capitol building and saw the flags of the 16 states of Palau.

We visited a traditional man's house similar to the ones I had seen when I was in Papua New Guinea.

Survivor, the reality television show, was taped here during one season. While they were taping, they built a bar for the participants and film workers to use. Now they use it as a restaurant.

The Etpison Museum in Koror had an extensive display of the various kinds of clothing used through the years, glassware, wood carvings, jewelry, and several examples of the stone money.

Now it is off to Yap for my last stop of the trip. This is a small town. From my hotel, the Manta Ray Bay Hotel, I could walk to the Supreme Court building, the Library, the hospital, and an outdoor museum. This island is also one of those where most of the people who come here do so for diving. This hotel not only had a dive shop, but its own brewery. They brewed three kinds of beer – light, medium, and dark.

Here I met some people who had come to dive. Two were from Belgium and one from the Canary Islands. Each day while I was there they would go diving. After I returned from my sightseeing, I would ask them how successful their diving went for the day. They would usually reply that they were a little disappointed as they had not seen very much that day. I showed them several photos of manta rays on my digital camera that I had taken at the aquarium in Koror. They agreed that I had better pictures from the aquarium than they had been able to take while diving.

The three of us were taken on a sightseeing tour of the island. One of the first sights was the remains of a plane crash that killed Joseph Edward Cox. We also saw the remains of a Continental Airlines plane that had crashed several years prior. We saw mangroves and a man's meeting house. However, one cannot visit this island without seeing all the large stone 'coins.' They are of different sizes shaped like a donut—round with a hole in the middle.

The Balkan Countries. I had been to Belgrade and Dubrovnik in 1976 on my trip to all the communist countries. It was then Yugoslavia. Now that Yugoslavia had been broken up into several other countries, it was time to return.

I must admit that being back in Belgrade I did not recognize a lot since it had been 36 years since my previous visit. I arrived a day or two ahead of our group departure and was able to walk all around the city and try to see if I could find something with which to associate my last visit.

The old railway station had not changed that much. For the first night I stayed at a hotel across from the station. It was interesting to note that old trolley-like vehicles operating alongside the new ones.

There were several buildings in ruins with many bullet holes as a reminder of the recent wars.

The next day I met my guide for the trip and the other travel mates. There were only four of us which made it very nice not only for sightseeing, but being able to ask many questions without feeling that you were holding up the group.

Our walking city tour that first morning allowed us to see the Residence of the Mayor, the Serbian Museum, and the opera house. We then boarded our small van and visited the Princess Ljubica's house, the Sava Cathedral, an orthodox church, and the old fortress.

Other than the sights themselves, there were some other memorable moments. One was a little boy sitting outside the Sava Cathedral with his accordion. Another was the children at play with their parents in a park adjacent to the cathedral. And, at the orthodox cathedral there was literally a line of couples waiting to get married.

We traveled across the river to the newer side of town. There were several boats docked alongside the river. We were told that these boats are actually night clubs and the younger crowd seems to migrate to this area in the evening. From this vantage point one has a really nice view across the way of the old city.

The fortress consists of a large park where families to for a Sunday outing. There was also a Military Museum inside the fortress along with a nicely sculptured garden dedicated to the French people.

Our group departed Belgrade the next morning and drove through the countryside for several hours. Our goal was to arrive at the Sarganska Osmia Railway in time for its 2 p.m. departure. Not only did we leave about a half an hour late we also were confronted with road construction along the way. Fortunately we made it just in time to get the train. If we had been ten minutes later, we would have just waved goodbye to those who made it on time.

The Sarganska Osmia Railway is a narrow gauge railway that crosses several bridges and goes through several tunnels on its picturesque journey through the mountainous terrain. It was initially built to connect Belgrade to other cities. Nowadays it is just an extremely profitable tourist attraction.

We entered the Republic of Srpska and drove to the bridge over the Drina River in Visegard. The bridge was built in the 16th century and was designed by the architect Sinan. The span is quite pleasing to the eye with its many large arch supports. Ivo Andric wrote a book about the bridge and he won a Pulitzer Prize for Literature in 1961.

We spent the night at the Staro Sele Hotel on Mt. Zlatibor in the Village of Sirogojno. The accommodations were quite rustic and each person had their own log cabin. Since we arrived quite late our dinner meal was wrapped in foil and placed in our kitchen. The weather was somewhat chilly, to say the least. The heater in my room didn't work. My guide was concerned, but I assured him that I would be fine without it. It actually brought back memories of my childhood in growing up in a house without central heat. To keep warm during the night one just threw on another quilt.

Our walking tour of the village the next morning included the local church, a small museum depicting life as it once was, and a shopping street here local ladies were selling their hand made woolen items.

During this part of the trip we visited several monasteries including the Studenica Monastery, the Sopocani Monastery, and the Decani Monastery.

In Pristina, the capital of Kosovo, we saw a large cathedral, several government buildings, a statue of Bill Clinton, a replica of the Statue of Liberty, and the business and shopping districts.

In Skopje, Macedonia we toured the Kale Fortress, the Mustafa Pasha Mosque, and the Church of the Holy Saviour. This church was particular interesting in that it was built below the ground level. It is dedicated to Goce Delcev, a revolutionary hero. Surprisingly enough it was quite elaborate. The wooden iconostasis was ornately carved and depicted stories of the Bible and several saints.

Crossing the stone bridge is the Holocaust Museum, a theater, an art school, and a museum of technology. Closer to the town center is a statue of Justinian I and of Alexander the Great.

The drive to Ohrid the following morning offered a memorable happening. Our guide had chosen a spot to stop for a quick lunch. In fact it was the only place we saw to stop. They weren't ready for us. We had to succomb to eating warm polenta and their local yogurt!

Ohrid is a beautiful city and our hotel was situated up the hill with a spectacular view of the lake and the surrounding area. There was a dance performance by the local high school students in the downtown waterfront park. This park had a statue of Cyril and Methode, the founders of the Cyrillic alphabet.

The tour of Ohrid included the Fortress, the Saint Clement Cathedral, and the Saint Sophia Church.

We began the next day by being introduced to our new guide that we would be having for Albania. From Ohrid our first visit was to the Monastery of Saint Naum. We then continued our drive toward Berat, Albania. As we approached Berat we visited the old castle situated high upon a hill overlooking the city.

After checking into our centrally-located hotel we had the remainder of the day free. I walked around the city and took my photos of several churches and mosques, the old harem, the old part of town, and the bridge over the Osum River. Our group had a surprise the next morning. A young boy introduced himself and explained that his grandfather had suffered a major heart attack during the night and our guide (this boy's father) had to return to Tirana to take care of the situation. As it turns out, the son was a university student and had conducted tours previously. So that situation offered him the opportunity to improve his tourism skills.

In Durres, which is a seaside town in Albania, we visited the old coliseum. I had visited this coliseum on my first visit to Albania in 2008. From here we drove to Tirana, the capital of Albania.

As though I had not been in Tirana before, I spent most of the remainder of the day walking around town and taking lots of pictures which I was almost sure that they would probably look just like the ones I had taken four years ago.

The next morning we drove to Kruja, which is located in the mountains with beautiful views. There we visited the Skanderbert Museum and the Ethnological Museum.

We spent the next evening in Budva, Montenegro. The hotel there was extremely modern. My room had a patio with a nice view of the castle and the beach. The patio was large enough to accommodate at least one hundred people!

Adjacent to the bed was a shower. Strangely enough the large shower area had a window in the corner that looked out onto the bedroom. (Yes, I thought this was a little strange!) The only time I had ever encountered this was the hotel in India, however, that one had the entire wall in glass. This one at least offered a little opportunity for some modesty.

Within walking distance of the hotel was a shopping area, several outdoor restaurants, the beach, the citadel, and several churches.

On our mountainous drive to Kotor we stopped in the small town of Centinje where we walked down the main street and were able to admire the many beautiful old homes that looked as though they had just been freshly painted. We visited the Palace of King Kokola II and the Monastery of St. Peter.

We were able to stop in several places before arriving in Kotor where we had perfect places to take pictures of the city and its surrounding waterfront. In our approach we could see several large yachts moored in the harbor. This had an uncanny resemblance to Monaco and its yachts of the rich and famous. There was also a large cruise ship in port.

Our hotel in Kotor was located in the old section of the city with extremely narrow streets. Inside the old city were several churches including St. Tryphon's Church (1166), the Church of St. Luke (1195), and the much newer St. Nicholas Church (1902).

We stopped in Trebinje the next day of our drive to Mostar. There we saw the World War II memorial and the large cathedral. Inside the cathedral the floors were elaborately tiled using various colored stones.

The major attraction in Mostar is the bridge over the Neretva River. The old bridge was built in the 16th century. In order to offer the tourists an extra opportunity to take pictures local divers periodically dive from the bridge into the river.

Our tour in Sarejevo took us to the building just down the street from our hotel where Francis Ferdinand and his wife were killed in 1914.

The city planners in Sarejevo had chosen a location for a new city hall—one that would be the first thing one would see upon entering the city. The only problem was that there was a family home located in the same place. The house was moved to a new location several blocks away.

One item that I remember in going through the bazaar in Sarejevo was that there were writing pens for sale that had been made out of old bullets from the war.

The Gazi Husrev-Beg Mosque in Sarejevo was built in the 16th century and is one of the most religious structures in the country. People are not called to prayer by a loud speaker. The mosque actually used a real person to do this chore.

In Sarejevo we also toured the madrassa (school), an old bath house, a Jewish Museum, and the Mother of God Serbian Orthodox Church.

At the end of our sightseeing here we had two of our group members who had previously planned to end their trip at this point. Therefore, the next few days our group would consist of only two people.

The next leg of the trip would probably bring back some memories. I had visited Dubrovnik in 1976 and today I was to return some 36 years later. Of course the old walled city hasn't changed very much since it is a UNESCO world heritage location. However, there was a chart of the walled city with dots showing where there had been bullet marks from the recent war.

The usual sights in the city included St. Ignatius of Loyola Church (1725) and St. Vlaho Church (1715). Most tourists who come here, especially for the first time take the walk around the city atop the wall. Since I had done this before, I decided I didn't need to do it again this time.

The main street had several entertainers—the usual ones who pose as a statue, various musicians, and one gentleman with a nice collection of colorful birds. He would place the birds on a tourists head, shoulders, etc. while their friends took photos of them.

In the afternoon I was scouting out a restaurant where I would have my birthday dinner. In checking out the menu at one particular restaurant, I told the maitre'd that I wasn't interested in lunch, but was trying to select a restaurant for my birthday dinner later. I told him that I had visited here 36 years ago to which he made the comment, "This restaurant wasn't here then."

I returned to my hotel to get a little rest before returning for dinner. To my

surprise upon entering my room there was a bottle of wine, wine glasses, a vase of white roses, and a letter from the management wishing me a happy birthday. I could only surmise that they had obtained that information from my passport which was left at reception upon checking into the hotel.

I did return to the aforementioned restaurant and the maitre'd remembered me by welcoming me with a warm handshake and by saying, "Happy Birthday." It turned out to be a nice birthday dinner.

The next day we continued our journey by driving to Split. The scenery on the drive up the Adriatic coast is quite pleasing to the eye. The highlight of the visit to Split was touring the Palace of Diocletian. The architecture is a mixture of Egyptian and Roman.

While we were going through the cathedral and the bell tower we were entertained by a quartet of singers. The cellar is gigantic and is now used as a museum. In the cellar one is able to get a better view of the support system used for the palace.

The one thing that surprised me was that there were still apartments in the palace occupied by the local residents.

Republic Square in Split reminded me a little of St. Mark's Square in Venice. There are several restaurants located in the square.

Our drive from here including stops in Trogir, Sibenek, and Zadar. Trogir is a medieval town and we walked through the city gate to observe the cathedral and loggia. In Sibenek we visited the Cathedral of St. James. Other than the St. Donatas Church in Zadar, I witnessed something that I had never seen before. Along the waterfront there were holes in the sidewalk. These holes were used as a giant pipe organ. The force of the waves produced the sounds.

We spent the night in a hotel adjacent to Plitvice National Park. The next morning we took a little train to one of the entrances of the park. From that point one follows the trails back to the starting point. We walked for almost five hours that day and saw many, many, lakes and waterfalls. The camera really got a workout that day!

From this point of the trip my only other travel companion left the tour and departed for her home. Therefore, I was again a 'group of one.'

In Zagreb I toured the cathedral, the old city wall, a walking street with many restaurants, and a local theater. I returned to the walking street in the evening where I would have a delicious dinner.

The next day my guide and I drove to Slovenia. On the way we stopped at the Lipica Stud Farm. The farm started in 1580 by Austrian Archduke Charles, son of Ferdinand I. The horses were trained here and then used in the Lippizaner shows in the Spanish Riding School in Austria. In walking through the stalls, the training areas, etc. it was obvious that the horses are pampered in every way.

The Postojna Cave System is a must-see 2,000 years old cavern and stretches for some 27 kilometers. Tourists are taken into the caverns on a small train. At a certain point you are requested to depart the train and walk. The guide then points out several highlights of interest along the way and ends in a large reception hall and gift shop (naturally). At that point you re-board the train which takes you back to the main entrance.

Ljubljana was a beautiful town to visit and I wish that I had had more time to spend there. The hotel was strategically located in the center of the city making it easy to walk around and take photos. I found it interesting in the literature of the hotel that showed the photos of the visit of Queen Elizabeth. When I saw this I knew that this must be 'the place' to stay in this city.

The main square of the city sits amongst three rivers thus the Three Rivers Bridge. There is a statue in the square of Preseren who was a well-known poet. Also in the square were the city hall, a large department store, the Franciscan Church of the Annunciation, and several restaurants.

Another large square within walking distance was the university, the Philharmonic Hall, more churches, and several government buildings.

Bled was my last stop and in some ways the most memorable. After having visited this small town, I couldn't fathom anyone visiting this area without coming here. I really enjoyed walking around the lake while seeing tourists riding in horse-drawn carriages. It seems that every restaurant here sells their favorite dessert, which is called "cream cake." Yes—I couldn't resist!

My guide and I walked to the top of the hill adjoining the lake to visit the castle. There is a small museum now located in the castle and the exhibits depict the way of life for this region through the years. The views from here were spectacular and well worth the hike to get there.

Included in my tour was a visit to the only island in Slovenia. Yes, it is located in the middle of Lake Bled. One takes a small boat to get to the island and the boat is powered by a person and not a motor.

The main attraction on the island is the Church of Assumption of Mary. The church contains many large paintings depicting stories of the Bible. Also inside you are able to have your picture taken while pulling the cords and ringing the bells of the church. While doing this you are supposed to make a wish and if you are able to make the bells ring your wish will come true.

On the return boat ride to the shore I couldn't resist in asking the rower if he ever dreamed of rowing at night in his sleep. He chuckled and responded that he had.

Something happened as I was waiting for my flight home that had never happened before and hopefully will never happen again. While I was waiting at the airport I was editing my photos. I was going to delete one. I chose the button to delete "one item". Then just as I was getting ready to push the button that asks you if you are sure, the other button in a split second changed to "delete all items." Needless to say it was an instantaneous hopeless feeling as you are sitting there watching your camera delete approximately 700 pictures.

Fortunately upon my return home I took the chip from the camera to a reputable camera shop. They were able to retrieve almost all of them. I learned my lesson. Now instead of editing as much as before I wait until the pictures are on the computer and do it then.

2013

Another Caribbean Cruise
Switzerland
Lampedusa, Sardinia, and Corsica
Azores, Madeira, Canary Islands

In 2013 I found another Caribbean cruise that had stops in places I had not previously visited—St. Barts, St. Lucia, St. Vincent, and Bonaire. On some cruises I choose to participate in one of the ship's excursions and on others, I prefer to just do things on my own or with other fellow travelers that I have met on the cruise. It depends on several factors – whether I have visited there previously, if the ship docks at a convenient location to a town, or the variety of things offered to do. For example, being of fair skin and not supposed to be in the sun, there are several options are usually eliminated automatically. Even though several things are not taken into consideration, I still enjoy being in a climate where the weather is nice and warm.

Several of the islands in the Caribbean give one the feeling that they have been there before as the saying goes—after a while, they all seem to be alike. An island really needs something that stands out to make it memorable. Some have volcanoes, some have mountains, some are flat, some are arid, and some are lush with rain forests and waterfalls.

St. Barts has the distinction of being the island for the upper crust or the rich and famous. Because of this distinction, there are several high-end places to stay and many French restaurants.

Our next port of call on this cruise was the island of St. Lucia. Here I decided to participate in one of the excursions planned by the ships company. The first stop on our tour was the St Marks house, which was owned by a wealthy merchant and his wife. It was a beautiful old house with a magnificent view of the island. Several items in the house bring back fond memories of the tour – the piano in the living room, the old globe bar, the mirror and crystal swans on the dining room table, and the many photos.

We visited a batik shop and were given a demonstration on the processes used in obtaining items which reflected island living using many vibrant colors.

In a gift shop we saw banana ketchup, banana barbeque sauce, mango pepper sauce, and hot pepper sauce. There were soaps using pineapple, cocoa, ginger, all spice, aloe vera, and papaya.

In driving around the island one begins to realize that at almost any place one has a view of the Piton Mountains. There are two – the Gran Piton and the Petit Piton.

The village of Marigot was most interesting with its small homes that were painted in various pastel colors and many of the porches and windows had a very lacy gingerbread-like trim.

At the Church of the Nativity of the Blessed Virgin Mary I took several pictures of the children who were either in day care or were actually in regular school classes sponsored by the church.

Barbados was one of the stops on the cruise where I chose to join a couple from Canada that I had met on the cruise to enjoy sightseeing together since they had also been here several times before.

I found St. Vincent to be one of my favorites! The visit to Fort Charlotte was most interesting. The fort was built in 1806 by the English in order to keep out any invasion of the French. The view from this fort was stunning. Inside one section of the fort is a museum which consists of several paintings depicting the history surrounding the fort and of slavery during this time. Our guide explained to us how the Black Caribs were taken to Balliceaux and to Bequia. In 1797 they were put on British men-of-war ships and exiled to Roatan Island in the Bay of Honduras. Their descendants may now be found in many Central American countries.

Looking down from the fort one could see a ship that was used in the recent movie ***Pirates of the Caribbean***. Looking west one could see an island that supposedly Donald Trump owns.

The botanical gardens were our next stop on the tour. Here we saw a large beautifully landscaped area that included banyan trees, cannonball trees, and breadfruit trees. There were many flowering plants and an enclosed area with large parrots.

In our drive back to the ship we saw many large homes which are owned by expats to the island, the airport, and a large sports stadium. In order to make our drive back more exciting, our guide gave each of us on the tour a number and we participated on a raffle. The winner won a picture made of seeds and pieces of plants by a local artist. What made it even more exciting is that I won the raffle!

Since Bonaire is considered a 'diver's paradise' and I don't dive, I didn't expect that there would be much to see or do. Was I wrong? Much of the island is composed of a gray rock and the island seemed more arid than some of the other Caribbean islands I had visited. We saw several wild donkeys and an area with flamingos.

There was a natural bridge which we were told was a bridge that one crosses in hopes that it will assure a marriage in the future.

Several Hollywood stars have made their home here on this island. One home we saw had belonged to Harry Belafonte.

There was a stone beach where small buildings had been erected. Each stone building had openings on the sides in order to allow the sea breezes to come through and make life more comfortable for the slaves who slept in them at night.

Nearby was an area for salt production. Here one could see several high pyramids of salt for export

The tour of Aruba began with a drive from the ship to an area where the surf is extremely strong. At that location we visited a natural bridge created by the pounding surf. The bridge collapsed in 2005 and was one of the largest of its kind in the world. Nearby is what is referred to as the Baby Bridge.

As one is visiting in this area one begins to notice that several large rocks have smaller rocks stacked up upon them. People are to make a wish and place a rock on another. If the stone isn't blown away, the wish is supposed to come true.

In a distance as we drove around the island we could see the Hooiberg Mountain, commonly referred to as the haystack. It is approximately 540 feet high and can be seen from almost any location on the island. Another large rock formation was the Casibara. We had time to walk to the top where spectacular views of the island were possible.

The California lighthouse was another one of the highlights to include while touring the island of Aruba. It was built around the beginning of the 20th century and was named after the Steamship California which wrecked nearby in 1891.

On our way back to the ship we drove through the area of the island where all the large hotels and tourist resorts are located. The shopping street near the ship contained the usual array of several diamond shops (the same as seen in so many of the other Caribbean islands).

Switzerland. I had visited Switzerland on my first trip to Europe in 1962. However, on that trip we merely drove through Switzerland to Austria via Lichtenstein and spent one night in Lucerne. Consequently I had not seen a lot of this country. I felt it was time to return to spend more time there and upon leaving have the feeling that I had now seen the country.

In searching for tours I found a 14-day tour, The Country Roads of Switzerland, that I felt was exactly the one for which I was looking. I had used this same company for several previous trips and was always pleased with their service.

I flew to Zurich and was immediately transported by bus to Lucerne. After checking into the Hotel Astoria I decided to take a walk and see if there was anything that I would remember from 51 years ago!! Of course, one can't ever forget seeing the Chapel Bridge.

That evening we had our welcome dinner at the National Hotel where we would be able to meet the other travelers we would be traveling with for the next two weeks. It was quite an international group. Several members of the group were from Australia and New Zealand. However, they had moved there from England, Poland, Switzerland, etc. They were surprised to hear that I had been to Australia seven times. Then they discovered that I had seen parts of Australia that they hadn't seen.

The city tour the next morning included the Chapel Bridge, the Water Tower, city hall, the railway station, and the Sleeping Lion statue. Chapel Bridge was built in 1333 and a fire in 1993 destroyed most of it. It has now been restored and the pictures on the bridge tell the history of the city. The Sleeping Lion statue was designed by Bertel Thorvaldsen in 1820-21. It is a memorial to the Swiss guards who were massacred in 1792 during the French Revolution. Mark Twain had great praise for this monument.

Since the afternoon was free for sightseeing on our own I was able to return to the riverfront where I was able to go into the Jesuit Church and witness its elaborately-decorated interior.

As one expects that while being in any part of Switzerland one is going to see many chocolate shops. Many of the window displays prove this through showing many candies, cakes, etc. with their intricately decorated items.

The remainder of the afternoon was used in exploring the Musegg Wall. Part of this wall was built in 1386 and is still intact and offers spectacular views of Lucerne and the river. The four towers that are open for visitation—Schirmer, Mannli, Zyt, and Wacht—each were built for various uses. For example, one is merely a clock tower.

In the evening several of our group participated in a Folklore Show and Dinner. The entire outside of the old adjoining building where this took place was ornately painted to match the typical Swiss style of architecture. Our menu consisted of Fondue, Salad, Veal Strips, Grated Potatoes, Meringue with applesauce, and strawberry ice cream. The entertainment included accordians, alpine long horns, yodeling, flag throwing, and bell ringing. Lucerne was absolutely beautiful as we walked back across the Chapel Bridge to our hotel in the evening with a full moon shining over the river.

The next morning we took a trip to Mt. Pilatus. The rain didn't seem to deter us in the least. We were inside a nice cable car for our ascent. It wasn't until we reached to summit and began walking on the outside that we realized just how cold it really was! – and this was happening in June!

The capital city of Bern was our next stop. Upon our entry to the city we stopped at a bear pit to enjoy taking photos of the bears, which are the symbol for the city.

The most significant remembrances of Bern for me were the many, many statues that are located in the street. As one walks toward the clock tower in the center, one passes several statues. Some are of people, some animals, and some maintains its own true identity.

The Bernminster is a huge Swiss Reformed Cathedral of Gothic architecture also located in the center of the city. It is well worth a visit. The tall spire can be seen from almost any section of the city.

Other points of interest would include the Capitol building, the Swiss National Bank, and the ever-present Casino. There was a large flower and plant market in the square. This area comprised several antique shops. I found it interesting that some of them had stuffed animals, old bicycles, old musical instruments, as well as the ordinary pieces of art and china.

Murten is a medieval city located alongside Lake Morat in the Fribourg canton. Our group had some free time here to enjoy the city on our way to Montreaux.

Chillon Castle is strategically located alongside the edge of Lake Geneva and almost screams out to tourists – "take photos!" In touring the inside of the castle one can see some of the old fireplaces, heaters, different pieces of furniture, tile medallions of family crests, baths, and even toilets built for two people.

The Counts of Savoy occupied the castle during the middle of the 12th century. The castle was used as a prison

The castle was also made famous by the poem by Lord Byron called *The Prisoner of Chillon Castle.* It is recorded that a gentleman who was a monk and a politician was imprisoned here from 1530-36. One of the stones in the lower part of the castle has an engraving on it with the name of Lord Byron.

Gstaad is a delightful little town with several interesting shops. It seems the main attraction here is the large hotel overlooking the town where the rich and famous come to escape.

Not far from Gstaad is another small town, Gruyeres, known for its cheese. There is a 13th century castle there for one to visit. The crane is the symbol for the city. One is depicted in a large floral arrangement located nearby the parking area for tour buses, etc. We had lunch here and my sandwich roll was grilled in such a way that it had a crane on it also.

The day trip to Geneva included a visit to the Reformation Monument and a drive where we were able to see the headquarters for the United Nations and the Red Cross. Several in our group walked together to go through St. Peters Cathedral, a large Swiss Reformed Church, where John Calvin attended.

There is a huge plume of water that ascends high in the sky from Lake Geneva—another place for photos.

Pianos are placed in various areas of the city and expect visitors to take advantage of them by playing. Pianos usually on display for tourists to see have a sign indicating that they are not to be played. However, the pianos in Geneva had a sign that said, "Please play me." I couldn't resist! I now have a picture of me playing Clare de Lune alongside Lake Geneva. (Does that make me an international pianist?)

After our visit to Geneva we took a boat ride back to our hotel in Montreaux. The Royal Plaza Hotel is situated alongside Lake Geneva and offers wonderful views of the snow covered mountains on the opposite side. A walking park adjacent to the hotel contained an eccentric display of artistry. There was a collage made of shopping baskets and another made of bathroom fixtures. Even an old car had plants and flowers growing all over it.

Our evening was spent driving to a vineyard where we had a nice dinner in the cellar restaurant. On the drive there we were able to see the city of Lusanne and also Mt. Blanc in the distance.

Our drive to Zermatt included a stop in Martigny to view the amphitheater and a stop in Sion to enjoy the large street market/festival. At a certain point the buses have to be parked and tourists are taken by a cogwheel railway to the Matterhorn Station. Battery operated taxies take tourists from that area to their respective hotels. No automobiles are allowed.

The Alex Hotel here is centrally located and the lobbies are filled with beautiful pieces of furniture, chandeliers, paintings, etc. From the small balcony of my room I could see the Kleine Matterhorn, where we would be going the next day.

Just up the main street was the St. Mauritius Catholic Church. From the left side of the front of the church one can get a nice photo of the Matterhorn. Unfortunately, that day the mountain was partially covered with clouds. However, the next morning just before our departure it was crystal clear!!

The members of our group departed just after breakfast for our ascent to Furi by way of a gondola ride. In Furi we were transferred to the railway that took us the remainder of the way. An ever popular St. Bernard was seen at the station. Upon departing the railway one must walk through a long tunnel in reaching your final destination. At that point one has now arrived at the Kleine Matterhorn which is 12,739 ft. elevation. During our stay there we were able to see several groups of people skiing. There also was a helicopter flying around. We couldn't decipher if it was a sightseeing trip for other tourists or if it was a recovery mission for someone who had had a mishap while skiing or mountain climbing.

The drive to Lugano took us through the Simplon Pass. Along the way we made a stop in order to be able to get some photos of the Giant Eagle statue erected to honor the troops of the 11th brigade who from 1939-45 worked to keep this area under Swiss control.

We spent one night in Lugano before continuing on to St. Moritz where we stayed at the Monopol Hotel. There was a clock tower just outside my room. My first thoughts were whether or not it would be sounding the bells at through the night. Fortunately it didn't!

We took the Bernini Express train from St. Moritz to Poschiavo. Along the way we had a lot of beautiful scenery to absorb. Poschiavo is a small town and it was a pleasure to be able to walk around to see how the villagers lived. I can't ever remember seeing a nun with a bicycle until I was here.

On our way back to St. Moritz several of our group members chose to take the cable ride to Diavolezza (She-Devil). The views on the way up were spectacular to say the least. At the summit we had an opportunity to capture some extra photos and partake of a nice lunch. This was my first experience of eating Blue Potato Soup. Others were not that adventurous. On several occasions of my travels I have been asked if I like a particular food. I usually reply, "Is it food? – If it's food, I like it!"

The one thing that sold me on this particular tour was that it included the ride on the Glacier Express. This is one of the world's great railway journeys. It ascends through the spiral tunnels of Albula Pass and crosses the Landwasser Viaduct. The trip takes 7 hours, goes through 91 tunnels, and 291 bridges.

We made our departure in Andematt where we would be rejoined with our tour bus. From there we drove to Interlaken.

The Royal St. George Hotel in Interlaken was one of the old grand hotels where one could stand in the lobby and just gape at the beautiful chandeliers, mirrors, and paintings. However, upon arrival, the section of the hotel where our rooms were located had been closed. It was about 90 degrees outside! After having been in the high mountains for several days with low temperatures, it really hit! Needless to say our rooms and the hallways were stifling!! We all agreed that we would open our windows and the hallway doors. We also opened the door at the end of the hallway. Sure enough, before long it was livable!

As we drove through the beautiful and lush Grindelwald Valley we were able to absorb the nice views of the Wetterhorn Peaks. We took a cogwheel train to the summit of the Jungfrau Mountain.

We follow the sparkling Lutschine River to Lauterbrunnen at the head of the Valley of Waterfalls where we saw the Staubbach Falls plunging some 900 feet.

Here we changed trains for our final approach. The mountain is 11,642 feet high. Needless to say, it was not only cold, but extremely windy!

The ice palace there is reached by walking through a long tunnel which is carved out of ice. The exhibits inside the ice palace include sculptures of bears, igloos, seals, and penguins.

At one point on the way down we had the opportunity of seeing all three major mountains at one time – the Eiger, the Monch, and the Jungfrau.

Trummelbach Falls is one of the few if not the only falls located inside a cave. Tourists are taken by way of a tunnel lift where upon exiting it is possible to walk back to the entry point. On the return you are able to witness one of the most unforgettable and powerful waterfalls you will ever see!

Ballenberg is an open air museum where one is able to absorb the traditional architecture of Switzerland. In the several acres one is able to see homes of rich people and typical homes occupied by farmers. There were several farm animals accompanying this area. In one of the houses there was a wine cellar and in another an exhibit of various clothing worn through the years.

There were craft demonstrations including weaving and pottery making. It was possible to see cheese-making and wine production.

The last segment of our tour was a bus trip to Zurich where we did a city tour. This tour included the St. Peter's Church and Clock Tower, Frau Munster Church where Marc Chagall had made the stained glass windows, the opera house, and a walking tour through small streets with various small shops including clothing and jewelry. At the end of the tour we walked by the Stork Hotel. On the top of this hotel is actually a large stork nest with two storks made out of metal.

There was a farewell dinner in a local restaurant on this the last evening of our tour.

Lampedusa. My flight on Blue Panorama Airlines to Lampedusa was early in the morning after having spent one night in a hotel near the airport in Rome. The view of the island upon arriving in Lampedusa looks as if a large rock has been dropped in the Mediterranean Sea.

The O'scia Hotel was centrally located in that it only took a short walk up a steep hill to the main street where most of the shops and restaurants were located. The staff at the hotel was very congenial and helpful.

Most people have never even heard of Lampedusa and when I would say that that was to be my first stop of this trip, they would ask where it is located. I would just say that it is a small island in the Mediterranean owned by Italy and is located between Malta and Tunisia. It was only a week or two after my visit there that a boat filled with immigrants from Africa capsized and more than 200 people were killed.

A travel mate who is also a neighbor and friend, was supposed to meet me here the day I arrived. However, due to complications with airline cancellations, he didn't arrive until late the next day. During this time the front desk staff learned that not only had I done a lot of traveling throughout the world, I had actually written a book in 2011 about my travels.

The one tourist thing a visitor should do in Lampedusa is to take a boat ride around the island. The hotel staff made a recommendation for a company which turned out perfect! I shared the experience with 14 really nice people and all from Italy. They all just referred to me as 'the American.' We left at 9:30 a.m. and didn't return until about 6:15 p.m. There were several stops where anyone who wished had the opportunity of swimming in the crystal-clear water. A nice lunch was served during the trip.

Between my hotel and the boat harbor was a large area with boats in a large pile. I learned that these were boats that had also capsized and had been placed there as a memorial to those who had died.

As I was leaving the go to the airport for my departure, I was pleasantly surprised when the lady from the front desk said that she had already ordered a copy of my book.

Sardinia and Corsica. My friend and I began our stay here by checking into the Regina Margherita Hotel which was located within walking distance to many nice restaurants and ice cream parlors!

We were to pick up a rental car. However, we had to take a bus from the hotel to the location where we were to pick up the car. We tried to keep in mind the direction because we knew we had to be able to get back to the hotel. There was one thing that we were a little hesitant about. For some reason the key for the automobile had evidently been submersed in water, therefore, the insides were corroded. We took the car and drove back to the hotel.

The remainder of that day was spent touring the old city which was also within walking distance of the hotel. There we took the elevator up to the upper part of the old walled city.

In the old city we saw the Cathedral, the archeological museum, the elephantine tower, and the Palace of the Provential Government.

Sure enough, the next morning upon checking out of the hotel, the car would not start. Fortunately, there were a couple businessmen checking out at the same time and were familiar with the particular automobile we had. I still don't know how or what they did, but it did start.

We drove directly back to the place where we had picked up the car the previous day. We explained our situation to the gentleman and said that we were going to be driving the car for the next 10 or 11 days and would not feel comfortable being in the countryside and not knowing if the car was going to start or not.

We opted to wait for about an hour for another vehicle to arrive. Needless to say, we were relieved upon leaving for our trip to be in an automobile that we had confidence in that it would start!

The first leg of our journey was to drive from Cagliari to Alghero. The GPS on my newly-acquired tablet with the map of Sardinia and Corsica was a god sent.

We stopped in a small beach town where we enjoyed the scenery of the beach while also enjoyed a nice lunch.

Alghero is a beach town where seemingly many people come to enjoy their holidays. Finding a parking spot anywhere in that area was extremely difficult as we found out the first evening when we were going to select a restaurant for dinner.

The old walled city contains many restaurants, several churches, a bastion, and a plethora of places for photography.

Neptune's Grotto was within driving distance from our hotel. We drove there early the next morning. There was a place for parking and a small gift shop at the top. From there one walks down the cliffs some 654 steps to arrive at the entrance for the caves. The views as one descends are absolutely spectacular and also offer many opportunities to get photos of the cliffs with the Mediterranean Sea in the background.

Since both of us had been through many caves before and decided that they are mostly the same, we opted not to take the tour. Anyway, at the opening where we arrived, there was enough to see and get some photos.

Now—the challenging part begins!—the walk back up the 654 steps to get to the car!

A nuraghe is an area consisting of several structures built of stone. Most of them were built during the early or middle Bronze Age. Some of the structures were supposedly used as religious temples, as a dwelling, as a military stronghold, and as meeting halls. It is somewhat difficult to determine exactly for what purpose each one was used. There are many nuraghi throughout Sardinia.

We were able to tour the Palmavera Nuraghe on our way back to Alghero from the caves.

We took the Moby Ferry from Sardinia to Corsica. The crossing only takes about 45 minutes. The approach to Bonafacio, Corsica is a site that one could never forget. The sheer high cliffs arising from the sea are a bright white in color since they are formed of limestone.

Fortunately our hotel, the Santa Teresa, was located adjacent to the old town and close to the cliffs. We walked through the narrow streets of the old section of town where we chose a nice little restaurant for dinner.

Early the next morning I took a walk through the old cemetery which was located just across from our hotel. Most of the family crypts and mausoleums are quite large and elaborately carved. Several had flowers at their entrances.

We drove through the countryside the next day to Ajaccio. Sometimes in the small villages the traffic would be at a standstill. It was then that we realized that our nice Audi diesel rental car would cut off when stopped in traffic and the brake was activated. As soon as the brake was released the car would start again. This was beneficial in getting a really good gas mileage.

Napoleon was from Ajaccio and everywhere one looks there is something else that is named for him. Even our hotel was the Hotel Napoleon. Yes, there was a statue of him in the lobby.

There is a large museum on the walking street in Ajaccio. It is called the Fesch Museum. It seems that he was an uncle of Napoleon.

Just beyond the walking street and the downtown area there was a large fort. The beach was adjacent to the fort. We were able to enjoy the beach for a little while on our last morning there.

There was one large market in the downtown area and another near the train station. It seems that the markets deal mostly with food during the daytime and at night they deal mostly with clothing, belts, wigs, and anything they think a tourist might want to buy.

Calvi, our next stop, is a harbor town. Our hotel was right on the waterfront overlooking a marina and many restaurants. The street in the front of the hotel is a walking street for part of the day. Fortunately upon our arrival we were able to drive to the front entrance. Once we were checked into the hotel we had to move the car to a parking lot outside the downtown area and walk back.

We got our exercise that afternoon by walking up the many, many steep steps of the Citadel. However, the views from there were worth the effort.

Our dinner that evening was at one of the restaurants across from our hotel. There was an art show that evening on the docks of the marina. While we strolled through the exhibits we were in awe of some of the large yachts there. Several of them were occupied and the lighting on some of the yachts for the evening was creative and unique. We were quite surprised that one of the yachts showed that it was registered in Delaware in the United States!

Bastia is located in the far northeastern section of Corsica. Our room at the L'Ariana Hotel was right on the Mediterranean Sea. It seems that what we saw most on the water there was the ever-present Corsica Ferry boats going back and forth.

After checking into our hotel there, we decided that we would drive further north around the Cap Corse. It was a pleasant drive, however, at some points the width of the road was hardly wide enough for one vehicle let alone two!!

There were small villages where the houses were built seemingly hanging on the hillside. Of course, each village had a large church with a tall spire.

Being a tourist sometimes reminds us of just how easily we are excited about something. For example, in driving the Cap Corse, the first Genoese tower that one sees, you must stop and take a photo. However, after you have seen five or six of them in two hours, they become less meaningful. These towers were built in order to offer protection from pirates.

We drove down the eastern side of the island to Puerto Vecchio for our next stop. Our hotel here was a Best Western. Breakfast here was served on the rooftop which was quite pleasant. This hotel was again within walking distance of the old section of town. There we found a really nice restaurant with a terrace on an upper level that offered nice views of the surrounding area.

The Moby ferry was taken from Bonafacio back to Sardinia where we then drove to Olbia. We toured the old town here.

We flew from Olbia back to Rome and then continued on back to the United States.

The Azores, Madeira, & the Canary Islands. This 14-day cruise started in Southampton, England on the Celebrity Eclipse. Ponte Delgado was our first port of call. Our bus excursion took us around the island in the pouring down rain!! However, we were able to visit the St. Nicholas Church in the Sete Cidades district.

The Church of St. Peter and a statue of Goncalo Vehho Cadral, an early explorer, are located on the city square in Ponte Delgado. Our tour ended with a wine and cheese tasting.

The highlight of the visit to Funchal, Madeira was the breathtaking toboggan ride almost 2 kilometers down the hillside. Two people occupy the toboggan and two locals with ropes guide the toboggan as it descends. At one point where the terrain in somewhat level, the guides pull the toboggan until it begins its descent again. It was interesting to note that at the bottom of the hill there is a bus waiting to take the workers back to the top.

Adjacent to the area where the ride begins is the Our Lady of the Mountain Church. It is a beautiful church overlooking the city. In the courtyard in front of the church is a statue of Beato Carlos de Hapsburg, the last ruler of the Austro-Hungarian Empire.

At the end of the toboggan ride one takes a cable car ride to the lower section of the city. There we went through the local market. Inside the market was a large fish section with black fish, salmon, and many other varieties. There was also a large section comprised of a large assortment of fruits and vegetables. Arts and crafts were located in another section.

Our group then visited a large winery where we were able to sample some of the various kinds of wines produced here.

The day in Tenerife was made special in that I was able to make an email contact with a person who resides there that I had met on the trip to Yap, Micronesia the year before. He is a professional underwater photographer and was in Yap on a diving expedition. He consented to be our guide for the day. My travel partner and I went to the side of the ship that morning and he was already standing there waiting for us.

The scenery was spectacular as we drove to great heights through the Esperanza Forest where we realized that we were actually above the clouds below. At one point we could see Las Palmas and Gran Canaria rising above the clouds. Mt. Teide was actually our destination. It is the highest mountain in Spain at the elevation of 12,198 feet.

On our way there we stopped for photos in the Canadas National Park. The landscape there gave one the feeling of being on the moon. It was quite barren with a scattering of large rocks. Near the foot of the mountain was a place where we were able to have a coffee while admiring the scenery.

Just outside La Oratavo we stopped to have lunch at a restaurant which was located adjacent to a large vineyard. The restaurant makes its own wine from the grapes in their vineyard.

My friend took us on a walking tour of La Oratavo which included the Conception Parish Church, Constitution Square, and the Botanical Garden. Nearby was another large landscaped garden with many varieties of flowers and plants. At the top of these gardens was a mausoleum for the Marques de la Quinta Roja.

Many of the homes here have large intricately-carved wooden balconies on the second or third floor. We chose a place to have ice cream which was known as 'the house of balconies.'

My travel friend and I expressed our gratitude to our guide for his excellent choices for our short visit. It was really a treat to see him again.

That evening our ship departed Tenerife and headed to Las Palmas in the Gran Canaria.

We took a walking tour of the downtown area which included the Cantenas Beach which was near the area where the ship was docked. From there we visited the Museum Canario. The exhibits included several skeletons, skulls, animals, and articles of clothing from different areas and periods of time.

Nearby was the large St. Ana Cathedral. In the street behind the cathedral was an outdoor street bazaar selling arts and crafts. I found a bird there for my collection at home. The bird was nicely hand carved from several varieties of wood.

The Igesia San Antonio Abad was a small church where supposedly Christopher Columbus had worshipped at one time.

Our ship excursion group drove by bus through several large vineyards on our way to visit the Bandama Crater. The volcanic eruption occurred many, many years ago. The crater measures approximately 1 kilometer in diameter and about 200 meters deep.

Our last stop was to see a local folklore dance presentation on the grounds of the beautiful Hotel Santa Catalina. The dancers were colorfully attired in period costumes.

On the grounds of the hotel were nicely landscaped gardens with many varieties of flowers, large fountains, and statuary. A large pond with many varieties of colorful fish was also enjoyable.

Visiting the volcanic islands Fuerteventura and Lanzarote completed our tour of the Canary Islands.

On our way back to Southampton we made one final stop in Lisbon, Portugal. I had been to Lisbon several times before and spent most of the day just revisiting places I had been to on previous trips.

2014

The Marathon of the Caribbean
Riverboat Cruise in the Netherlands and Belgium
Islands of Europe
Islands of the Southern Pacific

Marathon of the Caribbean. The first step in my 'marathon of the Caribbean' was to send an email to my travel agent with a suggested itinerary. He called me upon receiving the email to let me know that one of the things he likes about me is that I always offer him a challenge! Since all of the original suggestions weren't possible due to one ship being a charter and was already sold out, we reverted to 'plan B' and the following is what finally transpired.

I flew to Antigua for four nights. Having been to this island previously, I chose this opportunity to visit and explore a couple nearby islands.

The first morning after my arrival I had an early morning flight to Guadeloupe for a day trip. I took a taxi from the airport to the center of the city, Pointe-A-Pitre, where I would spend the day. I asked the taxi driver to drop me off at a tourist information office. Based upon my previous travel experiences while traveling alone, I have found that this is a good place to begin planning my day. The sign out front indicated that it would be opening at 8 a.m. and it was only 7:30 a.m. at that time. I decided that I would just walk around that area and come back. At 8:15 it still hadn't opened. I finally asked a local policeman if he knew what time it would be opening and he informed me that that information office was closed permanently and would not be opening at all.

My 'plan b' (or c as the case may be) was to find a nearby hotel in hopes that a person there would be able to give me some choices of what to do for the day. Unfortunately, I never was able to even find a hotel. Evidently all the hotels here are resorts geared to those travelers who come here for a week or two just to lie on the beach, dive, etc.

Since 'plans a, b, nor c' had worked, I went to 'plan d' by spending some time in a large park which included a large statue of Felix Eboue who was Governor General from 1884-1944. Many locals utilize this park for meeting with friends and relaxing.

I later visited the John Perse Museum, the Bascilica of St. Peter and St. Paul Cathedral, a local food market, and the environs of the downtown area of Pointe-A-Pitre before returning to the airport.

Since I had some time at the airport before going through customs and security, I chose to use it by taking advantage of the free wi-fi. I was able to send some emails to friends back home.

Something happened while going through security here that I had never had happen before. Upon exiting the radar check I was asked if I had anything in my back pocket. I responded by saying that I had a handkerchief there. I was not only asked to take it out, I was asked to open it up and shake it! (Interesting?)

The next day I went on yet another day trip to Montserrat. Upon arriving at the dock from which the boat was to depart, I was told that I wouldn't be able to pay by credit card! I didn't have enough cash with me! Fortunately, I was able to ask my driver from the hotel before he returned if he had enough money to loan me and that I would repay him later.

After receiving the money from him, I approached the departure window again to find out when I told the cashier that I had made a reservation the day before for a package deal that would include lunch and sightseeing, she then told me that I would actually need to see another person for that and that he would be arriving in a few minutes.

In the meantime I was told to walk to a nearby building in order to go through passport control. When I returned to the dock, the gentleman from the company through which I had booked the day trip had arrived and I learned that the day trip could in fact be paid by credit card.

Even though the boat had about 25 passengers, there were only two others who had booked through the same company as I had. Therefore, we spent the day together. He was from the UK and she was originally from Russia. They were traveling with Russian passports and had just gotten married a couple days before this. The lady was quite surprised when I told her that I had been to Russia five times. She was even more excited upon discovering that I had actually visited her home town.

Montserrat had suffered a major earthquake in 1995. When I told the lady at my hotel what I was doing for the day, she said that she could still remember the day of the earthquake.

We first visited a large 'community center' which included a very nice auditorium which could be used for local programs, concerts, etc. We learned that several world-known stars including Elton John and Paul McCartney had contributed to this cause and there were plaques with their hand prints on them displayed in the lobby.

Plymouth, the capital, was completed destroyed by the earthquake. It is being relocated in another area of the island and that area is referred to as Little Bay.

In an area near the old capitol we were shown a photo of a large house. Then, we were taken to the house and saw what it looks like today. The first two floors of the house are now underground!

Our driver took us to an area where we could still see the steam coming up from the mountain. In looking over the ashen terrain we saw what appeared to be a smokestack. That was all that was left of the former airport.

The next morning I checked out of my hotel in Antigua to go to the airport for my short flight to St. Maarten. As I was leaving the office, I heard the lady sing, "Blessed Assurance…" I immediately turned around and sang, "Jesus is Mine." She laughed and said, "You know this song?" and I answered, "Yes, we used to sing it in our church in North Carolina when I was growing up."

The front of my hotel in Philipsburg, St. Maarten was centrally located toward the end of the main street. The rear of the hotel was right on the beach.

Every day there would be several cruise ships arriving early in the morning. One day there was seven! It was quite interesting to see how busy the town was during the day. However, after 6 p.m. all the ships would depart and the town would become completely different–and very quiet!

The second day here I was transported by taxi to an area where I would get a boat for my day trip to Anguilla. Another day meant another day of going through customs and immigration.

Several taxis were there as we departed the boat offering deals for sightseeing. I selected one and was on my way. Seeing that my last name is Ashley, it was quite amusing that the first sign I saw when we started the sightseeing was for Ashley's Supermarket. Needless to say, I asked the driver to stop in order to get a photo. He did.

Anguilla is saturated with high-end resorts. We visited several of them. They are all nice and I am sure they are usually well occupied by tourists who want to get away, play golf, and just relax.

We visited Wallblake House which was built by slaves. There was a conference center and a church with a plaque in memory of Mother Teresa's visit here in 1998.

The next morning I went to the French section of the island where I would begin my hydrofoil ride to the island of Saba. I spent the day in Saba with two couples from the Netherlands. They couldn't believe that I was going to be in the Netherlands for a river boat cruise in a couple months from then.

While touring the island we saw the Sacred Heart Church. This Catholic Church was built in 1877 and has a lovely painted ceiling. It is located in The Bottom, which is the capital of the island. Near the church was a craft center which displayed many crocheted objects by local ladies. Christmas has always been a special time of the year for me and yes, I was able to purchase a red and green crocheted Christmas tree, which I plan to use in my decorations for many years to come.

The Queen of the Rosary church is located in the Hell's Gate section of the island. From this location one can look down at the shortest commercial landing strip in the world at the Juancho E. Yrausquin airport.

We took the Mt. Scenery Trail which takes about a half an hour or more to complete. In doing this, one is at the highest point of the island. This is a good diversion not only to see the scenery, but to get in a little exercise at the same time. There are approximately 1,064 steps!!

The five of us had a delightful lunch at a local restaurant. Located within walking distance of the restaurant was a nice little house that had been converted into a museum. The museum housed many pieces of period furniture and several photos depicting the life and history of the island.

I returned on the hydrofoil to St. Marten and had difficulty getting a taxi back to my hotel since this was the day that seven cruise ships were in port. Obviously all the taxis were busy taking care of the tourists from those. Fortunately a nearby police officer listened to my situation and was able to contact a friend of hers who just happened to be a taxi driver. Even though I had to wait for about 45 minutes, it was worth it. Without his help—who knows—I might still be waiting!

The following day I flew from St. Maarten to Ft. Lauderdale where I spent one night at a hotel near the airport. The next morning I got the shuttle from the airport to the cruise terminal where I departed on a seven-day Caribbean cruise. Remember, I said it was my 'marathon of the Caribbean.'–and we're not finished yet!

This cruise was on the Oasis of the Seas, which accommodates more than 6,000 tourists! Even though there are that many people, it never really felt that crowded since there was so much space. The boarding and departure procedures were handled in such a way that it took less time than I had encountered on smaller vessels.

Our first stop was in Labadee, Haiti. The entire area for this port stop is owned by the cruise company. I took advantage of one of the several excursions. We were taken to a private beach where we had to get off the small boat and wade through water almost crotch deep. We had an hour or so to enjoy the beach and possibly buy shells and other items from the local vendors.

We then were taken on a walking tour of what was an outdoor museum. As one walked through there were exhibits letting one know about life on the island. These exhibits included listening to music, seeing elaborate wood carvings, the preparation of food, and processing coffee beans.

On days at sea there was a plethora of choices of things to choose from in order to not be bored—i.e., playing trivia (which I like), all kinds of sports activities, speakers, etc. I never thought I would be on a ship with an ice skating rink and a wave pool for surfing!!

Jamaica was our next port of call. I had been to Jamaica once before, but it was in 1966! As mentioned in an earlier chapter, I mentioned how Negril at that time had no hotels and that now it is filled with them. On this day I would be returning to Montego Bay – would I recognize anything? I didn't think so – and I didn't. However, it was nice to go back and see how things had changed.

Since I had also visited the next port stop of Cozomel I tried to choose a ship-sponsored excursion which would be something different. Therefore, I chose the ride on the submarine where we would be able to see many different species of fish. It was similar to one that I did at the barrier reef in Australia.

Upon arriving back in Ft. Lauderdale I spent a few days with a friend in Boca Raton. I then drove to Miami where I was able to fly to the Cayman Islands.

The hotel there was really nice and located just outside George Town. From the rear of the hotel one could see all the cruise ships visiting here. In the lower level of the lobby of the hotel was an exhibit of underwater photos of Cathy Church.

Since my time here was somewhat limited I decided to take a land tour or the island. The lady at the front desk recommended one conducted by Cayman Safari Adventure Tours. I was picked up at the hotel the next morning. The gentleman who would be my guide for the day was very outgoing and extremely personable.

As we drove around the island he explained much of its history and local customs. We visited the Botanical Gardens where we were able to see blue and green iguanas, a mahogany forest, cacti, orchids, and many other flowering plants.

The Pedro St. James Castle was built in 1780. It was rather 'out of its place' in some ways. Most of the other nearby homes were on one level and had a thatched roof. This one was on three levels with a slate roof! Through the years it was destroyed by hurricanes, lightning, etc. Consequently it sat forgotten several times.

Through the years it has served as a courthouse, a jail, a restaurant, and now a museum. The initiation to this place is through watching an innovative presentation which shows the history of its existence. The presentation of several period pieces of furniture and home furnishings in various rooms allowed one to witness their way of life during that period of time.

Our guide chose a nice outdoor restaurant for lunch with a spectacular view. During the lunch he generated several questions which further conveyed interesting tidbits of information which clarified any misrepresentations we had developed.

All nine of our tour group members had once again climbed back into the jeep for the continuation of our tour. However, when the key was turned there were only a few clicks. The battery was dead! Fortunately there was another tour group there. We used their battery to get a jump start.

When we stopped at the blow hole for a photo stop the engine was left running just in case we had not charged the battery enough.

Just as we were stopping to visit the workshop of Doc Carey's Black Coral Clinic our guide reverted to habit and turned the engine off. I immediately said, "You forgot to leave the engine running." Oops! Too late now.

We continued on into the clinic to meet the gentleman and see all of his collections. There was the most visible collection hanging in the ceiling. He is trying to set a Guinness world record for the most thongs. There was a wall completely filled with jars of marbles. And, if that were not enough—he did have a large collection of beautifully-carved black coral jewelry.

Upon leaving, you guessed it! The jeep wouldn't start! Not a problem with this group. We just hopped behind and gave it a push and voila – we were on our way again.

For the next day I was to go on yet another excursion that would include the turtle farm and a visit to Hell. A grumpy lady appeared. Upon entering the vehicle she asked me where I wanted to go! I tried to explain that the lady at the hotel had said that I would go to the Turtle Farm and to Hell. This lady then told me that she would not have time for all that because she was to be at the airport at 11 a.m. to pick up someone else. My first thought was – well, why did she agree in the first place? She said that she could drop me off at the Turtle Farm and that I would have to pay extra for that, but she would then come back to pick me up. However, we would definitely not have time to go to Hell!

I then said that I would appreciate it if she would just take me back to the hotel. I conveyed all of this to the lady at the hotel. I don't think she will ever use that person again. I felt as though I had been to Hell and back!!

What a difference a day makes! On the day before I had had one of the most wonderful days of sightseeing with a guide who really loved his job and I was able to share that day with a group of other tourists who felt the same way.

Continuing my 'marathon' I flew back to Ft. Lauderdale, spent another night, and transferred to the cruise terminal the next morning for yet another seven-day Caribbean tour.

This time I would be on the Holland America's Nieuw Amsterdam with stops in Puerto Rico and St. Thomas both of which I had visited on several other occasions. However, it was nice to re-visit. There isn't much I can say without being somewhat redundant.

The highlight of this cruise was to be able to visit Turks & Caicos for the first time. Upon my visit here, I will have been in every place there is to go in the Caribbean! It did take a 'marathon.'

The day trip began by seeing the United States Air Force tracking base here. It was in this location that John Glenn splashed down in 1962. A replica of the Friendship 7 capsule is displayed just outside the base.

A stop in Cockburn allowed us time to see the museum, the post office, a couple churches, the prison, etc. There was a plaque commemorating the 50th anniversary of the Coronation of Queen Elizabeth.

The lighthouse here was built in 1852 in England and transported over. It is 60 feet high. Nearby the lighthouse was an area where there were several old buildings. It was a navy station at one time, but is now used as part of the university. Also near the lighthouse was a plaque giving information regarding the Trouvadore shipwreck. This ship was supposedly sailing to Cuba with 193 African slaves aboard. They were to become workers in Cuba in the sugar fields. However, the ship wrecked and many of the slaves were saved. They were allowed to live here and some of their descendants are still local residents.

Riverboat Cruise in the Netherlands and Belgium. A long-time friend of mine and I had an overnight flight to Amsterdam where we would have almost two days of sightseeing before leaving embarking on a 10-day river boat cruise.

Since he had never been to Amsterdam previously, it was my opportunity to be a 'tour guide' for a couple days. This allowed him to see the opera house, the skinny bridge, the Anne Frank house, and the Rijksmuseum.

He began telling me throughout the day especially in the later afternoon that his throat really hurt and that there was some pain in the chest area and at the back of his neck. We made it through the day and dinner. However, during the night I awakened and he was sitting on the edge of his bed in some discomfort and pain. I waited a while and then I saw him sitting in a chair in the dark with a blanket wrapped around him.

It was then that I turned on the light and began asking him questions. I said that I could call the front desk at the hotel and they could probably call a physician. This decision was based upon a similar situation at the same hotel that had occurred several years ago with another friend who was in the middle of a diabetic seizure—maybe I shouldn't stay here next time! Upon calling the front desk they told me that it would be best and less expensive to have them call a taxi and have the taxi take us to the emergency room of a nearby hospital.

The receptionist, the nurse, and the doctor at the hospital were all extremely nice and congenial even at 4 a.m. It just so happens that my friend is deaf and mute. Therefore I was helping to interpret with the information they needed to process him.

The nurse was asking questions in English. I would ask my friend for an answer and relate it to the nurse. However, in one question she was using English except for one word. She kept saying, "hoest." I looked at her questioningly and said, "What is 'hoest'?" She began laughing as she realized she had been using the Dutch word for cough.

After a thorough examination including blood pressure, fever, and an electrocardiogram, etc. they surmised that since all of these were normal he probably just had a slight ear infection. They gave him a couple pills to take and a prescription, but told him that it would probably work itself out in a couple days. Sweeter words could have not been spoken since we were to leave for the cruise the next day.

The Viking Bragi had approximately 80 passengers. Most of them were from the United States and Canada and most had traveled extensively through the years. It is always nice to be able to exchange travel experiences with others.

Our first stop was in Hoorn. There we began our sightseeing by doing a walking tour of the city. Not long after we began we had our first rain. It didn't seem to hamper anyone as we continued as though the sun were shining.

Several residents of Hoorn had volunteered to open their homes to members of our cruise. My group was fortunate to be able to spend some time in the home of a delightful couple. Even though we were soaked from the rain, we were welcomed with open arms! The gentleman of the couple had at one time been the calligrapher for the Queen. His workshop was located near their home.

We were served some nice refreshments and coffee while we toured the home and heard stories of their lives. It seems that coming from a somewhat small town, everyone knew them. They shared their wedding album with us. Several of the photos indicated that they traversed the city that day in a horse-drawn carriage. They were attired in such a way that they appeared to be royalty. All the calligraphy in the album of course had been done by the done by him. They spend their winters in South Africa.

The afternoon in Hoorn was spent visiting a tulip farm. Upon our arrival we were escorted into a room where we were given cookies and coffee to enjoy as we saw an introductory film and heard a speech explaining what we would be seeing later.

We toured the warehouse where the tulips were being processed for the auction house. We learned that the tulips grown in the greenhouses are used for the market and the ones grown in the large fields are grown for the bulbs.

Most of the participants enjoyed a few 'Kodak moments' before our departure back to the boat for taking pictures of the tulip fields.

Arnhem was our next stop. Our boat was docked near the John Frost Bridge which was the rebuilt bridge featured in the book and movie called A Bridge Too Far.

We were able to view the battlefields where the Battle of Arnhem was fought in 1944. We also toured the Airbourne Museum and saw several exhibits depicting this war. Many school children are brought here as part of their history lessons. There were several school groups here at the time we visited. Not too far from this museum was the Military Cemetery in Oosterbeek.

The afternoon was spent walking through the town of Arnhem. The highlight of this was visiting the St. Eusebius Cathedral where my friend and I were able to ascend by elevator to the top of the tower. This offered spectacular views of the city. Also at the top one was able to be amazed at the size of the bells in the tower.

The nearby Maarten Van Rossum house, also known as 'the devil's house,' carried the legacy that it was consumed by evil spirits. However, others felt that it received this name because of the unusual gargoyles.

The highlight of Kinderdijk, a UNESCO sight, is visiting the 19 old windmills there. Unfortunately, this was our second day of a rainy morning!! Not only was it pouring rain, the wind was blowing fiercely. Again, it didn't seem to deter any seasoned travelers like us – we just 'rose above it' and enjoyed!

While we traveled toward Belgium the staff of the boat took advantage of this time to indoctrinate us to how to make Belgian waffles. They first were asking for a volunteer to assist in this endeavor. They said that they wanted a person who knew absolutely nothing about cooking. Instantaneously a group of people pointed toward this one man. They agreed that he knew nothing.

As he completed his assignment he would take a short pause to have a sip of wine. This seemed to help. Once the demonstration was finished we were treated to a Belgian waffle that had just come from the kitchen below.

The name of the city of Antwerp is translated as 'hand throwing.' At one time there was an evil person who would make people pay a toll to cross the river. If they refused, he would cut off their hand and throw it in the river. Legend has it that Brabo accosted the ogre, cut off his hand, and threw it into the river. Because of this he is considered a hero and there is a statue of him in the main city square.

Steen Castle in Antwerp is located alongside the river. It has been used as a prison and a museum. Outside the castle there are several statues. One of them is called The Lange Wapper. Ladies who wanted to have children would come and touch this statue with the hopes that it would cause them to have children. At one time the statue possessed an extremely long 'private part' which has since been removed. Isn't it remarkable at how puritanical we become sometimes.

The Cathedral of Our Lady contains several paintings by Peter Paul Rubens. The intricately carved oak paneled confessionals date back to 1713. The choir was carved in a similar fashion. The stained glass windows in the cathedral were awesome.

It becomes obvious that we are now in Belgium because in walking through the shopping area one sees many shop windows filled with chocolate and lace.

In Bruges we toured the Our Lady's Church where one can see Michaelangelo's statue of the Madonna. Adjacent to the cathedral is the Gruuthuuze Palace and Gardens and a statue of Guido Gezelle, a famous Belgium poet.

There were many horse drawn carriages for tourists going through the narrow streets. Near the town center is an extremely high clock tower.

The major attraction to the visit in Ghent is to see the 15th century altar piece painted by Van Eyck. It has been stolen several times yet it always seems to show up again. Fortunately, for now, it has an appropriate resting place.

Arriving back in the Netherlands we were taken to a museum that depicts the large flood of 1953. Our guide explained to us how large cement containers were sent from England and how they are used in preventing this from happening in the future. On one exhibit in the museum there was a list of all the people who died from the flood. There was also another exhibit that listed various countries and what they contributed to the effort.

In making our way back toward Amsterdam we were able to have a pleasant stop in the quaint little town of Veere. There we saw the Great Church (1348) which had at one time been used as a hospital for soldiers by Napoleon and has been used also as a house for beggars.

As we walked through the residential streets it becomes obvious that everyone is particularly interested in maintaining their homes by keeping them clean, especially the windows with the lace curtains. Our guide pointed out that on the mail slot one can set to indicate that they do not want 'junk mail' or whether or not a newspaper is to be delivered to that address.

There were several quaint shops here. In one of them I was able to find a new bird made of tin for my collection.

One of the things that our guide told us that it was a must here was to try the snack food that is shaped to look like the dropping of a dog!! I chose not.

The boat arrived back in Amsterdam and the next morning we went by bus to visit the Keukenhof Gardens! These gardens are absolutely magnificent! They cover approximately 70 acres and contains landscaping for over 7 million bulbs. Needless to say, the camera really got a work out here. I think I took over 100 pictures in the time there.

This boat trip has come to an end and the memories of it will linger for a long time. One of the things that had subconsciously been on my 'bucket list' was to be able to stand and see large fields of tulips in bloom. That one has now been marked off the list.

Islands of Europe—The Isle of Man. On July I flew from Washington to London. After one day there I flew from the London City Airport to the Isle of Man. Upon my arrival I approached the tourist information counter in order to plan my day. The lady in command was most helpful. I took a bus from the airport to Douglas, the capital of The Isle of Man. The waterfront there is most scenic with an extensive beautifully-manicured garden which consisted of a wide variety of many colorful flowers.

As one scans the horizon from this area it is quite obvious that there is a small castle-like structure just off the coast. It seems that through the years many boats were surprised by a large underwater sand bank which caused them to stop abruptly. By building the castle the boat captains would be able to determine that there was land nearby and they would have to go around. It is aptly named the Tower of Refuge.

After taking several photos in Douglas I boarded another bus that took me to the other side of the island to a small town named Peel. The major attraction in Peel is the large castle. However, Peel has a very nice long beach area which I am sure is the busy part of the island during the major tourist seasons. This area also provides the island with a prosperous fishing industry.

After returning to Douglas from Peel, I took another bus that traveled in the direction back to the airport. I asked the driver of the bus if he would be able to stop on the way back so that I would be able to tour the Isle of Man Home for Old Horses and he indicated that it was possible. Yes, they actually have a retirement home for old horses. There are individual stables for the horses, many acres of grazing pasture land, and a guide that can show you around and answer any questions you may have. There is also a small café where one can get a bite to eat.

I boarded the next bus and instead of stopping at the airport I continued on to the small town of Castletown and yet further on to Port Erin. In the small town of Castletown there is Rushen Castle, a monument to those who died in World War II, and The Old House of Keys where their government affairs used to take place and is now a museum. Erin is quite scenic in that it is located at the extreme southern end of the island. One of the major attractions here is the old railroad station and the steam engine train. The train is a tourist attraction whereby one can take it from Erin back to Castletown or on to Douglas.

Across from the major church here, there is a set of steps that take you down to the beach area. At the bottom of the steps one would fine St. Catherine's Well. This was used at one time for baptisms.

My visit to this beautiful island had come to a close and it was time for me to return to the airport for my flight back to London.

Jersey. The next morning I made my way to the Victoria subway stop where I would be able to take the Gatwick Express train to Gatwick Airport for my flight to the island of Jersey. Again, as the previous day, I took a bus from the airport into the capital, St. Helier. It is a quaint little compact town which makes is quite conducive for a walking tour. After taking in the main street, I made my way to the east end of the town where I walked through the Howard Davis Park. Story has it that he was caught as a kid looking for chestnuts with a friend and was punished severely. In revenge he vowed to become a rich man which he did. This allowed him to return, purchase the property, destroy the former house, and use the land to donate a beautiful garden to the city. There was a statue of Mr. Davis at the entrance along with a floral exhibition for those who died in World War I.

Offshore from St. Helier is the Elizabeth Castle. It was built in the 16th century to be used in fortifying the city from intruders.

Guernsey. My next adventure was to visit the island of Guernsey and to do this I was able to fly on an airline that I had never previously used – Aurigny Airlines. I flew from Gatwick to St. Peter Port, the capital of Guernsey.

The waterfront of St. Peter Port is very picturesque with the harbor named after Queen Victoria and Prince Albert. They made a visit here in 1846 and to commemorate this visit, there is a statue of Prince Albert near the end of the harbor. Alongside the waterfront are several businesses, banks, information offices, restaurants, and churches all festively decorated with many, many beautiful flowers.

Across the harbor is Castle Cornet which was built almost 8 centuries ago and is now used to house several museums and also offers a dramatic setting for theatrical performances.

Victor Hugo was a resident here for almost 14 years while in exile from France. He wrote many of his works while living here. His home and gardens which is located within walking distance of the harbor is open to the public for tours.

After having a nice lunch in a nearby restaurant, I boarded a local bus which would afford me the opportunity of seeing the other parts of the island and finish at the airport.

Along the way I saw several cruise ships which accounted for the abundance of tourists in town for the day. The beaches along the northern part of the island are quite nice and were filled with people enjoying them.

Several towers and bunkers were erected toward the end of the 18th century along this area and were used for protection of invasion from enemies especially France. One of the most picturesque of these and one of the only ones still standing is the Rousse Tower.

The Faroe Islands. I flew from Copenhagen to the Vagar Airport where it was extremely mountainous and foggy which was an extreme contrast to the experiences I had just had in the other islands where it was sunny and dry!

The Hotel Foroyar in Torshavn, the capital of the Faroe Islands, was situated high above the city. The lower level of the hotel is partially underground. My room happened to be on the lower level which meant that the grass on the outside was at window level. To compensate for this, the floor was heated.

Many famous people and bands had stayed in this hotel. There was a plaque with their names listed. Included in these were the Queen of Denmark, Bill Clinton, Al Gore, and several well-known bands.

I walked from my hotel down the hill to the city where I was able to take photos of the waterfront, churches, and the smallest Parliament Building that I had ever seen and probably the smallest in the world.

The hotel arranged for an English-speaking guide/driver to pick me up at the hotel to give me a tour of the island and then drop me at the airport later.

The drive was extremely memorable in that at almost every turn there would be a beautiful waterfall. Yes, many waterfalls and lakes with many opportunities to take photos of cattle, horses, grass-covered houses and churches.

After two or three hours I mentioned to my driver that I needed to be at the airport for my flight back to Copenhagen. My how times have changed from my olden days of travel! He got on his phone, checked with the airport to get an update on flight information, and related to me that we had plenty of time. In fact, he took me to the airport at one point just to get checked in and get a boarding pass. Then, he said, "Now, we leave so that I can show you another part of the island that you must see." We left and thankfully so, we did see scenes that I had not seen before! And, he did get me back to the airport in time for the flight. It really worked out great because upon my arrival back at the airport, the other passengers had already gone through security and were waiting at the gate. I was able to just zip right through.

Aland Islands. There are approximately 6,700 islands making up the Aland (pronounced Oh-lund) Islands. They are owned by Finland and are located between Sweden and Finland. Mariehamn is the capital of the Aland Islands and is one of the only ones that is inhabited.

Mariehamn is a quaint small town with a walking street that contains several clothing shops, gift shops, souvenirs, and restaurants. Nearby is a City Hall and Parliament Buildings. In front of the City Hall is a statue of Marie Alexandrovna of Russia from whom the city received its name.

The major tourist attraction is the Maritime Museum. There are exhibits over three levels including tools and items used in loading and unloading ships, original pirate flags, and many photos. There are several mastheads on the second level. Captain's quarters and sleeping areas are also shown.

Adjacent to the Maritime Museum is Pommern, one of the world's only four-masted sailing ships in its original state. Admission to the ship is included in the admission to the Maritime Museum. The Pommern was used at one time to shipping grain from Australia.

Just in front of the Pommern is located the terminal for the ferries coming from Stockholm and Helsinki.

This trip was finished by revisiting Oslo. I had been to Oslo in 1971 which was 43 years prior to this visit. I was wondering if I would recognize anything! The one thing I did remember was the Vigeland Sculpture Gardens. These world-renowned gardens cover several acres and contain hundreds of statues by Vigeland along with glorious fountains.

Statues of Sonja Henie and Oscar Mathisen are located just up the street from the entrance to the gardens. They of course were famous Norweigians noted for their achievements in sports. Sonja Henie not only was well decorated with many titles in skating, but was in several movies as well. One of the treasured awards given to male skaters today is the Oscar Mathisen trophy.

Included in my walk around the city included the Parliament, the National Theater, the Munch Museum, and the Royal Palace. The new Opera House –at least since my last visit – was spectacular. It is located near the central railway station and is designed so that one can walk all around the roof to the very top! From here it offers grand views of the city.

Living in Washington DC with not only its Smithsonian Museums, but many more, one can become a little jaded when it comes to visiting museums in other places. However, The National Gallery in Oslo was first-class! I really enjoyed walking through and seeing the works of Munch (the scream!), Matisse, Gaugin, Cezanne, Monet, Picasso, Steen, and Rubens.

The large rooms in the City Hall are used for the presentation of the world-renowned Nobel prizes. A Nobel Peace Center is adjacent to the City Hall.

Outside the city center I visited the Viking Museum which had exhibits of several large boats and the Kon-Tiki Museum with its exhibits relating the adventures of Thor Hyerdahl.

The Holmenkollen National Arena is the site of the 1952 Olympics. Even though the ski jump has been updated, it is possible to ascend by elevator to the top of the new one. This allows one not only to witness exactly how high it really is, but an opportunity to see the city of Oslo in the background. For a fee I chose to take a ride on a simulator which offers the feeling of coming down the slope. It was well worth it!

Islands of the South Pacific. A neighbor and travel friend of mine and I departed in mid-September for a 29-flight trip to visit several of the islands in the South Pacific of which we had not previously visited.

We began by flying to Honolulu. From there we flew to Christmas Island which is part of the Line Islands and also part of the country of Kiribati. We were to be in Christmas Island for only an hour before continuing on to Fiji. However, there was a problem with the paperwork for the flight that the captain explained was highly unusual – something he had never experienced before. Because of this we needed to take five people off the plane. This needed to happen within one hour because it would be dark and there are no lights on the runway at this airport. With the added weight, we would use more fuel and would have to stop in Apia, Samoa to re-fuel. Finally, five employees of the airline were asked to depart and we were on our way. What was supposed to be a one-hour layover turned into being a four-hour layover. We arrived in Fiji in the middle of the night.

After a couple hours of sleep we were up bright and early the next morning for our transfer to the airport for our flight to Tonga. We were met at the airport and taken to our hotel. My travel agent always makes my hotel reservation when I am traveling with a friend for a room with two beds for two people. Upon our arrival to our room here we discovered that there was only one bed. We were told that the reservation didn't specify two beds and that there was not another room available with two beds. We were further told that for them to put another bed in the room there would be an additional fee of $70. Upon a lengthy discussion with the person in charge we were able to come to an agreement whereby we did get the extra bed and were not charged for it.

We departed the hotel for a walk to discover the waterfront across from our hotel and the small town of Nuku'alufo. Just down the street from our hotel was the royal palace. There were several churches of various denominations in the downtown area. Nearby was a large area that contained the tombs of some of the previous kings.

A travel agency was found here in the downtown area and we were able to make arrangements for a tour of the island for the next day whereby we would be picked up at our hotel and dropped off at the airport at the end of the tour.

Promptly at 11 a.m. the following day the van arrived. Our guide was extremely knowledgeable and had no problem communicating with perfect English.

We visited an area with several blow holes along the shore which was extremely picturesque. We stopped at an area depicting the place where Captain Cook came ashore. A plaque displayed here also recognized the visit of Queen Elizabeth II and Prince Philip in 1970. Our driver led us through quite a large cave where we were able to get some choice photos.

Our guide pointed out what she called 'flying squirrels' but to my friend and myself, they looked like bats hanging on the limbs in the tops of several trees. The other phenomenon for us was to see 'fishing pigs' – yes, they were in the shallow part of the water and were catching fish!!

The Ha'monga A Maui monument consisted of two large stone pillars with another stone lying across the top. It was built about 1200 AD and was probably used as an entrance to the royal compound. However, some historians have posited that it could have been constructed in such a manner that it could show the longest and shortest day of the year. Another large rock shaped like a seat on one side was probably used for the king to sit while welcoming guests.

We were dropped off at the airport for our flight to Suva where we would spend the night and be ready for our flight to Funafuti, Tuvalu the next morning.

However, the next morning we were told that the flight had been cancelled. This created somewhat of a dilemma since here we were in Suva and had hotel reservations for that evening in Nadi. They flew us back to Nadi. Then, the next morning we flew from Nadi to Suva, Suva to Funafuti, Funafuti to Suva, and Suva back to Nadi. Yes! Only four flights in one day, but thankfully they were short ones.

Tuvalu is merely a long strip of land and the runway for the airport takes up about half of the island. We were on our approach to land and the captain came on the PA system to announce that we were going to have to circle and come back to land because there were dogs on the runway!! As we did land, we could see that there were no fences on either side of the runway. Families were living on both sides.

The airport terminal was quite small. Even the duty free shop was merely a small kiosk outside at the back of the airport. We had about an hour or so to walk about the small town where there was some shops, a government building, and a hotel.

The next day we flew from Nadi, Fiji to Port Vila, Vanuatu. A gentleman who is a member of one of our local travel chapters had been working in Vanuatu for some time. Prior to our departure I was able to get in touch with him by emails and let him know that my friend and I were indeed going to be in Vanuatu. Upon checking in at the hotel, I called him. He came by the hotel that evening and picked us up and took us to a very nice restaurant for dinner.

The next day we took a tour of the island. We were joined by another traveler who had signed up for the same tour. First we visited the Blue Lagoon. Here the waters were crystal clear. Several of the local children were enjoying this location because a rope had been attached to a tree and they could swing out on the rope and release themselves into the water. Our next stop was not only to see the beach in that area with lava rock, etc. but while we were sightseeing and taking photos, our driver and guide was busy preparing papaya, bananas, and coconut for our mid-morning break.

Continuing around the island we stopped at the Taka Castom Village where we were serenaded by local dancers in their native costumes. Another group played music while we had lunch at the village.

Several World War II sights were included on our tour. One was an old air strip that was used during the war. Alongside the runway were three large U-shaped mounds of dirt. They were built so that planes could be hidden behind them. We saw several old tanks in the water nearby.

One of the locals had a large glass collection including old coke bottles from the time of World War II. He gave us a commentary as to their identity and how he was able to collect them.

The next day we flew from Port Vila, Vanuatu to Noumea, New Caledonia. Here we took a local bus from our hotel into the downtown area where we were able to see the Central Park, the Chinatown, St. Joseph's Cathedral, the City Museum, and a large memorial recognizing the United States for their contribution during the war.

We flew to Brisbane, Australia for one night before flying out yet again for another island!! Yes, we flew to Honiara, the capital of the Solomon Islands.

The cost of our hotel in Honiara was quite expensive since there was not a lot of competition. There literally was only one decent hotel for tourists. We noticed a photo of Prince William and Kate who had stayed at this hotel.

Not long after we were settled in our room, I decided to go out and take some photos of our new lodging. When I returned to the room, I couldn't get the door to open. We called maintenance and were told that the lock would have to be changed. This put us in an awkward situation because we couldn't leave our room until the lock was changed. After a while I went to the front desk to find out how long it was going to take. At that point the front desk was not able to locate the maintenance department. Needless to say, I complained to the point that we were asked to move to another room which meant repacking our bags, etc. Then, the first room they took us to was a room with one bedroom and we were promised that there would be two because of the trouble we had encountered. So, we then moved to another room that no only had two bedrooms, but had a kitchen, a washer and dryer, etc.

The next morning we met a gentleman who would be our guide for the day visiting the World War II sites around Guadal Canal. These battles occurred between August 7, 1942 and February 9, 1943. There were several monuments recognizing the United States influence during this time.

Adjacent to the airport was a garden-type monument and cemetery dedicated to the American Marines who gave their lives here. Included in our tour was a visit to the area for the Battle of Bloody Ridge and the Solomon Peace Memorial Park.

The standard of living on this island could be determined by the structure of their homes and the lack of a wide selection of shops for purchasing items and for food. A couple times while we were sightseeing, young kids would appear to hopefully sell us an old coke bottle that they said was from the World War II era.

We flew back to Brisbane and here at the airport was where my friend and I would go our separate ways. My friend had visited a couple of the places that I wanted to visit. Therefore, he followed a different route to include some places that he had not previously visited.

During my two night visit to Brisbane I saw several places in the city that I had not seen on my previous visits. This included several government buildings, statues of Queen Victoria and Queen Elizabeth II, a section of old homes that had been restored, an art museum, and the botanical gardens.

From Brisbane I flew to Norfolk Island. One of the things that anyone would remember about this island is that has Norfolk Island pine trees everywhere and some of the old ones are gigantic! Another fond memory is that this is one of the few places I have visited that a free tour of the island is included! The first morning I was picked up at my hotel for a wonderful tour of the island with a delightful gentleman as our informative guide.

We toured the area around Kingston, the capital of Norfolk Island, which had been restored. Not only is one able to view the old jail, an old cemetery, etc. but at the same time take in the exquisite scenery—other small islands, the sea, etc. There was a stop at an outdoor theater where the happenings of the Mutiny on the Bounty is presented. History correlates the fact that there was indeed a connection between the Bounty and descendants of the island.

One has to be alert as to where they are walking on this island because there are a lot of cows and yes, they have to 'go to the bathroom' somewhere! I certainly enjoyed my short visit here and will never forget the kindness of everyone in assuring that your visit is a good one.

Lord Howe Island was next on my list. This island is quite small and because of this it makes walking around enjoyable. I love to take pictures and this island offers many opportunities for that. During my walk I saw the local school, the post office, a museum, the hospital, and several churches. On one sign there were arrows pointing to the direction of the liquor store.

In years gone past, I am sure that it was difficult for small businesses to purchase any item they needed for their home or the business. Even today, they have a boat that comes in every two weeks with supplies. This includes food, gas and oil, the mail, everything. However, now with the internet, items can be purchased from almost any place in the world and then delivered. The owner of my hotel clarified this. He had just received new tables for the restaurant. He had ordered them from a company in Chicago. They were delivered to the port in California and were received in Lord Howe Island about two weeks later. Years ago this would not have been possible. However, the night before I had to be taken to another restaurant for dinner since the food had not arrived for this restaurant. And, being a small island, that restaurant gave me a shuttle ride back to my hotel when I finished my dinner.

After two days and nights of rediscovering the city of Sydney, Australia I began my last leg of the journey and felt as those I was on my way home. I flew through Auckland, New Zealand to Papeete, Tahiti where I would spend one night and then go to the Marquesas Islands.

I arrived at the airport the next morning and boarded the plane. After a few minutes we were told that there was a mechanical problem and that we should gather all our belongings and depart the aircraft. However, after a few minutes of standing, we were again instructed that the problem had been fixed and that we could now take our seats again! The flight to Nuku Hiva had a short stopover in Hiva Oa just to drop off several passengers and to collect some others.

The drive from the airport in Nuku Hiva to the hotel took almost an hour and a half. At one point of the drive there was rain. Then, at the higher levels of the mountains, there was heavy fog where one could only see a few feet in front of the vehicle. As we came over the mountains and began our descent into the small city the weather cleared and it was really spectacular scenery.

My hotel in Nuku Hiva was really nice! It was strategically located on the side of a hill overlooking the entire bay and town. After getting settled into my own little cabin, I took a walk down the hill to see what the small town had to offer. I walked for a while on the beach and I was the only person there – talk about secluded. There was a small museum and another building that exhibited crafts that had been made by the locals.

The long drive from the hotel back to the airport was nothing like the ride had been on our way over. That day it was sunny – no rain, no fog.

The flight from Nuku Hiva back to Papeete, Tahiti was again to include a short stop in Hiva Oa where we would stay on the plane, drop off some, and pick up others. However, upon landing, we were told that we would deplane.

It wasn't until later, we were told that the reason for this was that there was a person on the island that was sick and that the small plane at the airport was needed to fly and pick up this person and take them to a hospital. However, our pilot was the only available one to do this. So, we waited at the airport for almost four hours while he performed his extra duty. The staff at this small airport was very congenial and offered us free drinks and sandwiches while we waited.

Needless to say, my flight home wasn't a quick one! I flew from Nuku Hiva to Hiva Oa, on to Papeete, then to Los Angeles, to Charlotte, NC and finally into Washington DC.

2015

Puerto Vallarta, Mexico
South America Cruise
Germany, Slovenia, Bulgaria, Serbia, & Romania
Michigan

The year began by leaving behind the snowy and cold weather of Washington DC and spending a week with friends in Puerto Vallarta, Mexico. Fortunately these two long-time friends of mine had indicated at dinner one evening that they would be in Mexico for three months and that I should plan to come to visit while they were there. I said to them that I just might do that since I had been to Timbuktu and back, to over 200 countries, but that I had never been to Puerto Vallarta, Mexico.

It was a wonderful week there with great weather and fantastic restaurants. One day while there we boarded a bus and went outside the city to the Botanical Gardens. The gardens especially the orchid house was a real treat. We had lunch there and the setting was delightful.

Having traveled as extensively as I have through the past 50 some years, it has become a regular habit of mine to ask people where they are from. For example, I remember asking a waiter. He looked at me as though most Americans aren't aware of world geography and there would probably be no way that I would even have heard of his country. He was pleasantly surprised after he said, "Bangladesh" that I responded, "Are you from Dacha, Jessore, Bogra, Kulna, etc." He couldn't believe it! Another time I ask a waitress where she was from and she said, "Do you want to guess or should I tell you?" I said, "I think you are from Ethiopia." And she was.

At the Botanical Gardens outside Puerto Vallarta, my friends and I had been talking to a lady that was working there. It seems that she had been working there for several years, however, she said that her place of residence was California. I asked where in California and when she said, "Northern," I said, "Near Mount Shasta." She couldn't believe it, but that was exactly where she was from.

Another day we participated in a house tour. It seems that this organization there sponsors these tours and the money is given to a charity that helps in defraying the costs of operations for children whose parents can't afford the operations.

The first place wasn't a house, but a penthouse apartment in a condominium building located right on the beach with a wonderful view of the city. Needless to say, all the places were show pieces and were decorated extremely well.

South American Cruise. In February I flew to Buenos Aires for a few days before joining a cruise. It was nice being back in this city again. However, the last time I was here, the opera house was closed for renovation. This time I was able to take the opera house tour and it was well worth the time and effort.

The first stop on the cruise was Montevideo, Uruguay. Even though I had been there once in 1969, I decided to participate in one of the excursions from the ship. We were given an introductory talk about the buildings around the main square. Afterwards, we had time to meander for a while in order to take our photos. While waiting, I told the guide that I had been here once, but is was in 1969! She began looking around the square and saying, "Well, I think that building and that building might have been here then, but everything else would be new.

The cruise continued on to Stanley, the capital of the Falkland Islands. This was one place that I had not visited and was able to check off another place on my list of countries/places visited. The architecture of the buildings was quite typical of an island country. One of the things I remember about being here was the statue of Margaret Thatcher and the adjacent street that was named after her. Of course, she was a strategic person during the conflict in the mid 80's.

Puerto Arenas was our next stop and what a quaint little town it was! The cemetery there was unlike any other I had ever seen. Many of the tombs were elaborately constructed and on the lanes separating them in a street-like fashion were extremely large shrubs shaped in cone-like figures.

There were different kinds of crosses at the top of several gravesites and we were told that indicated whether or not that person was catholic, protestant, etc. Also in the cemetery was a long columbarium where remains had been stored and many flowers accompanied several of them.

Also in the cemetery was a monument to the first settlers of the area.

We continued on to visit an outdoor museum. This contained several pieces of farm equipment, railway cars, farming instruments, etc. There was also several homes that had been transported to this area to give one an idea of the types of homes the people had lived in through the years. One building also contained several old cars, an ambulance, and a fire truck.

In the downtown area we walked through a large museum that contained many, many interesting exhibits.

Germany and the Balkans. Now that I have visited almost every country in the world that is safe to visit, I am beginning to re-visit. My first time in Germany was in 1962. It had also been 20 years since I had been to Munich, Frankfurt, and Berlin. It had been 50 years since I had visited Cologne and I had never been to Hamburg. Therefore, I decided that it was time to return. I traveled between cities using their excellent train service and spent three wonderful days each in Munich, Frankfurt, Cologne, Hamburg, and Berlin.

I enjoyed having time in the city of Munich to see and remember all the wonderful churches in the downtown area. While there I was able to visit a friend who lived outside the city and that area had beautiful views of the nearby mountains.

In Frankfurt I spent some time in the old section of town where I had been two times previously.

I had not been to their botanical gardens. I walked there from my hotel and it was well worth the walk! My camera got a workout as many of the various flowers were in full bloom!

A new opera house had been built since my previous visits and I was able to get a ticket to see Der Rosenkavalier. I had been a supernumerary for that opera with the Washington Opera several years previously and it was nice to sit in the audience and re-live the opera even though it was a completely different production.

My only visit to Cologne had been in 1962 on my first visit to Europe and we only spent a few hours in Cologne seeing the Cathedral before we departed on a boat for a Rhine River cruise. This time I was able to not only spend more time seeing the cathedral, but walked the 530 steps to the top of one of the towers that is open to tourists. The views were spectacular!

By being there for three days I was able to get a much better feel for the city and its people. Again in Cologne I walked from my hotel to the botanical gardens and also visited several churches other than the major cathedral.

This was my first visit to the city of Hamburg and what an impressive city it is!

One of my reasons for this visit was to go to the Miniature Wonderland exhibit and it was even more than I expected. I had read some information prior to my visit regarding the difficulty of obtaining tickets for the exhibit and that some people have to wait for hours before they are allowed entry. I was prepared for this in that I left my hotel early that morning and arrived before the opening hour. By doing that I was fortunate in being able to enter immediately.

The exhibits are located in what evidently was once huge warehouse buildings and takes up all of three floors. I must have taken over 100 photos there and could have easily spent the entire day just looking at the marvelous exhibits. Some of these were of landscapes, some were cities with apartment buildings where you could peer into the apartments and see furniture and people, sporting events, concerts, castles—unbelievable! There were multiple exhibits of railways – terminals, through mountains, through villages, etc.

There was a large exhibit of an airline terminal. One could see the planes flying in or taking off. There were fire trucks going around the terminal. Everything was planned in order to include almost everything one expects to see at an airport.

There was a section for the United States which included Las Vegas (day and night), our space program, and the Grand Canyon.

Other than the miniature wonderland I was able to tour the City Hall, St. Michael's Church, St. Catherine's Church, and the walked from one end to the other of their botanical gardens. These gardens were a delight and I was able to do it early in the morning and there wasn't a lot of people around. Near the end of the gardens was a group of buildings which housed their courts. Also nearby was a Russian Orthodox Church and they were having a service at the time. Being inside reminded me of several of the same types of churches I visited when I was in Siberia on the Trans-Siberian Railway trip. And one could never miss the huge statue of Otto von Bismark. It was in need of attention in that it contained a lot of graffiti and seemingly had been ignored for some time. Even the grass that surrounded it also needed some attention.

My first afternoon in Berlin I walked from my hotel to the central part of the city where the Parliament building is located. I had seen the old building before but had not been able to see the new glass domed structure now adorning the top.

On my way there I was able to walk through the Jewish monument for the Halocaust. It covers a large city block and consists of concrete squares in rows and are of varying heights. One does begin to have a certain empty feeling as one walks through and realizes what happened. It was quite moving.

Also before I reached the Parliament Building, I was able to see the Brandenburg Gate. My first time here in 1976 I was able to go through Checkpoint Charlie and that was a memorable experience....and my how things have changed since 1992!

I had the lady from the hotel make a reservation for me to visit the glass dome structure. However, when I arrived there I was told that the reservation had not been sufficiently completed. Consequently, I stood in line for an hour or so and obtained a ticket for the next day.

Since I do like to walk, I then walked in a different direction back to my hotel. However, the next day I did take the bus for my return.

It was definitely well worth the wait and was everything that I had expected it to be. While touring the dome, there was a couple from Brazil that was touring at the same time. I asked if I could take pictures of them together and they heartily agreed. Then they insisted on taking several photos of me.

The next day I decided that I would check out the large department store that was only a few blocks from my hotel. The name of the store is KaDeWe and covers an entire block and is about six or seven stories high. Needless to say, it was amazing! One entire floor was nothing but food. I saw a crystal statue that was on sale for $32,000! The top floor was mostly glass and had a large buffet where one could take a break from shopping and re-energize themselves for another round!

I purchased some chocolates there in interesting containers to give to my friend in Bled, Slovenia that I would be visiting a couple days later.

Most of the next day was spent going through Charlottenburg Palace which I had also been to but it was in 1971. It was just as exciting this time as it was before. While going through and taking photos, there was another couple following along at about the same speed. Later I saw them in the gardens and said hello. I couldn't believe it when they said that they were from Baltimore which is only about 40 miles from my home.

I flew from Berlin to Ljubljana where my friend picked me up at the airport. We spent most of our time driving through the beautiful Julian Alps which are picturesquely portrayed among spectacular evergreen trees with snow covering the tops of mountains made of rock.

It was amazing to see and read about the influence of Russian people who were there during World War I. There were several monuments to those who died while building highways, etc. One such monument was a miniature Russian church.

In this area there were many ski resorts and lodges for the multitude of tourists who come there in the winter for skiing vacations.

We had breakfast one morning sitting by a lake surrounded by the snow-covered mountains—absolutely beautiful! As we drove through these Julian Alps there were many, many waterfalls.

So now it was time for me to continue my journey by leaving this utopia and flying from Slovenia to Sofia, Bulgaria where I would join a tour group.

I was picked up at the airport and transported to my hotel. I couldn't believe it as we turned the corner and drove up to the hotel – it was the same hotel that I had stayed in 39 years before in 1976!! It was comforting to realize that it had had a complete 'face lift' and had a new name. Yes, this was the same hotel that I mentioned earlier in the book where I left the hotel and upon my return that night I was informed that my friend and I were at the wrong hotel and they proceeded to take us to another hotel.

The first evening our group had an orientation meeting. This allowed each of us to get to know each other, meet our tour director, and to hear about the details of the tour. When I introduced myself I also let the other know the story about the hotel from 39 years previously. They could hardly believe it.

One of the first things I noticed as we began our tour of Sofia that had changed drastically since my previous visit was the number of automobiles in the street. On my earlier visit one could literally walk down one of the main wide streets and hardly see an automobile. Now there are many more!

Our city tour included the National Museum of History and our guide gave us a short synopsis of the history of the country. We walked by the impressive Neo-Byzantine golden-domed Temple Sveti Nickolay, saw the ruins in the Roman Rotunda, and toured the huge Cathedral of St. Alexander Nevski.

In the afternoon most of our group visited the Rila Monastery. It was named after St. Ivan of Rila, who was a hermit and at one time lived in a cave nearby the present location.

Through the years the history of the monastery is quite interesting in that it was originally begun in the 10th century. It was upgraded in the 14th century, had raids in the 15th century, and a fire in the mid-19th century. The large building which encompasses the Bishop's Throne is quite impressive with the gold altar and elaborate gates.

A museum is located in the lower level of one of the many buildings in the complex and the most treasured item in the museum is Rafail's Cross, which was carved from one large piece of wood and contains many religious scenes as well as hundreds of religious people.

Photography is prohibited in the museum. One of our members continued to take photos even though there were signs and there had also been oral announcements. Yes, he was finally screamed at and almost had his camera knocked out of his hand.

We drove across the border into Serbia the following morning. We had a nice lunch at a local restaurant in the city of Nis. However, the lunch didn't include a dessert that actually whetted the appetite. I excused myself and as usual when I travel – within a few steps from the restaurant, I found a nice ice cream place. When other members began leaving the lunch room, they saw me with the ice cream and questioned me as to where I was able to find it. Of course, our departure was delayed several minutes until all the others were able to satisfy their sweet tooth desires.

One claim to fame for the city is that Constantine the Great was born here. We also saw the ruins where there had been a large concentration camp here during World War II.

After a long day of driving we arrived in Belgrade. My last time here had been only 2 years previously. Our first night we walked to a nearby restaurant in the Old Bohemian Quarter of Skadarlija. It just so happened that this was the same restaurant I had been taken to on the previous trip. While our group enjoyed the wonderful beers of Serbia and a nice dinner, we were serenaded by local musicians and singers.

The one segment of our city tour the following day was to drive through the newer part of the city. My previous tour only crossed the bridge and pointed out all the boats along the river that serve as discos and night clubs for the younger people in the evening. It was nice to be able to see a lot more of this area than I had been able to see before.

The two major places visited was the Old Fortress and the Saint Sava Temple. The fortress is built high above the confluence of the Danube and the Sava Rivers and is quite impressive. The Sava Temple, one of the largest Orthodox churches in the world, is still under construction yet one can visit the interior and enjoy listening to recorded music.

Our hotel, the Moscow Hotel, was centrally located and made it convenient to walk from the hotel down the walking street which has many, many shops and restaurants. Along the way, one can sit and listen to the locals performing music.

Novi Sad was our first stop the next day. The major sightseeing feature of this city is the Petrovaradin Citadel perched high above the Danube River. Of course during its earlier years it was used as a fortress for military purposes. Today it is mainly a museum, however, incorporated in it is many shops and a nice hotel.

We had time there to enjoy lunch on our own on a walking street that had many choices of places to eat outside. At the end of the street was Liberty Square which is where the City Hall and other important buildings were located.

Continuing north we arrive in Timisoara. A lot of this city is under construction, however, the buildings that have been completed are absolutely delightful – very cheerful in vibrant pastel colors. Our hotel was centrally located which made it nice for an evening stroll through the city. In the evening the hotel as well as the opera house next door were very impressively lighted. One street nearby was filled with brightly-colored umbrellas!

One couldn't help but to notice all the extremely large homes on the highway between Timisoara and Sibiu. It seems there are 'gypsy' people who live in this area and make their living by selling items along the roadside. We were able to see some of them. They must be successful at what they do in order to be able to have such large homes.

Another item of interest on our drive was that at several places we were able to not only spot stork nests on top of some of the homes, but some of them were actually occupied.

We had a guided walking tour the next morning in the Bohemian Old Town that still remains the grandeur of its earlier days with a medieval wall guarding the historic area where narrow streets pass by steep-roofed 17th century buildings. We walked through the Great Square, Little Square, and the Evangelical Cathedral.

Our journey then continued on to the city of Sighisoara, which is one of the best preserved medieval cities in Southeastern Europe with its fortified walls, cobblestone streets, and old houses. The highlight of this stop was the Clock Tower Museum and the workings of the magnificent clock with its moving wooden figurines.

The city of Brasov is aesthetically surrounded by the Carpathian Mountains. This offers several nice places for photos. Our guide was from this city and one could tell by the exuberance he showed in depicting the history of the city and its many cathedrals, museums, etc. At one point of our tour his son appeared. We were told that it wasn't so much that his son wanted to see him but that just like any teenager – he needed money!!

The highlight of this tour for me and for most of our group was that the next day we would be driving to Bran Castle, commonly known as "Dracula's Castle."

Originally a medieval fortress in the early 13th century the castle changed ownership many times through the years. It was completed in 1388 and was occupied for many years with military personnel and mercenaries. It was used as a Royal Residence by Queen Maria in the early 20th century. Vlad the Impaler occupied the castle from 1448 until 1476.

Even though Bram Stoker's novel, Dracula, depicted a fictitious character it is somehow believed that it was based upon the real-life character from many years previously. Thus, Bran Castle, is commonly known as Dracula's Castle.

Continuing our journey from this area to the capital city of Bucharest we had a stop at Peles Castle. This enormously large and extravagant castle was actually the home of Carol I, the ruler of Romania. He was born in 1866 and died in 1914. He was married and had one child who died at three years old.

It contained 160 rooms that were exquisitely decorated. Many of the rooms had hand-carved wooden panels which were used as the walls and sometimes the ceilings for the room. There was an ornate wooden spiral staircase, interior balconies, many large mirrors, statues, military weapons, offices, apartments, and several large dining areas.

Pelisor Castle was erected nearby in 1889 and was to be used by Ferdinand, the nephew of Carol I, who would become the next ruler since neither of Carol's brothers accepted the authority.

Also on our way to Bucharest we stopped in Sinaia where we had a tour of the Sinaia Monastery. The monastery was founded by Mikhail Cantacuzino. He had visited St. Catherine's monastery on Mount Sinai and was so impressed with it that he used it as a basis for this monastery.

The monastery consists of two major churches – the Old Church which was built in 1695 and the Great Church in 1846.

We finally arrived in Bucharest which is sometimes referred to as the Paris of the East for our final stop of the tour. They even have a replica of the Arc de Triomphe.

I had been in Bucharest in 1976 when it was still under communist rule and couldn't wait to see if I actually recognized anything from my 1976 visit.

Upon revealing to several people before my departure for this trip that I would be in Bucharest, the first question that I would usually get was whether or not I had seen 'the large building' there. Of course, they were referring to the new Parliament Building, which had not been erected in 1976. Therefore, it would have been impossible for me to have seen it.

This Parliament Building, better known here as the Palace of Parliament, was the first stop on our tour of the city. It is enormous! It is the second largest building in the world next to the Pentagon just outside the city of Washington, DC. The building has 8 levels below ground, 12 floors above ground, 1100 rooms, and several large conference halls.

Construction began in 1980 while the country was still under the influence of communism and was completed in 1989.

Our walking tour included the Stavropoleos Church, a Greek church which was built in 1724, the opera house, and the old part of the city.

We then drove to the Open Air Village Museum where we were able to see such things as a half-buried house with a thatched roof, old windmills, farmhouses, cottages, and artisan workshops. There was a delightful indoor museum where one could see the costumes worn by the local people through years past.

This tour as many others do concluded with a farewell dinner which also included entertainment.

Michigan. After having visited all of the 50 states of the United States and almost every country in the world that is safe to visit, I have begun to look at the map and try to find places that I have visited before, but haven't seen certain areas. Thus, Michigan.

I had been to Detroit, but had never seen any of the rest of the state. I had originally thought that I would fly to Detroit where I would rent a car and drive to the areas I wanted to see. However, I found a group tour that went to those places and decided that would be much better.

The one place that had been on my subconscious 'bucket list' for some time was the Grand Hotel on Mackinac Island and this tour included that.

The tour began with two nights in Traverse City. I must admit that before I began researching information for this trip, I had never heard of Traverse City.

We visited a Music Museum there. My initial thought of going to a museum here after having lived in Washington, DC for 50 years with all its museums was a little apprehensible to say the least. Was I ever surprised! It was fantastic!

The lady docent who gave us the tour was a delight! She gave us demonstrations using several of the pieces including player pianos, pipe organs, and other several others.

One piece that was situated on the 2nd level was the 1922 Mortier Dance Hall Organ commonly called the Amaryllis. It was built in Belgium and is 18 feet by 30 feet. In other parts of the museum were old juke boxes and record players with the large brass horns for amplification.

While in this area we visited The Sleeping Bear sand dunes. Having almost no knowledge of this area of the country prior to my visit, it was undoubtedly an eye opener to witness sand dunes that went as high as 200 feet.

Later in the afternoon we visited a winery where were able to participate in a wine tasting which was followed by a delightful dinner accompanied by some of their tasty wines.

On our drive north the next morning there was a huge display alongside the highway – the world's largest cherry pie!! Yes—we're still in cherry country!

There were several things that made the visit to Charlevoix memorable. One of the things that one first notices is that the residents of the town plant petunias every Thursday before Memorial Day on both sides of the road from one end of town to the other. There are approximately 60,000 of them! The other thing would be the 'mushroom houses' of Earl Young. He was an architect from this area and built several homes that have curved roofs that are indicative of some of the work of Gaudi in Barcelona, Spain. He used a lot of large rocks also in these houses.

Our journey north then took us to the delightful town of Petosky. There we had time to walk around the town and observe some of their quaint shops. We then went to a local inn where we had a delightful lunch. The owner gave us a little talk while we had lunch. We learned that he had worked at an entry level job at one time, but through the years and marriage, he actually took over the inn and had been there ever since.

We took advantage of the bridge that connects the lower part of Michigan to the upper part for our group tour photo. Nearby was an old lighthouse.

Now it was time to board the ferry to take us to Mackinac Island. This for me was to be the highlight of the tour. It had for a long time been on my subconscious 'bucket list' to not only visit the island, but to stay at the Grand Hotel.

Prior even to getting to this point, our guide had taken time to give us some insight as to what to expect in regards to the hotel. She said that we probably had visions of what it would be like, but she wanted to remind us that it would not be like a regular Hyatt or a Four Seasons – the hotel was built over 100 years ago. She said that as we walk in our room or down the hall, the floor would probably creak a little. She also let us know before we arrived that our rooms would probably be on the back side of the hotel and not on the front with a view as those rooms sometimes go for up to $2,000! It is good that we were told these things before we arrived—then there was no surprise.

I must say that the experience of staying at the hotel was well worth the whole trip. I thoroughly enjoyed everything about it even down to the coconut ice cream in the little shop on the lower level.

The movie Somewhere in Time with Christopher Reeve and Jane Seymour was filmed here at the hotel in 1979. As with any hotel of this grandeur and prominence many famous people had stayed at the hotel through the years.

There are no automobiles permitted on the island. One travels by horse-drawn carriages. As part of our group tour we were able the next morning to take a horse-drawn carriage ride of the island which would finish at the fort. We were told that the week before the weather had been almost 90 degrees and the morning of our ride, it was much colder. In fact, the high for that day was 57 degrees.

While on the ride I was surprised at the number of huge houses here as well as many large Bed and Breakfast places to stay. The fort was well worth a visit and the views from the fort are priceless.

There is a very nice museum in the downtown area which exhibits items depicting life on the island.

We had a stop in the afternoon in Midland where we were able to tour the home of the son of the founder of the Dow Chemical Company. It seems that he went off the college and his parents just thought that he would exceed in the sciences and eventually take over the business. That didn't happen. After a couple years of college and having the feeling that this just wasn't working out, he decided to go to another school and change to architecture.

His home is now a museum and it was a treat to be able to go through it. He also built several other homes and buildings in the town. Even though several things remind you of Frank Lloyd Wright, he did know and study with him. However, he also had many disagreements with him.

After spending one night in Bay City we departed the next morning on a tall ship which made its way out into Lake Huron. Upon our return we proceeded south to the quaint Bavarian town of Frankenmuth. This was another part of the tour that had been on my subconscious 'bucket list.' Not only did I enjoy seeing the various buildings here and having a scrumptious lunch at the Bavarian Inn, I was able to visit the largest Christmas store in the world.

Christmas has always been a big part of my life – summer Christmas parties for 25 years and winter Christmas parties for over 20 years. One of my email addresses even incorporates 'xmas' in it and my automobile license plate is also 'xmas.'

Our group stayed at a lovely hotel in Dearborn which is a suburb of Detroit. We did a tour of the downtown area where we were able to see the major buildings which included the Renaissance Center, several old theaters, Motown headquarters, and being able to look over into Canada (on the south side.)

The highlight of the stop here was of course the tour of the Ford Museum and Greenfield Village. One could spend hours and hours at the Ford Museum. There were limousines from former Presidents of the United States, old railroad cars, and many other exhibits.

At Greenfield Village we took a ride on a steam engine and also took a ride in an old Model T. Here one was able to see the house that Ford had lived in and there were several other structures depicting the lifestyle in that era.

2016

Kashmir

The only trip planned at this point for 2016 is to visit Kashmir in April. It has been on my subconscious 'bucket list' for some time that before my travels are finished, I will be able to go to Kashmir and spend a night or two in one of the luxury boat hotels.

My friend and I plan to fly through Delhi and continue on to Leh, the capital of Kashmir. While there we will tour the palace and several monasteries. We will have a day excursion to Khardongla pass which is the highest motorable pass in the world at 5600 meters where we will see several snow-covered mountains.

From Leh we will fly to Srinagar for three nights and one of them is to be on a boat hotel. While in Srinagar we will have a tour of The Mughal Gardens including the Nishat Bagh (the garden of pleasure), Chashmashahi (the Royal Spring), and Shalimar Garden (the abode of love).

In the evening there will be a romantic ride by Shikara to visit the Floating Gardens and the Lotus Gardens at the lake.

We will have a full day tour to Gulmarg, a resort in the valley, where we will have a cable car ride to Khilanmarg to have scenic views of the area. There we will have a pony ride to see the open fields to seven springs and a lake which stays frozen until June.

There will also be a full day excursion to Pahalgam in the Lidder Valley which again will offer more spectacular views of snow-covered mountains.

It will now be time to fly back to Delhi for one night before we begin a short extension of the trip that will include a visit to the Andaman Islands and Lapshadweep. The Andaman Islands are on the east side between India and Myanmar and Lapshadweep Islands are on the west side north of the Maldives.

I have been fortunate to have been able to do my travels at a time when it was much safer to do so than in today's world. Fortunately fifty years ago one did not have to be overly concerned whether or not a quaint little bistro would be blown up before one could finish a memorable meal with friends or fellow travelers.

Based upon the aforementioned state of the world it is now time for me to look at a globe and determine where there is a place to which I would enjoy visiting again. For example, I have visited Greece several times, however, I haven't seen the northern part of that country. Also, having visited France several times yet there are areas of France that I haven't seen and look forward to adding them to my future travel plans.

Summary

Traveling in some ways can be equated to a residence that it is never completed—there is always something else that needs to be accomplished.

When two travelers get together, there is never a lull in the conversation. It is always nice to be able to converse with others who have visited the same places you have and to be able to compare visits.

One way of accomplishing this for me is being active in the Circumnavigators Club and the Travelers Century Club. The Circumnavigators Club is an international organization for individuals who have been around the world in a single trip. The Travelers Century Club is an international organization for individuals who have been to more than hundred countries.

My circumnavigation to celebrate my retirement in 1994 qualified me for the Circumnavigators Club. I have circumnavigated the world four times since then.

The Circumnavigators Club bestows the Magellan Award each year to a deserving person at their meeting in New York. I was fortunate to be able to attend the one where Steve Fossett received the award.

The Travelers Century Club just started a chapter in the Washington area about two years ago. In their list of over three hundred countries and places to visit I have been to 259 of them already.

There seems to be a certain segment of society who doesn't agree with these clubs' assessment of countries. For example, Hawaii and Alaska are listed as separate entities. If I am ever questioned regarding these regulations, I use this as an example. I say to the person that if they take a trip to Tahiti, they don't return home and tell their neighbors that they just went to France.

Many years of my life were spent getting an education in classrooms from elementary school through graduate school. However, it seems that most of my education has come from the many years of travel. The travels have not only helped to educate me as to the geographical locations of countries, their customs, etc., it has also helped me in my teaching career, to be able to realize that all students are different and have to be treated in different ways. It is never too late to learn from someone who is from a different culture and that their way and my way of seeing things are not always the same. This doesn't mean that either of us is right or wrong.

A day never passes without my realizing that none of these travel experiences could have been accomplished without having been extremely fortunate to have been in excellent health. My philosophy is that I should continue to pursue my dreams of travel while I am in good health and can enjoy it. There will come a day when I won't be able to do this. I don't want to have any regrets of thinking about places that I would like to have visited and didn't.

It is my hope that this diary of my travels will motivate someone to follow their dream in traveling to other parts of the world. If it indeed does this, it will make this endeavor worthwhile.

About the Author

Bill S. Ashley was born in rural Yadkin County, North Carolina. Upon his graduation from high school, he further pursued his education by receiving an Associate in Arts from Gardner-Webb Junior College (now Gardner-Webb University), a Bachelor of Science from Appalachian State Teachers College (now Appalachian State University), a Master of Education in Business Education from the University of Maryland, and a Doctorate in Education from the International Graduate School in Saint Louis, Missouri.

He was a secondary education teacher in the state of Virginia from 1960 through 1993. He was a vocational coordinator of the work training program for students in the business department.

Even though most of his early life was consumed through his education in the classroom, his most meaningful education has been received through his compulsion for traveling.

He belongs to the Circumnavigators Club, which is an international organization comprised of those travelers who have circumnavigated the globe in a single trip. Since his retirement he has circumnavigated the globe four times.

He also belongs to the Travelers Century Club, an international organization whose members have traveled to more than 100 countries. In their list of more than 300 countries and places to visit, he has already been to more than 250.

One of his traveling goals was achieved in 2003 when he visited all seven continents within one year.

CPSIA information can be obtained
at www.ICGtesting.com
Printed in the USA
FFOW04n1246120516
24034FF